To my best teachers:
Hattie and George, parents
Jay, husband
Daniel, Emma, Apple, Hannah, children
Jane Lazarre, dear friend

Contents

Acknowledgments

But I must do what I believe in or nothing at all. Life's so short.

Sylvia Ashton-Warner
Teacher

Teaching Children to Care is a book about teaching and about teachers doing what they "must." The ideas represent what I have learned from the practice of many teachers and the writings of many educators. With this book, I hope to acknowledge the courage and inspiration of those who dare to teach and to persist in their best hopes for children.

I am indebted to my first colleagues: their guidance, modeling, and endless hours of conversation and relief. In particular Corinne Price, Naomi Gutheil, Juana Culhane, Ann Green, and Rose Thompson.

I am especially grateful to the founding members of the Greenfield Center School and Northeast Foundation for Children for the opportunity to construct and grow together:

To Chip Wood, for his vision, his leadership, his trust in children and teachers, his sometimes booming voice, and his always yearning and learning self.

To Jay Lord, for his effusive energy, affections, and capacity to play; for his noticing and attention to the very best efforts and strengths of others; for his ceaseless support and encouragement of my work and of me.

To Marlynn Clayton, who makes a classroom beautiful, safe, and fun; who brings structure, the richness of activity and a gentle joy to childhood; and who is not afraid to mean what she says and say what she means.

I wish to give thanks to all my colleagues at the Greenfield Center School whose ideas and passions infuse this book. Particularly:

To Ellen Doris, who helped me see birds, and for opening closed doors.
To Terry Kayne, whose infectious kindness matters.
To Debby Porter, who is ever inventive and committed.

To Bob Strachota, who teaches pride and poetry to sevens.

To Mary Beth Forton and her extraordinary appetite for learning.

To Timmy Sheyda and his delicious room-smells of cooking and paint.

To Paula Denton and her unabashed promotion of the academic curriculum.

I also want to acknowledge the teachers at the Savin Rock Elementary School (West Haven CT), who openly and enthusiastically share their work with me, and have allowed the use of so many quotes and photographs for this book. Especially, I want to thank the initial Drop-Out Prevention Team: Joan Bomadier, Pamela Daddio, John Deppen, Rosalea Donahue, Jan Doyle, Patricia Fusco, Catherine Iaccarino, Dawn Jordan, and Deborah Roth. I appreciate the support of Prinicpals Peter Florio and Bill Fournier.

I am indebted to the many people who have edited and worked on this manuscript:

To John Clayton, who edited the first drafts. His skillful editing, patience, vehement criticisms and compliments made it happen.

To the deep and loving reading by friends and colleagues — Zina Steinberg, who littered the manuscript with corrections, references, and good ideas; Jane Lazarre, who often gave me both right words and the stamina to go on; Jay Lord, who knew how to untie the knots and find the flow.

To Apple Lord, who took the pictures, documenting the essence of the book with her photographs.

To Jan Doyle, who took the wonderful cover photograph.

To Steven Finer, who sifted the text for errors.

And I am deeply indebted to Al Woods for his insights on how to tidy and clarify, and his determination to bring this manuscript to publication.

Finally, I want to acknowledge the many teachers I have met at workshops, and recently in the Washington D.C. Public Schools, who have the courage to defy the overwhelming odds facing some of their children. They counter it with their own hopes and powerful caring, which promises an ongoing revision of this book.

Foreword

This is one teacher's story. It is largely anecdotal and personal. Yet it is more than a compendium of experiences. It is an outgrowth of a search for explanations.

In the course of writing, I struggled with doubts and uncertainties. I questioned my credentials and authority. I doubted my perspective and ability to convey that perspective clearly. After all, I was paraphrasing the ideas of mentors and authors; I had been given so much by other teachers who shared their wisdom through conversations. I had little training as a writer or academic. Certainty and contradiction kept a steady pace.

However, there was also another, less personal, source of the uncertainty and doubt. Teaching is by definition an uncertainty. We leave our classrooms still "running the tapes" of the day, wondering who or what we forgot. Our shoulder bags are heavy with the past and future — papers to correct, plans for the next day. Our heads are stuffed with children, crammed full of problems to resolve and next steps to identify. Our bodies are pumped up with the success of the day or pressed down with the failure of a single moment.

I know teachers who drive children to the eye doctor to make sure that those glasses are repaired; teachers who keep special stashes of peanut butter and crackers for the ones without breakfast; teachers who provide extra outings to museums or camps to extend horizons in one more way. A friend recalled the need to periodically bunk children in her own house when their parents went on overnight drinking binges.

And even with the most loving care and the best teachers, children fail. They mess up, they defy parents or teachers and go their own, sometimes self-destructive, way. There are no assurances — "no-fault" insurance isn't available. Despite tireless efforts and exceptional talents, we have only partial control over the results that are our children. Teaching is, by definition, uncertainty.

I attempt with this book to reconcile these uncertainties through the ordering of my experiences, an ordering which, by necessity, places the integrity of theory against the immediacy of the classroom. The theories concern what is known about how children learn and how they develop.

I hope with this ordering to confront my own uncertainties with honesty, to share my struggles, and to pass on an affection for moral and ethical behavior.

I See You, I See Everything

Introduction

"Good morning"

The children drift into school in the morning and make their way into the classroom. The teacher stands by the entrance and welcomes them. A message is on the chart next to her.

"Good morning Leah . . . Hi Andy . . . Morning, William . . . Morning, Renee. I like your new scarf."

Leah mumbles a response. Andy nods and scurries off. William waves, sort of. Renee continues, head down, into the room. The teacher, feeling like a piece of furniture, realizes that she is now getting cranky.

At morning meeting time, she informs the group, gathered in a wide circle, that she looks forward to seeing them and she likes to show this with a "Good morning." What is she to think, she asks in a somewhat joking way, when she says hello and someone says back, "mmf" or "grrr," or pulls back — she imitates a turtle receding into a shell. Giggles. The children enjoy the pantomime. How nice it feels, she tells them in a more serious vein, to hear a hearty round of "Hello" or "Good morning" or "Nice day." Perhaps we just need some warm-ups, she suggests!

"Good morning, Eddie." Eddie smiles and looks around. "What might Eddie say now?" the teacher asks.

"Good morning, Ms. Charney?"

"Yes. I'd like that. Eddie?"

"Good morning," Eddie manages in a quiet voice.

"Good morning, Justin."

Justin replies with spirit, "Good morning Mrs. C."

"I like that nice strong voice, Justin. I also like hearing my name."

Then Justin is asked to greet someone else in the circle, until there is a full round of "good mornings" and every single person in the class has been named. Every student has been greeted, and has named and greeted another. In this "game," each child is spoken to, named in a friendly manner, and is responsible for continuing that manner. The mood of the circle is now awake and even gay. "Yes," the communication implies, "we are glad to be here. Yes, we are glad to see each other."

3

The "good morning game" initiates each morning meeting until there is a spontaneous flow. Weeks later, the teacher bends over the very quiet Eva. "Good morning, Eva."

Eva, with a shy, crooked grin, looks up, and with her face almost touching her teacher says, "Good morning." In a sudden gleeful gesture, the two rub noses and then go off to work.

The water table

The group at the water table has been instructed that water stays in the water table. Water may go in buckets, in funnels, in vials, but not on each other. That is the rule.

The class has practiced good ways to keep the water in the table. They have demonstrated ways to pour. They have also practiced using a mop. They have been eager to try out this new area in the room for a "choice" activity.

Ricky is quick to garner vials, buckets, and hose-like extensions for his work. He deftly hooks up a pump to a hose and with proper pressure releases a stream of water through the hose and into a bucket. Ricky casts a furtive eye about the room. Next there is a high-rising spout, then a minor geyser, and finally a predictable eruption cascading out of the bounds of the table, drenching the floor and his neighbor's feet.

"Ricky, you wet me!" cries the offended child.

"I didn't mean to. It was an accident," he retorts, with an equally indignant stare, looking for the whereabouts of the teacher. I observe that Ricky, with his furtive glance, is not merely exploring the force of his instruments, the thrill of seeing water travel a distance. He is also testing out the limits of his force, the distance between him and the teacher.

"Ricky. I noticed that you were doing some interesting experiments. I also noticed that you weren't using the rules. You need to leave the water table now. Perhaps, tomorrow you will choose to remember to use our rules."

Sherill

The fifth grade class is writing. Sherill has been looking about, putting occasional marks on her paper, erasing, crossing out, staring out the window. For a while she appears to study her friend, who is busy, writing and writing. "Did you see Jesse's haircut?" she whispers, trying to start a conversation.

Rachel looks up from her writing and nods, but quickly loses interest in Sherrill's comments and returns to her own story. Sherrill gets up and flounces across the room in the direction of a pencil sharpener, weaving in and out of the tables, her arms swinging recklessly. The inevitable happens. A folder goes flying off a desktop, its pages scattering across the floor.

"Can't you watch out," cries Beth, as she gets up to collect her sheets of writing.

"I'll get you," Sherrill hurls back and stomps over to her seat.

"Sherrill," the teacher says softly. "You seem to be having a hard morning. Perhaps you'd like to tell me about it ... or maybe even write about it. Sometimes when I'm in a lousy mood or having a bad day, it helps me to write a letter to a friend even if I don't send it. And some people like to write in their journal or make up a scene for a story. What do you think would work for you now?"

Sherrill shrugs. "I don't have a friend to write to."

"You could write to me."

"Maybe."

"See what happens. I'll check back in a few minutes."

Sherrill laboriously smoothes a fresh piece of paper, selects pencils, and, head close to the page, begins to write. Gradually, the tension in her face and her fingers relaxes. She writes continuously until the period is over, then carefully folds her paper and slips it into her desk. As she gets up to go to her next group, she calls over to Beth, "Wanna' have lunch?"

◆

This book is about managing a responsive classroom and teaching children to care. It draws on my many years as a teacher in inner-city schools and, more recently, in an independent school which was founded in order to apply a developmental point of view. The most important thing I have learned is that discipline is a subject to be taught, just as reading or arithmetic is taught. It is taught year after year without apology. It is taught with the conviction and affirmation of the teacher.

I started out knowing so little. I was ill-prepared to succeed in the classroom, but I learned. What I have learned will always need to be refined and revised, but it has given me focus and courage. I hope that readers will gather strength and renewed vigor from this book so they can face the endless list of challenges: unruly Jerome, "Make-Me Annie," Sean of the Spitball Hall of Fame ... the fights before and after school, the lunchroom frenzies, the boots that Lee denies he put in the toilet ... the pencil that belongs to Chris that Jenny insists she found in her desk ... the notes, the secrets, the cliques ... the ragged transitions, the minimal effort on assignments, the no-effort excuses ... the tattling, the teasing, the sneaking ....

Teachers face enormous pressures. It is a struggle just to survive as a proud teacher of today's children in schools which may lack even the basics. It is a challenge to help children grow up to be decent and kind, and to retain our faith in ourselves, our children, and our expectations. To meet these challenges, we need to know how to manage a classroom and how to teach our children to behave. We need to know how to pass on an affection for moral and ethical behavior in a difficult world.

Twenty-five years ago I was applying for my license as a New York City public school teacher. There was an oral exam. I recall my innocence uneasily and the scene vividly. I entered a dimly lit classroom. In the rear of the room sat three crouching figures. In my mind, they were all in black cloaks! One of the figures was making a rasping sound as she filed her nails. The filing stopped only as the question was read in an absurdly slow and nasal voice:

"Imagine that you are teaching a lesson. From the back of the room, one of your students tosses a paper airplane. You ask him to stop. He does it again. What will you do?"

I answered the question with all the cockiness and confidence of one who has never taught. It was actually so simple. In my mind, there were two choices. I could take the "Tough Authority" approach and invoke a chain of command which would end in a punishment for the misbehaving student:

"Either you stop or I will take away your paper and book."

The student is on a roll. Quietly, he extracts page 37 from his geometry book and folds it neatly into a 747 design, which swoops and crashes only moments after I have made my decree.

"That's IT! Jane, go get The Principal."

The Principal will call his mother. His mother will call his father and then he'll get in trouble, which will assure his future cooperative behavior in my class.

Or, I thought, I could assume that the student was simply not interested in the geography lesson that was underway. If properly motivated, no child misbehaves. Thus the answer would be to refocus the lesson. I pick up the airplane and begin a brilliant lesson on aerodynamics:

"What is it that makes planes fly?"

"I dunno'."

I hold up the paper model. "What is it that makes this plane fly?"

"I threw it."

I am not to be put off with such wit. I take out a flat sheet and ask, "If I threw this paper, would it fly?"

"Nah."

Soon the recalcitrant student and others in the class are enthralled and productively exploring the mysteries of flight. They are comparing model planes. They are observing and calculating the flight patterns of different wing designs. Robby is making a graph. Christine is measuring distances to the quarter inch. Our previously disruptive student has just left on a mission to the library to research books on airplanes.

I use the second approach for my answer. When I finished, the examiners thanked me. I left feeling confident and righteous. The rasping had stopped and I had passed the exam. I went on, with license in hand, to teach my first class. Later, I discovered that I was not being graded on the content of my response. I was not graded on my educational expertise. My examiners were attending, not to teaching skills, but to my syntax. Because I spoke in English sentences, I passed.

I also later realized that my answer was a daydream, a fine fantasy. It wouldn't happen like that. It could happen that such a wonderful exercise would infuse the classroom, but not without what I had yet to learn: classroom management.

I went into my first classroom knowing about curriculum, interesting new ways to teach math and reading, and how to get terrific materials. I spent a lively summer in a workshop, building, planning and collecting. I set up my first grade room in centers, with tri-wall dividers I had constructed myself. I had an easel in the art corner. I had a salt-water aquarium in the science center. I had over twenty new books in the library and all different shapes and colors of pasta in the math center. On the first day of school, I surveyed an inviting and rich learning environment. I was proud of it all.

I will never forget what my Grady and Jerome and Michelle did to that room in the first week. The paint from the easel went straight from the room to the principal's office, along with Jerome. Pockets were heavy with pastas, which were eaten raw, thrown and stepped on, but not sorted or classified. The salt water aquarium soon resembled the Meadowlands Swamp, a repository for just about everything. Books were torn in an effort to speed-read, and rather than the eager and busy sighs of intent learners, there were whines and whimpers:

"Teacher, LOOK."

"Teacher, he broke my pencil."

"Teacher, what do we do now? Is it time to go home?"

It was a disaster. I felt personally wronged. I blamed the children. I blamed the school. I blamed everyone and anyone. I cried and was ready to quit. I knew that I had to quit or I had to learn to run a classroom. In that crisis, I decided to learn. I cleaned up the mess. I junked the dividers. I observed other teachers, experienced teachers who still smiled. I began again. From that awful beginning came the greatest insight of my teaching life — a teacher can teach children to behave.

With time, patience and determination, I could get Jerome's paint on the easel. After two years, Grady stopped puncturing materials and people. The books were being read. The pastas were sorted. The children made choices. It became a learning room. I understood that children didn't need to come to school knowing how to behave. But, they had to have a chance to learn it deliberately, slowly, and with encouragement. I realized that I can teach it — that *we* can teach it. I can look at my next smart aleck or menace and think confidently, "I'll get you. You'll learn!"

In my living room, there is a painting. It shows a world of red and green and yellow. Circling the world are children holding hands. Carefully etched in and out of the circle is a bright blue sky and a radiant sun. It was painted in June by Jerome, my most careless painter in the fall. It was a present to his teacher.

In this book, I share techniques which I used with Jerome and others. I describe approaches and tools I use to set up rules, expectations and significant consequences. These ideas are based on my own experiences and the insights and work of many, many teachers. The book is strongly influenced by my work for the past ten years with the Greenfield Center School, a unique collaboration of teachers working toward a functional, caring community for both children and adults.

These teaching approaches also represent what I have learned from the work of educational and developmental theorists. Their words are liberally quoted throughout the text and their ideas are etched into, and between, the lines of the book. (A selected bibliography is included.) I did not invent this material, but patiently collected and collated what I understood from observations and readings, until it felt like my own. I hope teachers will treat this book the same way. It is meant to be a living and livable guide. If some of these approaches don't work for you, I hope you will find yet another way.

The aim of every chapter and every technique is the creation of self-controls and community, which I define as the capacity to care about oneself, others and the world. A single, basic goal is to teach children in such a way that they gain affection for ethical behavior.

"I'll try myself"

"Jessica called me a bad name."

"Did you talk to Jessica?"

"Yes. I tried but she wouldn't listen."

"What do you want to say to Jessica?"

"Not to call me names."

"Show me. How will you tell Jessica that you don't like names?"

"Jessica! I don't like when you say I'm stupid."

"I wonder if you did something to make Jessica mad? What do you think?"

"Well . . . 'cause I didn't want her to take the markers 'cause she keeps them too long."

"Oh. So maybe you should have shared the markers. Do you want to try to talk to Jessica again by yourself or do you need my help?"

"I'll try myself."

◆

In this section, I introduce and describe the basics of managing a responsive classroom:

- The goals of self-control and community — Ch. 1
- The techniques of the first six weeks and their extension through the rest of the year — Ch. 2
- Some basic classroom rules and how children can be involved in their creation — Ch. 3
- A system of logical consequences for children's actions which includes problem-solving class meetings and a time-out procedure — Chs. 4, 5, & 6
- Some approaches to children who engage in power struggles — Ch. 7

1

Intentions

*The development of a child's potential depends on the
ability of the teacher to perceive the child's possibilities,
to stimulate the child to learn, and thereby, to make
the child's latent potentiality a reality.*

Rudolf Dreikurs
Maintaining Sanity in the Classroom

We need to approach the issues of classroom management and discipline as much more than what to do when children break rules and misbehave. Rather than simply reacting to problems, we need to establish an ongoing curriculum in self-control, social participation and human development. We need to accept the potential of children to learn these things, and the potential of teachers to teach them.

The best methods, most carefully planned programs, most intriguing classroom centers or exciting and delicious materials, are useless without discipline and management. The children can hurl the Lego's and crash the blocks, or they can build fine bridges. They can ingeniously combine rubber bands and paper clips to bombard unarmed classmates, or they can construct mobiles and invent robots. The critical difference is the approach to discipline and management. It is not enough (and not possible) to motivate students continually with dazzling demonstrations of paper plane aeronautics or new adventures. We spend too much time looking for gimmicks and catchy topics

9

to teach, when we should be looking for something else. Children don't learn by being entertained. They learn by doing, and finding success in the doing.

We go into teaching prepared to teach reading, math, writing, and social studies. We prepare for subjects. When I have to stop a lesson to remind Cindy not to interrupt, to discipline Patty for sarcastic remarks to David (who gave a wrong answer), or to quiet the voices of students not part of my group, I clench my teeth and mutter about "wasting time." Incorrectly, I start to feel that discipline is a time-waster, a symptom of problem students and poor teaching. If only I had the good class!

I *do* love to teach reading, writing and math. I love to help children decode new words, to share discussions about evil fictional characters, or to help them compose a thoughtful essay. But I've come to love being a "disciplinarian."

I have grown to appreciate the task of helping children learn to take better care of themselves, each other and their classrooms. It's not a waste. It's probably the most enduring thing that I teach. In a world filled with global violence, threats of nuclear and environmental devastation, where drugs and guns are available on nearly every street corner, learning to be more decent and to build caring communities is hardly a waste of time. Safe and effective communities in the classroom are rarely by-products. They are built through our commitment and conscious design; they grow from our best energies, time and attention. My strongest hope is that we will begin to envision our schools as centers dedicated to social growth and ethical behavior. We need to prepare in order to teach children how to behave, and we need to know it is not a waste of time.

Taking the time

Time is golden. How we use our precious classroom time defines our priorities. Our schedules often become a battleground for conflicting interests.

In a public school in Connecticut, a number of third through sixth grade classrooms in the school began conducting "morning meetings" as a half-hour ritual each day. The class gathers, gives greetings, shares important news and enjoys a game or interesting group activity. Teachers, students and parents overwhelmingly agreed that it contributed to a friendlier, more relaxed atmosphere. "You get to know other people better and find out things about them," wrote one student.

Both teachers and students looked forward to their morning meetings to hear each others' news, play together and get set for the day. But two years later, the school's writing mastery test scores (tested in early fall) were low. There was a school-wide mandate for more writing instruction. Teachers began to ask, "Is it OK if I just do my meeting for twenty minutes?"

The meeting time, which helps children and teachers look forward to school, was put in competition with instructional objectives. Could these teachers squeeze more writing into an already heavily-scheduled day? To squeeze in more, they had to squeeze something out — or burst!

In this battle for time, we need to remember that academics and social behavior are profoundly intertwined. In this case, the opportunities to talk and listen in morning meeting provided some of the conversation and confidence critical to the writing process. A responsive audience of teacher and peers offers a powerful incentive to share through writing, and to care about school. The more children care about school (because of friendly feelings, the chance to be heard, or things they want to find out) the more likely they are to grow academically as well as socially.[1]

A social curriculum, one which permits us to teach self-control and social participation, takes time. Time to stop lessons when the tone of the room is awful. Time to discuss what went wrong out at recess. Time to tell others about the baseball game, the new baby sister, the death of a pet. Without time in our day to talk to children and to allow them to talk to each other, there will be no discipline, only disciplining.

Discipline as learning

The word discipline is derived from the Latin root *disciplina*, meaning learning. It needs to be associated with positive acts and feats of learning, rather than negatively associated with punishing. Teaching discipline requires two fundamental elements: empathy and structure. Empathy helps us "know" the child, to perceive her needs, to hear what she is trying to say. Structure allows us to set guidelines and provide necessary limits. Effective, caring discipline requires both empathy and structure. This approach to classroom management involves the systematic teaching of discipline — it is a basic curriculum which flows through every classroom activity. There are two basic goals for this approach:

1. Creation of Self-Control
2. Creation of Community

Creation of self-control

We need to strive for the creation of self-control in children. It is the first purpose of classroom management. This purpose is summed up by a quote

---

1 See *Social Skills Rating System* by Gresham and Elliott and *Circles of Learning: Cooperation in the Classroom* by Johnson et al.

from John Dewey in his pamphlet, *Experience and Education*:

The ultimate aim of Education is creation of the power of self-control.

The key word for me in this quote is "power." Power, says Dewey, is the ability to "frame purposes, to judge wisely . . ." The power of self-control is the power to assert yourself in a positive way. It involves the capacities to regulate yourself, anticipate consequences, give up an immediate gratification to realize a long-term goal. It includes the ability to make and carry out a plan; solve a problem; think of a good idea and act on it; sift alternatives; make decisions. For children, it is the ability to enter a new group and say hello, to make new friends, to choose activities, and to hold fast to inner thoughts and beliefs. It isn't an innate power, says Dewey, but one that is "created."

I see children demonstrate this power daily. I observe five-year-olds during their first week of school trying to sit still in a circle, a clutch of wiggles, wagging hands and babbling voices. Six weeks later, there is a real semblance of order.

They are working on "being the boss" of their own bodies, staying "parked" in their spot, keeping their hands only on themselves, listening. They have learned songs, poems, numbers and everyone's name in the group. Mikey is telling a story about his bike. Maggie's hand starts to go up. She sees a slight shake of her teacher's head and remembers. Her hand goes down. She will wait — wait until Mikey is done talking to tell about her bike, " 'cause the same thing happened" to her on her bike. Self-control allows listening and waiting.

Dewey refers to the "creation" of self-control. We are not born with self-control. It is not inherent, a given attribute or gift. It is a creation. Teachers can engage their students in that creative process through a step-by-step sequence of instruction. The sequence is interactive and contextual. Teachers and children interact through conversations and shared experiences. The subjects of learning come directly from the context, the immediate environment. We do not need to import or invent dilemmas because we live them. We use what we experience in the school environment: the squabbles and rejections, the fears and failures. The process engages all children, and all of us, in the course of a lifetime.

Merely removing external controls, Dewey stated, is not "a guarantee for the production of self-controls." Instead, it often leaves children at the "mercy of impulses." I have witnessed tense and troubling scenes when teachers abdicate their authority, leaving children without the protective guidelines of clear limits, boundaries or strategies.

"How will you decide who goes first?" Left on their own, children may decide on the basis of who is biggest and most threatening, who has the loudest voice or most expensive clothes. But proposing and modeling some alternatives (odd finger, pick-a-number, cut the deck, "eenie-meenie-minee-mo") imposes the reins of justice where either tyranny or anarchy might have governed.

"You have five minutes to see if you can figure out a way to work together and get along; otherwise you'll have to work by yourself. I'll be back to see what you decided." Teachers provide choices, even time limits as a natural constraint, so that children don't keep "spinning their wheels" and to assure them that the teacher will help them out of the rut, if necessary. But they need opportunities to make the ruts.

The process of creating self-controls reflects the diverse temperaments and personalities in each class and involves stretching children's potentials. Some children have an easy time with body controls, but those same children may struggle with mouth-control. The clumsiest boy may be the most generous playmate. The most patient girl may have a hard time controlling her giggles or secret-telling. The student who works with diligence in view of the teacher may flounder and daydream with independent tasks. The child who seeks endless approval and flattery from teachers or peers gropes for self-esteem. As we build self-controls, these children will explore more of their potential.

If self-controls are established at one point along the continuum of growth, it doesn't mean that problems, conflicts and stunning bursts of impulse and disobedience will be erased. Getting older is not a promise of getting better, especially if "better" is to be even-tempered and of predictable mind. Getting older means encountering difficult, and often painful, issues of growing-up, separation, and identity. The cheerful five and spirited six may evolve, at seven, into a child troubled by change, clinging to routines, fearful of risks and worried about criticism. A headache attends every new math lesson. Tears follow the loss of a game of tag. Then the fretful seven becomes the gregarious, easy-going eight, who bounds into school until she decides to join the boys' kickball game at recess and gets banned from the girl-clique and jump-rope games.

Our best management techniques will not eliminate these issues from our classrooms. They will only help us deal with them in ways that promote self-control and ethical conduct. I've described three main points in this assertion that the first purpose of classroom management is the "creation of self-controls:"

- We need to teach self-control in the same way we teach our academics, as a recognized and valued part of our school curriculum.
- Creating self-control involves teachers and children in ongoing interactions which draw on the experiences and context of day-to-day life in school.
- The acquisition of self-control leads to a more fully engaged and purposeful school life. It fosters positive self-assertion, and allows children to plan, make decisions, and carry out purposeful activities. They can become more productive and successful in school.

The creation of community

What good is academic learning if young people don't learn to become contributing members of society?

Jane Nelson
Positive Discipline

In today's world, it is particularly urgent that we extend beyond the domain of self and the lessons of self-control. We need to find connections to others, and to feel ourselves members of many groups — intimate groups, community groups, and a world group. These connections and responsibilities need to be taught as well.

We need to teach children to give care as well as to receive care. In today's society, our children are often victims of adult attitudes of communal neglect and individual entitlement. We must help them learn to contribute, to *want* to contribute.

Belonging to a group means being needed, as well as needful, and believing that you have something vital to contribute. Every child can contribute care for others in many ways — by listening and responding with relevance and attention, by showing concern for the feelings and viewpoints of others, by developing a capacity for empathy.

There is an inherent need to be useful and helpful to others. But because it is inherent doesn't mean that it automatically flourishes or is tapped. In our society, there are vast numbers of people who suffer from a lack of meaningful work. Children, too, suffer from a partnership of neglect and indulgence that results in a lack of meaningful responsibilities. They are not expected to demonstrate care, not accustomed to taking care of others. Creating community means giving children the power to care.

My thesaurus shows that the word "care" has some interesting and varied connotations. It can mean "to take care" — to trouble oneself, give thought, forethought, painstaking attentions. Or it may mean "to care for" — to provide for, to look after, show regard. It can also refer to worry, as in "having cares" or "cares and woes." Thus, caring is a burden, a commitment, hard work. When we teach children to care, we ask them to accept this burden, to commit themselves to the hard work of caring.

Teaching children to care often means helping them find ways to express their care. When confronted with a classmate's loss and sadness, what can they say? What can they do? "You can say 'sorry'," we tell them. "You can make them a card or keep them company."

I see children struggle to make a place in their group for newcomers. How can they reach out? I know that the new girls are lonely, miss their old friends, and need new ones. I see that the other children are unaware, comfortable in their old groupings and familiar routines. They are only eight, I remind myself, still awkward in social behaviors. Yet, they can learn to take notice and respond. With help, they may offer, "Want to join our jump-rope game?" or "Want to have lunch at my table?"

"You have a gift to give," I sometimes inform children, as I seek their help in including someone new, or someone it's easier to avoid. There is a clear sense of self-worth, well-being, and pride when children show the "ethic of caring." Even though it's seldom spontaneous, it improves the world and "I," at six or ten or forty, *did* that improving.

To create community and to teach caring is an on-going challenge. My group of tens and elevens (4–5th graders) were planning a party day for the successful completion of their school store. It was a day earned from the proceeds of their work. They had shopped each week, ordered merchandise from catalogues, kept account books, computed prices and learned to be kindly shopkeepers. They had given over recess times and stayed after school. They had cleaned up. Some complained of overwork and some got headaches, but they had kept it going for a year and now they could celebrate.

At first it wasn't clear how to celebrate and how much of the profit might be used for a party. After several discussions, there was a proposal to divide the assets into three chunks. One chunk would be reinvested in the store, but what about the other two? As I listened, I was sorely tempted to manipulate the outcomes. I was queasy during their discussions when the percentages for the "good cause" and "their cause" were tilted in favor of the latter.

Figure 1.1

BUILDING COMMUNITY

We build community each day when we expect children to:

- Know names — know and use each other's names, get to know each other's interests and feelings
- Take turns — without arguing, pouting, or quitting
- Share — the center of attention, private time with the teacher, space at the sandbox or computer, snacks, crayons, markers, etc.
- Make room in the circle — for late comers, or children who aren't "best friends"
- Join activities — join small groups in a constructive way
- Invite others to join
- Be friendly — greet and include others (not only friends) in conversation and activities
- Cooperate — on projects, to solve problems or play games with input from everyone
- Solve conflicts — by talking about problems, sharing points of view, reaching mutually acceptable decisions without name calling or hurtful behavior

These community expectations are balanced by respect for individual needs — there are times during the day when you don't have to share, you get to pick your favorite, you get what you really need.

The end-results were not the most generous. Still, they were stretching. They were giving some of their earnings to others in the community: the homeless, who they read and heard about but didn't really see, and the "battered," who were also a faceless presence in their lives. These problems and others were largely abstractions — and these children are still concrete learners. Their intellectual grasp of these issues had a fragile foothold without input from direct experience.

To themselves, they gave a party: video, pizza and soda. They accepted, with grumbles, the teacher's ruling of no R-rated movies. They accepted, with resignation, that everyone wouldn't get their first choice, but no complaints were allowed. They enjoyed their morning movie, their midday pizza lunch and their afternoon soccer game. Then there was a request for ice-cream.

"We still have some money left."

"No. No ice cream," I replied.

"You're mean," said a whiny voice.

"No fair," said another.

"It's our money," joined yet one more.

This went on for a few minutes until I lost patience and felt that a sermon was inevitable and irresistible.

"What a privileged day," I began. "You have enjoyed so much. When you continue to ask for more and use those whiny voices, you sound ungrateful. When you try to manipulate and complain, you sound greedy. I don't like it. It's time to appreciate what you had and stop asking for more."

It was time for an adult to reset the boundaries, provide limits and expectations. It's still hard at age ten or eleven to locate those end-points. Sometimes a teacher has to simply yell, "Enough, already!"

There were certainly other "stretch-marks" to this experience. Even with its last-second deterioration, the celebration capped a positive learning experience for the group. They had made group decisions and abided by them. They shared in the enjoyment of their party, and held their positions in the soccer game. They kept to the limits of their spending and honored their pledge to give away one third of their earnings to help others. I recall one student saying persuasively in class discussion, "Our parents will support the store more if we give money away to a good cause." If that is not the crux of virtue, it still indicates that generosity is *expected*. It is part of a caring community.

A few years ago, my daughter shared a dream. In the dream, she was invisible. No one could see or hear her. She alone could see and hear everyone else. What she could see were frantic attempts to escape, and what she could hear were cries for help as bombs dropped into her school. "Let this be a nightmare," she screamed. "Let me wake up."

I didn't know how to comfort and reassure my daughter, how to erase her nightmare. I didn't know how to assuage her fears. Should I have lied to her, promised her that the world is safe? That children are not in danger, that violence is not real? Or should I tell her the truth, that her nightmares aren't much different than many adults' because our world is often circumscribed by violence?

Yet I don't dare be discouraged. I am invigorated by the dedication of so many colleagues and students to a safer world. Part of our mission is to create communities with fewer nightmares, where self-control and care for others minimizes the possibilities of violence.

Allison

A group of three children in the second grade class were seated around a table busily shaping and molding chunks of clay. Their chatter kept pace with their hand work. The teacher, moving about the room, stopped to observe the threesome.

Allison turned to Bobby, "After school, I'm gonna' get you . . . and then I'm gonna' punch your head in."

Bobby ignored her and turned to Juan, "Look at mine. It's a flying gorilla."

"Blood will come out of your nose . . ." continued Allison.

The teacher approached Allison, knelt next to her and cupped one hand over her clay and the other around her shoulder. "Stop your work for a moment and listen to me."

Allison reached for her clay, but turned back to her teacher, "What?"

"I just heard something that I really don't want to hear in our classroom. I heard some threats. Threats talk about ways to hurt people. You have a much more important job here. Do you know what that job is?"

"No . . . doing your work?"

"Yes. Doing your work of taking care of each other. That's a very important job that you have here. Not to threaten each other . . . to take care of each other. I know that you can do that."

"She won't," announced Bobby suddenly.

The teacher nodded firmly, "She will!"

2

I See You, I See Everything

I spend the first six weeks of school teaching my children how to behave. It rarely takes less time, sometimes it takes more. It takes six weeks even when many of the students were in the same class last year, and have been in the same school for several years. I cannot presume that what was so clear last year is remembered and accepted this year. I start again.

I do not apologize for this use of time. It is not a waste, not a waystation along a more important course of educational mastery. It is the critical foundation of learning. It is the first curriculum. I call it "classroom management." The emphasis is not on the 3R's of "readin', ritin' and 'rithmetic," but instead "reinforcin', remindin' and redirectin'."

In the Introduction, I described my initial teaching disasters. From my colossal mistakes grew important insights. The first and perhaps most important understanding was that to feel safe, children must feel *seen*.

A first classroom

I had participated in a stimulating summer workshop for teachers. In the workshop, I learned to tie-dye, make musical instruments, play logic games and build simple structures with tri-wall carpentry. I proudly and enthusiastically fashioned my classroom in Harlem, NYC from all I had learned that summer. I organized my room in centers, each wonderfully partitioned (with MY dividers!) for definition and privacy. I littered the areas with "goodies" I had made or salvaged.

I soon discovered, however, that when I was watching the group in the art area, I couldn't see the math corner. When I concentrated on the library, I couldn't see the easel or the science corner. And when I was working at the blackboard, I couldn't see anything at all!

Frequently, as I skirted the room, or disappeared into one of my centers, the children couldn't see me either. I quickly turned into a whirlwind. They tested the durability and scaling- potential of my tri-walls, and chased after me with a constant bleat:

"Look at me, Teacher."

"Look at my drawing, Teacher."

"Teacher, look what Jerome did to my book."

"TEACHER! LOOK!"

It was worthy of one of the classic primers: "Run Teacher Run. See Teacher Run. Run. Run. Run." I became weary and suffered serious headaches.

I was not a quick learner. After several weeks of wiping up spills, re-gluing bindings on books, making excuses to the principal for the disorder in the halls, blaming everything and everyone — from "*these* children" to "*this* system" — I had had enough. I swept the room clear of partitions. I removed three fourths of the materials. I plunked my chair down in the middle of the room and me down with it. In a fine, firm, clear (maybe even loud) voice, ripe with conviction, I announced, "I see you. I see everything."

♦

I realized that children need to be seen. It was a simple matter of safety and a more complex matter of recognition and trust. Developmental studies tell us that six-year-olds need to be seen so they will not climb walls. Fives need to be seen so that they can be free to venture off, leave the enclosure of the teacher for experiences with play and work. But I have also found that seven-, ten-, and thirteen year-olds need to be seen, just as they also need their private nooks and crannies. They need the encouragement and validation that comes from our best attention to their efforts. They need the safety that comes from the belief that their teacher sees them, *knows* them. Mutual trust grows from this security. When all children feel seen, they are released to work.

"I see you" is not a threat, but rather a message of caring and regard. When we say "I see you," the "seeing" is not always literal. We may "see" our children and trust them, at times, to be quite on their own. But not during the first six weeks.

"I see you" — noticing what children do right

My chair, my table or desk is where I can see the entire classroom. When I work with a small group, my chair is turned so that I see the room. I often gather the whole group in a circle so that everyone sees everyone else. I walk in the back — not the front — of the line. I see everyone. And everyone knows that

I see because I let them know with my comments, over and over. The keys to the first six weeks are:
- Seeing behaviors and individuals
- Commenting positively on what you see by reinforcing, reminding, and redirecting.

Seeing your children

"I see you." I see Devon struggle with his writing, puncturing holes in the paper in frustration. I see Lisa avoid the expected routines in her scramble to make contact with her friends in the morning. I see Ricky test limits. I see Molly waver in her new role as a friend of boys as well as girls. I see Chris "forget" his "have-to's" so he can play games. I see my students enter our room, heads down, neglecting common courtesies.

But primarily I see the efforts, persistence and desire of the children to please. They *want* to meet the expectations of their teachers, follow the rules correctly, execute each new skill, and succeed in their new class. To sustain that hope, I must focus on their positive energy and accomplishments:
- "I see that you are remembering how to keep your bodies still."
- "I see that you remember to raise your hands."
- "I notice the way Patty looks at Jamie when he speaks."
- "Jessica and Tim wiped off the paint jars and got the lids nice and tight."
- "Monica, I see you worked hard to make your butterfly sketch so realistic."
- "Thank you for fixing the pencil sharpener."
- "I notice that you are waiting so patiently for your turn to drink, Angie."
- "I notice that you are ready so quickly today for math group."
- "I like the way you included new people in your project."
- "I see that you are really trying to make those letters even. It looks hard."
- "Andy, I see that you've helped Laura a lot. I think you need to do your own work now."
- "I notice that a lot of people in this group are interested in the news."
- "I see . . ."

Commenting on what you see

> . . . for children, hope is as important as breathing.
> Sara Ruddick
> Maternal Thinking

Each time you comment, your tone and language are extremely important. They set the tone for the positive accomplishments which we often think of negatively as "discipline." For example, when a child runs down the stairs, you might say, "Jimmy, don't run down the stairs," or "No running, Jimmy, that's the rule." But rather than catching and correcting Jimmy, you could remind and redirect him instead, "I see too many steps, Jimmy. Show me again how you walk down the stairs." Appropriate comments are:

- Encouraging — they support children's efforts
- Specific — they name a behavior or accomplishment and avoid general labels of "good" and "bad"
- Positive — "Show me what you will do . . ." rather than "Don't do that"

Some examples of positive attitudes and language are provided in Figure 2.1 I concentrate on reminding, reinforcing, and redirecting. Remember that the focus of this entire approach is noticing what children do *right*.

Stages

Classroom management is, in part, a process of instilling expectations, routines and skills which allow children to work with competence on their own, in a group, or with a partner. Among other things, they need to learn to use materials, make choices, lower their voices, take care of themselves in the coat area, and respond to others even when we don't see them. To accomplish these tasks, we first must establish that we see them take care of the classroom. It doesn't work to try to rush or condense the process. Rules and skills need to be explained, demonstrated, modeled and practiced, then tried. I want to be able to say, "I know you know how to do . . . how to take care of . . . how to manage yourself during . . . And I know that because I've *seen* you do it."

But how can I do all this seeing?

How do I begin to teach a group to understand place value, trade seventeen ones for one ten and seven ones, and still keep track of that bunch in the library corner? How do I see if Jeffrey bluffs or reads? How do I have a conference with Kate about her story, if I stop every two minutes to remind the group working on their spelling to "spell" rather than chatter?

How do I notice who is remembering to put caps on the markers, put crayons carefully back in their box, put the gluepot lid on and return it to the shelf? How do I notice all that when I am instructing my group to blend consonant sounds with a short vowel "a"?

I DON'T! When I am immersed in teaching a group new skills, or concepts, I need to give them undivided attention. So, I do *not* begin the year teaching new skills or critical content lessons. I do not begin with intensive writing conferences or math assessments. I spend six weeks teaching children how to choose books, find supplies, set up their writing, monitor their own voice levels, make efficient transitions, ask for help from classmates, work cooperatively, and many more "how-to's." This instruction takes patience and a certain determination. It takes confidence that it is important work.

It is my practice to "open" the classroom gradually. Only some of the areas will be used the first week. Only some of the materials are out on the shelves.

Figure 2.1

COMMENTING ON WHAT YOU SEE

Here are some examples of commenting on what you see.

Reinforcing
- "I notice the way you remembered to carry the scissors point down."
- "I notice that you remember where to put your work so I can find it."
- "You are really scrubbing the brushes."
- "I notice that many of you like to share your drawings. The nice comments I hear really help people want to share."
- "I notice lots of different ideas and ways to draw trees. I like that people have different ways to do things."
- "I notice that most of you are taking time to read the directions and are now figuring out things for yourself."
- "Nick and Jimmy worked hard to solve a problem on their own this afternoon . . ."

Reminding
- "Before we go to our next period, remind me what you will need to do."
- "Who remembers what you will need to get for writing? Show me."
- "Remind me, what do you do if you can't think of how to spell a word?"
- "Who thinks they remember where to find a dictionary in our room? Show us."
- "If someone asks you to play a game, what are friendly ways you might respond? Remind me."
- "Remind us, what happens in our class if someone makes a mistake?"
- "Jackie, I see you walking around the room. Remind me, what's your job right now?"
- "Denise, remind me, what happens if someone needs to use the markers you are using. What can you say?"

Redirecting
- "Pencils are for writing, Stephen . . ."
- "I hear a lot of talking. This is your time to get your folders."
- "I see a lot of paper on your desk. Think about how many sheets of paper you will need. What's a good thing to do with the rest?"
- "I hear conversations about television programs. What do you need to be thinking about now?"
- "I want to hear quiet voices . . ."
- "I see a lot of silly-looking stuff at this table. I'll hold your papers for now. Tell me when you're ready to begin work."

New materials are introduced slowly. New expectations and responsibilities are also introduced gradually, in three stages. Each stage has its own objectives and criteria for moving to the next stage.

Stages One and Two take place largely during the first six weeks of school but are reinforced the rest of the year. Stage Three begins towards the end of the first six weeks and continues through the rest of the year.

Stage One focuses on the class, as a whole, learning expectations for behavior. Stage Two introduces the responsibilities for working in small groups, and for working independently while the teacher concentrates on a small group. Stage Three initiates new skill and content instruction.

These are broad, overlapping categories, but they do outline a progression which will vary with the unique character and rhythm of each class. Some of my classes, for example, need more time to establish whole group routines and coherence, while others "gel" as a group but take more time to build independence and interreliance in small group situations. The pace is adjusted by the teacher's assessment of the learning, rather than enforced by any strict time guidelines.

Stage one: whole class learning

The basic goals for this initial stage are listed below. In general, children are evolving the work habits and behaviors which create competence and promote respect. They are learning to:

- Listen
- Use kind language
- Ask questions
- Share solutions to problems
- Put things away
- Have fun and enjoy jokes (that don't rely on teasing)
- Get ready in a timely way
- Know everyone's name
- Follow the rules of the classroom
- Carry out orderly transitions

Stage One is a time when the tone for the whole year is established and basic classroom routines are introduced and mastered. Positive accomplishments are stressed. The following examples are activities directed toward the goals for this stage.

Choosing a book

When I send children off to the library corner to select their own book for independent reading (an important decision for active readers), I know that prior instruction has to take place. A few fluent readers would have no trouble picking a book they want to read. But many are accustomed to having books selected for them. So how do they choose? How will they know they want to read a particular book? We need to discuss ways to select and choose.

We talk about criteria. For example:

- Interest: "Will I like it?" "How do I find out without reading it first?"
- Readability: "Can I read it fairly easily?"

I send a group of students to select a book and to practice using these criteria. I watch. I notice children checking bookflaps, illustrations, skimming the first pages or conferring with each other.

I also notice that others grab the first book they touch, as if they got a prize for being the first done. Jeffrey glances at the cover, satisfied, and trots off quickly to stuff the book in his bin. "I'm done. What do I do now?" he asks. Choosing a book and reading it are clearly not related for him.

"I noticed you picked your book out quickly," I say. "I'd like you to show it to me." Reluctantly, he extracts it. He tells me he picked it because he likes horses. Horses are on the cover. He has met the first criterion. But the book is too difficult for Jeffrey to read and he has gotten into a habit of bluffing. I ask him what else he likes about the book. He tells me he likes thick books. I ask him if he prefers fiction or factual accounts of horses and point out a few more books on easier levels. "Check those out," I say, and walk away.

From the corner of my eye, I see him look through the book with photographs. He studies one of the pictures intently, exclaiming aloud, "I know about Arabians!" He takes the book to a desk and gets involved in the pictures, sometimes attempting to read the text. Later, he takes both the "thick book" and the picture book and puts them in his bin. It will be a year's work to help this ten-year-old read with honest and serious intent, overcoming resistance, fears, and painful issues of self-esteem. This was just a start, a message that involved seeing and commenting on his positive work. It helped Jeffrey and the whole group understand some of the expectations for the new year.

Class writing expectations

A group of sevens and eights are concluding morning meeting. The next thing on the schedule is class writing time. We review what they will need to begin writing:

"We need folders and paper," offers Martin.

"We might want drawing paper," adds Ramon.

"We could bring two pencils, 'cause sometimes one breaks," suggests John.

"Fine remembering. What else?"

"A clipboard if we want to sit on the rug?" wonders Matt.

"Good idea. When do you think is a good time to get a drink or go to the bathroom? Are you going to sit down — jump up — sit down? Watch me, tell me if you think I'm really going to accomplish my writing?"

The teacher acts out taking her seat . . . oops, forgot paper. Back to her seat . . . oops, need a ruler, jumps up to get a ruler. Sits back down and starts to

write and then — oops, waves her hand to ask a question about a lunchtime errand. The performance is a tad exaggerated, but the disruptions are ever so familiar to the children, judging by their broad smiles.

After modelling what not to do, the teacher demonstrates what concentration might look like. She gathers her supplies, sets up her work space and begins to initiate her story. She then phrases her expectations, "I know it's pretty hard to concentrate for a full half-hour. But I think your bodies and minds are ready for the challenge and I do want to find out about all those topics you talked about writing. Let's see if we can get close to a full half-hour writing time today. Have a nice writing time."

The children disperse from the meeting area and go to collect their materials. I know that just because Matt and Stephanie said (just minutes ago) that they will need pencils and notebooks doesn't mean they will sit down with both. I know that the reality of sitting for thirty minutes and staying on task is far from established. It's a stretch. Hands will go up:

"How do you spell . . . ?"

"Is it good?" — after only the second sentence.

"Can I get a drink of water?"

Minds will drift — out the window, to neighbors and inner worlds. My students are in the process of developing work habits, learning independence and extending their attention span. Some write with abandon, documenting every meal, every article of clothing, every action they can recall about a family camping trip. Others can't decide whether to write about their baseball team or space invaders. And some have stories that just don't come out of their heads, or make it to their hands or past the pencil!

"I see you," I say. I sit at my table, my chair turned to face the room. I watch the transition. I comment:

"I see you did remember to bring two pencils today, Joey."

"You found your folder so quickly today, Katie."

"So many quick starters!"

"Good idea Mark, to bring a cup of water to your desk. Now you won't have to get up at all." (I'd bet he'll figure out another way!)

"I see many busy writers."

These comments, addressed to Mark, Katie and Joey, are also intended for the group. What does the teacher notice? The teacher notices the positive efforts students make to get ready for their work. Her comments encourage these efforts by pointing them out.

As the group settles into their writing, I may circulate. I am still attending to the *how*, more than the what, of the activity. I primarily want to see the way children are going about their writing, rather than the specific details of *what* they are writing.

"I notice the way you helped each other with some spelling words."

"I see that you are really concentrating."

"What a fine start to your story."

"Interesting idea to start with a picture."

"It looks like you have decided on your topic."

"How's it going?"

"It sounds like you had quite an adventure and are excited to write it all down!"

"I see you are trying out the mapping strategy to get started today. How's it working?"

There are no magical words. I want to let the children know that I am interested and that I see their positive efforts as writers. A smile, a nod, a pat also reinforces that I know they are hard at work. I will also remind and redirect the "wanderers" gently:

"I wonder if that conversation is helping you concentrate?"

"I notice that you've worked a very long time on the illustration. Will you be ready to start your writing soon?"

"Remind me, Jess, what do writers do if they forget something about their topic?"

"Is this the time to figure out about lunch arrangements? What do you need to be thinking about now?"

"I notice so much erasing. What's an easier thing to do if you don't like something you've written?"

"In just five minutes, I want to come back and find that you have picked one of your topics and are ready to write today."

"Remind me, what helps with the jump-ups, Josh?"

At the end of writing time, I compliment the group on their work. I let them know that I saw many writers concentrate for close to thirty minutes. "How many of you found it hard? How many found it easy today?" I remind them that it would not be easy for me to run for thirty minutes unless I practiced. Everyone will get a chance to practice again tomorrow.

◆

Stage One is devoted to whole class activity. It is a time to set a tone and expectations, and create a positive group ethic. Simple procedures, which we often take for granted, help set that tone: group meetings, signals for quiet, "circling-up," choosing a partner.

"Circling-up"

We are about to go outside to play a group game. Week One. Day One. I give the class two directions: "I want you to hold hands and make a circle when you get out on the field. I will count and see how quickly you can do that." Curiously, I have found that the older the children, the harder this will be. I am prepared to be patient.

I walk in the back of the line. The children are ahead of me. As they reach the field, they form a loose huddle. Some take hands. Many race about looking for just the "right" hand. I am counting "1 . . . 2 . . . 3 . . . " Jed won't hold a girl's hand. Marty is trying to find her best friend's hand. "18 . . . 19 . . . " Sam is exploring the limits of arm-spans till bodies jerk and tumble. "35 . . . 36 . . . 49 . . . 50" and there is a collected mass that is holding hands, an approximation of a circle. I am still counting. Their faces show puzzlement. Why am I

counting if everyone is holding hands?

"Does this look like your idea of a circle?" I ask. "How will you make it a circle?" Some move out, some move further in. Back to counting. After almost five minutes, they are standing still, holding hands in a circle. They have achieved the simple directions.

"Well," I say, "you did it. It took to the count of 250, a long time. I expect you to do this to the count of 20. Last year's class record was 10. I noticed that some of you quickly took a hand. Some of you stood still and waited patiently. Some of you helped create a circle. Let's see everyone help this time. I will say 'scatter.' At the signal, 'Allee-allee-in-free,' I will expect you to circle-up and hold hands. Twenty seconds! Scatter!"

This technique conveys a tone. Does the teacher mean what she says? Does she care *how* something is done, not just that it gets done? Are there expectations about care and treatment of others — refusing to hold the hand of someone of the opposite sex, only holding hands of your "friends?" When all children are expected to hold all hands, the message is that we are all friends in this class. Period.

◆

The process also reinforces that behaviors need to be taught and learned, and that learning them is not a waste of time. The smooth transition, the "good circle," the quiet line-up, or the responsive class meeting won't happen the first time, but they will get better the next time. They will be even better the third time.

A safety signal

Inside the classroom, a bell rings. It's the class signal that means "freeze." "When you hear that signal you stop — you stop everything. You face the

person who gave the signal. You are ready to listen."

The bell rings. Children freeze . . . somewhat. Matt is still finishing his drawing. Cathy continues to drink from the fountain. Angie moves over to get next to her friend. A clutch in the library area continues to read their books.

"I see that many of you know just what to do when the bell rings in our class. I see Jonathan has stopped and is looking right at me. I see that Jessie has put down his pencil and looks at me. I see that the group working at the math table is still and ready to listen. I don't yet see EVERYONE. Go back to work. I will ring the bell again. I hope this time I see everyone freeze."

The quick response to the bell improves, but when the teacher begins her message, talking and distractions resume. It will take more than one practice and more than one day to work on "staying frozen" until the "melt" signal is given. This is an essential safety system. The teacher must be able to get the attention and hold the attention of the entire class, even when groups are deeply involved and scattered about the room. Or, in the rare case of an emergency the teacher needs to silence the room, make an announcement, and begin the transition. Later even students may ask to use the signal: "I can't find my book. Did anyone see it?" or "It's kinda' noisy here. Would people please be quieter?"

Morning meetings

This daily gathering of the class builds the principle of group and develops the ethic of an attentive and responsive group. Children count on and internalize the consistent and predictable events which become morning meeting rituals: greetings; time to share personal news; a repertoire of games, chants, and songs; classroom news for the day. The strength of a morning meeting also depends on the capacity of children to take responsibility for the routines of the group: active listening, relevant comments, enthusiastic play, sitting still, raising a hand. There is a lot to learn.

Meetings vary from teacher to teacher and class to class. Each meeting incorporates the character and flavor of the group. Each teacher evolves her own rituals.

"It's time for meeting . . . It's time for meeting . . . " is the melodious signal in Ms. Porter's kindergarten-first grade class. The tune passes spontaneously as children drift over to the rug, their meeting area. "Where is Rosie, where is Rosie . . . there she is . . . there she is . . . " they go on to sing.

In Mr. Deppen's fifth grade group, they begin morning meeting with naming, without the melody. Every student is named, everyone included in the circle with a resonant "good morning," and everyone has the responsibility of greeting and including others. Noticing who has yet to be named takes keen attention and watchfulness. No one gets left out.

In Mrs. Jordan's fourth grade, the children enjoy shaking hands, sometimes in a bashful manner, sometimes with a strut, but everyone is smiling.

My group makes number sentences for the calendar date. It is September 20th. We will need 20 sentences for the number 20. Who has one? "I hope we don't have school on the 30th!" someone whispers.

Molly says, "1/5 of 100 is 20." Molly loves to be first and loves to demonstrate her superior skills. Danny is next. "100 take away 80 is 20." Patty's turn. She says with hesitation, "9 and 9 is 20." I notice Molly smirk and nudge her neighbor.

I say with strong feeling, "I like people to contribute in our circle. It's pretty easy to do that when you feel very sure of what you know. It takes courage to speak when you don't feel so sure. I want this to be a class where everyone feels they can contribute, their math ideas, their singing voices, their stories — their sure things and their not-so-sure things. That's what's most important."

Often during meetings, someone gives an answer that is not correct. *It's an opportunity to teach "right behavior," not "right answers," a critical moment to set tone and group ethics.* I am easily reminded of the childhood fear that lurked in my stomach every time I had to give an answer, so afraid to be wrong that I rarely volunteered. I dreaded "those looks" and barely smothered giggles. I was afraid to be wrong — to forget 7 times 8, the capital of Maine, the longest river, the last verse — but I was not afraid or hesitant to ridicule others. Such fear stifles and hinders learning. I give a clear, direct, emphatic message to my students, *"I will not allow it in my classroom."*

It is something that needs repeating, year after year. A mistake is made and someone laughs or shows-off by blurting out the right answer. Someone else provides "the look" which says, "You should know that. That's stupid." But, children do learn. They learn first at morning meetings, then transfer the learning to other parts of the day. "Workers never laugh at each other's mistakes," is a favorite class rule. It allows children to become an honest, yet gentle audience for guesses and presented work. They become empathic listeners.

In our morning meeting, there is a time for sharing events and experiences which occur outside of school. Morning meeting serves as a transition, connecting lives at home to lives in school. In our routine, a student makes a brief report and then asks, "Any questions or comments?"

The rest of the group then becomes active. They may ask for more details, probe for more information, make reactive comments. They *learn* to respond with attention and authentic interest. When we permit the outward appearance of indifference (bodies turned away from the speaker, whispering to a neighbor, staring out windows, even wandering away), we encourage disinterest. When we expect the outward appearance of attention (looking at the person speaking, sitting still, a verbal response), we provide conditions for interest to develop.

On this day, Willie shared a story about a bike mishap. There were lots of questions for Willie.

"What part of your knee was hurt?"

"What kind of wheels do you have?"

"Don't worry, your bike can be fixed pretty easy 'cause that happened to me."

"When I fell off my bike, I was scared to ride it and my Dad said I had to. Are you scared to ride now?"

Then Alice showed the class a calendar of cats that her Grandmother had given her. "Will you pass it around?"

Deidre reported that her mother got a new job. Deidre wasn't sure just what the job was, but her Mom starts today.

"Any questions or comments?" No hands. Deidre is a quiet nine-year-old, apt to hang-back and give a sour appearance. I raise my hand. Deidre calls on me shyly, "Mrs. C."

"Are you glad your mother has a new job?"

Deidre replies uncertainly.

Janie's hand (at half-mast) "My mother got a job recently. She comes home tired and grumpy." Deidre smiles at Janie.

"What kind of job?" someone asks Janie. Before Janie can answer, I intervene in order to redirect the sharing back to Deidre. I do that by selecting a student and asking him for one more question for Deidre. He complies.

"Thank you for your interesting sharing. I'd love to hear more about your mother's new job so let us know what you find out," I conclude.

In this case, I tried to model a response with a question and comment. I also redirected the meeting when it began to shift away from the original sharer. Some children are naturally more outspoken and popular. Some command more attention from their peers. The group dynamics can be quite complex. The more comfortable and secure the group becomes, the more our quiet, reserved, or less popular children can risk coming forward.

◆

It is my goal to create a responsive tone, not to rearrange personalities. My expectations for a responsive classroom include the obligation of the group to respond to each other. Later on, I might speak directly to the class to discuss the reasons underlying this obligation, using both discussion and role-playing techniques.

Discussion in morning meeting

"I really like the ways that you show you can listen and care for each other. That is an important way to use The Golden Rule. How did you do that today during this meeting?"

"When we ask questions?"

"When we share."

"Yes. What are some examples of that sharing this morning?"

"When we told Willie we were sorry that his bike got broke?"

"Yes. I think that shows real care for Willie. You also listened. You remembered that he told you about the broken spoke. You remembered he skidded on rocks. You remembered the name of his bike. That must show Willie that you paid careful attention to his news." Heads nod in agreement.

I often use myself as the example for unpleasant situations so children aren't put on the spot. "Suppose I tell you about something that happened to me. Suppose when I ask for questions or comments, no one raises their hand. What would I think?"

"That we're not interested."

"Maybe that we don't like you."

". . . I know that sometimes you might be interested and you even might like me, but you are waiting for a good question to pop into your minds. Yes?" (It's important here to avoid judgment.) "But while you are waiting, it's quiet and I'm just sitting there. I don't feel very comfortable — do I? How can you help me?" Again, I want to move quickly towards a constructive and active tone, not a blaming one. The first encourages and engages my children. The second is apt to create a defensive resistance or even hostility.

Role-playing in morning meeting

I role-play frequently with children, ages five to thirteen, particularly for social issues. The children are quick to get the picture, and a role-play quickly builds excitement. "I need a volunteer." There is an eagerness to be "It," and I choose one of my more confident and assertive students. Whispering a plan and sending her momentarily out of the room, I explain to the rest of the group that when Jill shares her news, we will be silent. Jill returns and quickly improvises a sharing. It doesn't take her long to get into the part. The class gets into their part, too; they sit mute! We see Jill's cheerful face constrict into a scowl. After just a minute or so, she droops and we stop the "play."

"How do you think Jill feels?" I ask the group.

"Bad" they unanimously recognize. Jill feels bad.

"How did you feel?" I ask Jill.

"Lonely" she replies.

"Now, let's see how you might help Jill, help her to feel good and not so lonely." Immediately, the group provides soothing and supportive comments. In some ways, the activity has taken on the flavor of a game. There are more volunteers to be "Jill" and an excited plea to do the play again. But in another way, these nine-year-olds are gaining a sense of their own power — the power they have to affect others for good or ill. As we help children use their power to accept each others' mistakes or affirm others' sharing, we nudge them in a positive direction. The power that children exert finds a positive outlet in the construction of community.

◆

During Stage One of the first six weeks, I introduce the areas of the room, and establish routines and ways to use materials. We start a routine called "quiet time." Children need to choose an activity that they wish to do alone and quietly for a sustained period of time: puzzles, sewing, drawing, reading, independent math sheets. I observe as some students do elaborate things, others dream and a few watch the clock.

During this stage, I set up an art activity or a new technique for using the pastels. We may go outside and sketch a tree in the school yard. I urge them to look at shapes, textures, colors. I ask, "What part of your sketch do you like the best? What part do you think you might want to do differently next time?" I am teaching children to self-evaluate, to survey their own work before asking, "Teacher, is it good?"

The children have to know the place for the stapler, know how to carry scissors, where to find the bin for lined paper, the place for finished work, the proper storage for the paint brushes. I demonstrate. I explain. I model. One technique for opening the room is called "Guided Discovery."

Guided discovery

The process of "guided discovery" opens the areas of the classroom and prepares children for different aspects of the curriculum. It isn't necessary for every material or every activity, and it may present both familiar and new resources. One year, I started fourth graders with new techniques for using the number two pencil (in pencil sketching). Learning to work with care with a crayon — or a microscope — enhances its use and potential for individuals and groups.

Guided discovery lessons may introduce the entire class to areas of the program, such as how to use the library area or a "choice" period. They may establish routines for an entire group or for independent working. Certainly, as children develop their facilities with materials and routines, they become better able to manage them with minimal teacher supervision.

In any guided discovery lesson, there may be the following objectives:

· Motivate and excite by exploring possibilities
· Stretch individual students toward involvement in new or extended areas of learning
· Give information and ideas to guide and deepen the understanding of materials and activities in the classroom
· Give instruction in the techniques and skills needed for effective use of tools and materials
· Establish a common language and vocabulary
· Share ideas and procedures for independent use of the material or area (this goal may be prompted by children who have invented alternatives or found new ideas)
· Teach or reinforce social or cooperative guidelines
· Teach and reinforce care and clean-up routines.

The box of crayons

I often introduce a box of crayons or a large set of markers with more than thirty different colors during the first week of school. Even with older groups, I deliberately start with a common material, one that is taken for granted. I want to extend possibilities, as well as model a considered approach to the resources of our classroom.

I have covered the box of crayons with a wrapper. "Who can guess what I have? I'll give you a clue—it's something we regularly use in school." Quickly, this six-year-old group, feeling and shaking the package, guesses correctly.

"Yes. It's a box of crayons. But how many? A few or a lot?"

"A lot," replies a chorus of voices.

"Well. What's a lot?" I write down some of the numbers, enjoying the ideas of quantity that vary so with this age. One thousand, some say. Twenty-hundred is another possibility. Eighty-eight, a more precise fellow suggests.

"How will we find out?"

"Open it," come the excited answers.

I unwrap the package, but don't open the box. "Where does it tell us exactly how many?" As I hold up the box, different children try to locate and distinguish the numbers. Finding them easily, they are satisfied. And some will read them. But is it 46 or 64?

"Sixty-four crayons. That is a lot. Think now — are they all the same color? Are there sixty-four blue crayons. Sixty-four red crayons?" A quick poll shows that most are pretty sure there are sixty-four different colors. "Do you think you might be able to name 10 . . . 20?" Lots of nods.

Remember now, what we are exploring is a standard box of crayons, not a jazzy new product! By the time I actually open the lid in order to display sixty-four different colors, there is considerable interest, even drama. "Let's see if you can figure out ten of these fancy colors. I wonder . . ." The children eagerly begin to name, first the obvious, and then silver, gold, turquoise. I put their inventory on a chart, locating the crayon with each given label. They name ten, then twenty, and are pleased with their own knowledge, excited by their discoveries.

Perhaps I will add one new color. "Here's a very fancy one . . . magenta, it says on the label. Can anyone guess what color magenta might be?" I wiggle it in the box, keeping it hidden. Guessing adds to the final pleasure of discovery.

"It's sort of like reddish-purplish-pink" someone says.

"It's like Kim's shirt."

"Magenta . . . magenta," someone else sings.

The concept that there are shades of color, that magenta is a shade of red, would be an interesting one to develop in another lesson or might be the focus for an older group. Now, I move on to using the crayons. I explain that later in the morning there will be a drawing time. They will have a chance to use these special boxes of sixty-four crayons. "Where do you think we should keep them?"

"On the art shelf."

"Why would that be a good place?"

"Cause you use them for drawing and art."

"Yes. They are things that artists use."

"How do you think artists take care of their crayons?" I tell them that I've noticed how full the box is and how hard it can be to take out the crayons and find where to put them back. I demonstrate. "Should I just dump 'em all out, cause I'm in a hurry?"

"You gotta' be careful," someone tells me.

"Show me how you would be careful." A student comes up and gingerly extracts a single item. I make it "tricky" and shake the box, challenging her to then replace it. She does. "How did you know to put it there?"

She smiles. "I could see."

"What could she see?" I ask the others. The rest of the class peers into the box, intrigued with this mystery. Others want to try, but I remind them that they will all have a chance when it's time for art (or "choice").

"I've noticed something else about these crayons. I've noticed that they have a pretty sharp point."

"It's kind of roundish, too," someone observes.

"What do you think will happen if I need to press down hard to make it dark?"

"It will break?"

"You shouldn't do it so hard."

"It gets flat."

"Suppose I want to make a dark sky and I press hard and it does break, but I want it sharp again. Does anyone know a way to sharpen a crayon? Can you sharpen crayons?"

"They get stuck a lot."

"They do get stuck in pencil sharpeners. Is there another way?" We might experiment with different types of crayon sharpeners at another meeting — a group of seven-year-olds once took off on a study of crayon sharpeners! But for now, I just introduce the tool.

Before finishing the day's discovery lesson, I may need to talk about sharing. As one of the children finds space on our art shelf, I ask someone to count how many boxes we have in our class. There are six. "Will that be enough for everyone? Suppose more than six children want to use them at the same time? Suppose the whole class wants to use them for drawing later? How will we do that?" This may be a good time to introduce, or reinforce, behavior and language for sharing. Both are accomplished with modeling and role-playing:

"If I want the black, do I say, 'gimme it!'? What should I say, remind me . . ." I ask a child to demonstrate. I may propose other dilemmas. "What happens if the box is out of my reach?" or "What if we both need the same crayon at the same time?" I find that children need to go through this, even when they have heard it before, and even when they are ten years old. It is an important achievement to manage these courtesies. It helps children be polite, kind and helpful to each other, to visitors, and to teachers.

"Show me that you remember how to ask someone to pass over a marker," I say. "Who knows what to do if you have been waiting for the brown crayon for a long time? Is it OK to grab?"

As the children go to work with the crayons, or the math manipulatives, or their new readers, the role of the teacher is to watch. She can reinforce the discoveries, notice the careful handling of the material, observe the social behaviors.

"I see that you are trying both light and dark coloring."

"I like the way you are passing the box around the table."

"What nice words I hear . . ."

"You found another new color. What other color do you think it's like? Would you like to add that to our chart so others can look for it?"

And, of course, the teacher must remind and redirect when children "forget," because the process will always break down — for sixes and eights and tens. (See Appendix E for more information on Guided Discovery.)

Establishing routines

Efficient transitions, good clean-up, and friendly partners evolve during the first six weeks. It is important to remember that groups seem to have their own sore points and strengths. What might be a major drama for fives (like going to the bathroom) is a simple routine for the eights, while grouping-up may take more work for the eights (so the boys are not all on one side of the circle and the girls on the other).

The bathroom routine

Bathrooming is a basic and fundamental piece of management. If routines are established, it reinforces a sense of autonomy and self-regulation. Few classrooms have their own bathrooms, so unless children go on schedule, they must take care of themselves. But if a child doesn't follow the rules, you must say, "You'll have to wait until a teacher is able to go with you. It's *your* choice." Children can quickly assume this responsibility, but we shouldn't take it for granted. Establishing this routine increases the potential for self-controls — even when the teacher isn't watching.

Of course, there are lapses. Six-year-old boys may attempt a mad dash into the girls' bathroom. Six-year-old girls come back giggling or in a snit to expose this outrage. Eight-year-olds need reminders that bathrooming is not a social event — "You do not need to go every time a friend needs to go." Many tens also love to congregate for social purposes, to tell secrets or gossip, out of the eye of the teacher (they hope). Restless students make numerous forays especially when the subject matter befuddles them. Graffiti and petty vandalisms are common bathroom misdemeanors.

I recall when Maurice's mother came to school to find out how come I never let Maurice "go." Maurice, it turned out, was afraid to go to the bathroom by himself. A small, reticent child, he was picked on and teased. "Baldy-bean" they called him and snatched his protective cap off his head. And it was Jerome and Grady who proposed confidently, during class meeting, that they escort Maurice to the bathroom, "so he don't need to be scared of nothin'." They were class bullies, apt to exploit classmates cheerfully — for a nickel they would ensure a safe passage from school to home, mostly safe from them. This partnering accomplished several important changes in our classroom. It helped Maurice go to the bathroom. It also helped Maurice feel he had friends in school. And it helped Jerome and Grady be friends instead of bullies.

◆

It may seem easier to take children to the bathroom (although terribly time-consuming). Many schools still do. It avoids hassles and problems. Or does it? It is my strong contention that the routines of our classrooms (from bathrooming to helping a classmate master a times table) must be used as opportunities to teach decent behavior, not constrict it. The time we spend establishing those behaviors during the first six weeks of school is essential to a responsive classroom.

So we practice with our fives going to the bathroom, walking down the halls, first together and then in pairs. We teach our sevens to put up a name card on a "Bathroom Out" hook and to remember to remove it when they return. We are prepared to reinforce and remind, because if they "forget" the rules or choose not to follow them, they may lose the privilege — at least until they are ready to show they are able to remember and choose to follow the class rules. There are consequences, but they aren't consequences which release children from their job — safe and proper bathroom conduct.

Moving on from stage one

Although there are always slips, times when even the most basic routines and expectations need to be re-established, I know when a class is ready to move on to Stage Two by five simple criteria:

1) They group up quickly for meetings, story time, games, work periods.
2) They can locate and replace materials in the room.
3) They listen and make relevant comments at meetings.
4) They can stay with an activity for the expected and appropriate period of time (there will be a few exceptions).
5) They can make simple choices.

"I see everything" — extending expectations

During Stage One, we need to see what is right in front of us, as the whole group learns expectations and routines. During Stage Two, we need to "see everything" so that we can expand the expectations of the classroom beyond our line of sight. We need to see if children are beginning to internalize those expectations.

Stage two — "paradoxical groups"

Stage Two of the initial six weeks establishes expectations for group work. It's a time when children learn to function in two ways:
• In small groups, with the teacher

- Away from the teacher, with independence.

It is the second which allows the first to happen. I call them "paradoxical groups" because I pretend to teach the small group, while I am actually continuing to teach the whole class.

It is essential that children work effectively in small groups, as well as a whole class. Some classrooms work extensively in small groups, most have at least some portion of the day when children are in a reading or math group. Small groups and independent work are ways to meet the different levels and rates of learning. Small groups can generate interest and participation, and they allow me to teach in greater depth, to pursue individual questions and divergent lines of inquiry. As I teach a small group, I provide a model for cooperative, peer-directed groups as well.

When the teacher is teaching the group, the rest of the class still needs to work productively. I will not be able to concentrate on my group if I need to attend to disruptions and interruptions coming from the other corners of the classroom. If the rest of the class idles or can only handle "busy work" without the teacher's undivided attention, a great deal of learning is missed. A primary objective of Stage Two is for children to learn to be productive while the teacher teaches her group.

The basic goals for independent work away from the teacher are explained to the children, and regularly repeated:

- You plan ahead what you will do.
- You decide what to do from clear choices. It is your job to know the choices. They may be posted or they may be announced at morning meeting.
- You talk quietly.
- You keep your mind on your work.
- You stay in the area you have chosen to work in (fives and under may change areas more often).
- You try to solve problems on your own or with the help of your classmates.

My strategy for teaching these behaviors is to provide the small group with work that needs little of my attention while actually focusing on the rest of the class. At first, the teacher appears to be teaching a small group, but the real agenda is "I see everything." While the teacher meets with a small group, her chair always faces the class. Her eye is towards the other students.

Establishing independent skills outside the small group

The bell chimes, signalling that it is time to get ready for the next class period. Ten of the twenty-six third graders have a math group. Others have a choice of reading or copying and illustrating a poem. It still takes five minutes for many to make a transition. There are reminders:

"I notice that so many of you get ready quickly."

"I see students ready with their notebooks."

"Jeffrey, you've chosen a good place to read today."

"Alice, will you really be able to see the poem from there?"

"Everyone needs to be settled now," I say. "Last chance — THINK. Remind me, what do you need so that you will be able to concentrate and work for this entire period?" There is a quick review of work habits. "Do I have everything I need? What will I do if I finish early? Have I found a good situation to do my work?" In this case, children have choices about locale — it is one of their responsibilities to find a comfortable place to read, or a good spot to write where they can see the chart with the poem.

My math group is seated around the table. There is a single box of manipulatives on the table. A few children start to grab objects from the box.

"How do you know what you will need?" I ask. Most shrug and remove their hands. "That's a serious question," I repeat. "How will you know what you will need to do for math groups?"

"You'll tell us?"

"Any other way?" I ask. My goal for this group session is to introduce written directions as a prompt for an activity. On the blackboard next to our table, I have written out directions. Someone notices and begins to read aloud. "When you think you know what to do first, show us by doing it." I have made the directions simple and easy to read. I observe the ease of response for different children in the group. Some go right to work, some seem cautious and hesitant, one student looks puzzled. After a few minutes, I ask, "What could you do if you're not sure how to read a word, or if you don't understand the directions?" I take time to affirm the many resources available in a group. "You can ask a friend. You can read it again. You can ask the teacher."

We will also talk about what it means to be helpful. I will ask some of the children to model asking for help and giving the help. This takes only a short time and soon the children have the materials they need and clear directions. They are ready to explore on their own. Now, I can do the essential task for Stage Two. I can watch the students outside the group as they follow through with independent reading, copying or illustrating the poem.

As my math group figures out different ways to combine and arrange the pattern blocks I have distributed, I reinforce the efforts of the others to work independently.

"I see very good concentration."

"I like the way people are using quiet voices."

"I notice the way you helped Paul find an eraser."

"Kyle, I see you are being very careful with your writing today."

Usually, I need only a quiet voice from my perch. But sometimes I get up and circulate, intent on affirming and confirming what I see. My attention is necessary to validate the importance of independent work. No matter what we say, there is a sense that the real business is in the group, the place where the teacher is. It *must* be clear that the work that is done outside the teacher's circle is also serious and has purpose. Otherwise, children will be all business in the group, while outside of it, children will fiddle! Our goals point to the essential learning that should be going on outside the group: planning, choice, sustained attention, problem-solving.

First, we need to pay attention to the work the children do outside the group. We need to make sure it is real work — not "busy work" which we give children largely to keep them quiet. Busy work is mechanical, repetitious and long. Real work is relevant, takes skill, provides a challenge, and may be interesting or fun. Copying and illustrating a poem that the class recites and enacts together has meaning. Writing it beautifully, centering it on the page, and illustrating its message takes skill. It certainly poses a challenge for many eight-year-olds. Marcie wants to do the title in cursive. Jess wants to do it fast, be done first. Carla is fascinated with Emily Dickinson's line, "The rose is out of town." She is working hard on drawing the rose.

Some of the children are already into the tempo and rhythms of their own industry. There is a cluster copying the poem. A few recite it, practicing with each other. Others draw the gentle autumn scene evoked in the poem with ease and pleasurable concentration. Comments and spontaneous utterances create a wonderful hum. I never object to talk. Instead, I want to teach children the distinction between distracting and productive conversation. The group reading on the library rug, for example, chatters about a "cute boy on TV." Distracting conversation, I decide. They need reminding ("What do you need to be doing?") or redirecting ("Find another place where you will be better able to concentrate"). Some return easily to their reading.

Others flounder. Mark erases over and over as he works on his poem, then stops and stares at the wall. Meg writes one word at a time, looking around, flicking her braids. Her gaze wanders over her paper and about the classroom with an abstract, dreamy look. Jimmy has created his own hockey arena with select crumbs of eraser and pencil. The goal is now Meg's adjacent paper. She becomes a willing goalie. Andrea monitors the room. "Teacher, someone's at the door," she informs me, seconds after a visitor arrives.

I remind and redirect Andrea:

"Andrea, you planned to finish the poem. If you are looking at the door, your eyes can't see the chart. Where will you keep your eyes? I want you to try to concentrate for the next ten minutes. Eyes staying on your own work. Think you can manage that? Show me."

I redirect Jimmy and Meg:

"I expect to see the poem finished. What do you need to do so you can accomplish that goal?"

I continue to reinforce and encourage the class:

"So many of you are working on your poems. I see fine concentration. I see lots of people keeping their minds on their work. The quiet voices help us work. I notice the way Carrie found something to do on her own when she finished her poem. I liked seeing people help each other recite. You look happy with your illustration, Carla."

I have not abandoned my math group. When I see they are ready for a new activity, I demonstrate a simple attribute game already known by these students. The objective of the game is to guess the general category that someone has in mind by asking if certain shapes belong to the set. "Pick a shape. If it's in my set, I will say 'yes.' If it's not in my set, I will say 'no.' After you have five 'yes' answers, see if you can name my set. Let's try a round." They are quick to catch on and soon generalize from the collection of small, yellow, red, green and blue circles (both thick and thin) that my set is one of small circles. The next set is a bit "trickier," and involves three attributes.

They go around the table, taking turns, with questions and taking turns inventing new sets. I am able to monitor both the activity of the group and class. I see that this group is able to categorize by three attributes, and to identify categories. I see they are anxious to get their turn and need reminders to go in order. When I change the game and assign them partners for the activity, I find they are more focused as pairs than as a small group.

Most of the other children have sustained their work and conduct for the period, though a few had trouble and it got more ragged near the end. At the close of the group, we talk about other ways to use the math materials for independent activity. We also go over clean-up, placing the objects in the container (not pitching them), checking the floor, and putting the bin back in its place on the shelf.

The bell rings again, signalling the end of the period. I again compliment the class on their independent work. I remind them that if they didn't get to finish their poems, they will have another chance after lunch. I ask everyone to think about what they have next on the schedule. I am satisfied that we have made progress during this Stage Two work period in both small group work and independent work.

Working in small groups: Self-Portraits

I use Stage Two to establish both work and social habits: how to look up a word in a dictionary, make a straight measure with a ruler, revise a first draft composition, or study with a partner. During this stage, my instructional objectives in reading groups, for example, concern *how* children choose a book to read and a time and place to read, rather than tackling what they know about main ideas or digraph blends.

"Self-Portraits" draws on a variety of skills that children will use all year long. It's a project that may be done by kindergartners through sixth graders and may be repeated year after year, with minor adaptations. Even a class of seventh and eighth graders produced a wonderful portfolio one year, using a detailed interview procedure and precise portrait drawings.

In the "portraits," children will record facts, events and personal feelings. They will tell about siblings, pets, and middle names, and describe likes and dislikes. They will narrate a summer experience or reveal interests and hobbies. And they will study their image in a mirror, carefully noting shapes of eyes, shades of hair color, contours of lips and textures of skin. They will draw themselves.

The project, adapted to each age level, involves a range of familiar activities and skills. It involves composition, art and research. To do their research and answer their questions, children learn to use a number of sources, from a phone book to a parent — "How do you spell Grandma's name?" — and learn to think about whether their answers make sense.

They also discover the satisfaction of sharing work in process, as they read and compare results. "I hate getting stung by jellyfish," Anthony writes, reading aloud as he works.

"You got jellyfish stings?" Christopher asks. Anthony tells Christopher about his day at the beach with jellyfish. Later, he expands the sentence into an entire story, prompted by the interest of a friend.

"I hate spinach and throw-up" a younger child notes, to a gleeful consensus that erupts around the table. An appreciative audience is a powerful motivation for work.

Jessica shows others how she blended the pastels to get shades of color for her portrait. Justin helps others punch the holes to bind the sheets of paper. The proficient readers will help the uncertain ones. The skillful artists will demonstrate ways to etch the eyes. The good spellers supply a word or two. The quick workers may help the slower ones. The group works on working together, a primary objective of the project.

As always, I remind, reinforce, and redirect:

"I notice the way Anita is helping Joey read the directions."

Some pages from an eight-year-old's Self-Portrait

Facts sheet

My age: _8 and a half____

My address: _Upper St._____

_Buckland, MA_____

My Mom's name : _Janice_____

My Dad's name: _John_____

My size: _4 Feet 3 inches + 4 half an inch_

I have _0_____sisters.

I have _2 Brothers_____.

There are _5_____people in my family.

One other fact: _I Wear Size 6 and a half in Womens Shoes.___

My family:

"What a good way to make a mouth. Will you share this idea with the class?"

"Remind me, how do the 'guide words' in the dictionary help us find a word?"

"If you're not sure what to do next, how can you find out? Show me."

"How is this conversation helping you with your work right now?"

"I notice the good listening I see when people are reading their stories to each other."

Along with the other objectives, I see something else from the self-portraits. I see my children. I find out who likes horses, who likes to invent, who loves to draw. I find out about big brothers and new babies and special grandparents. I discover the things that intrigue children, their particular fascinations and expertise. I notice the *way* they do things — who helps others, who is first to talk, who is in a hurry and who takes their time — as well as *what* they do. I have much more to learn, but this foundation will help the building.

It is still important that the demands of the small group do not absorb the entire focus of the teacher. As groups work on their self-portraits, the teacher continues to monitor the rest of the class, which may be busy with portrait work or may be doing another task. They are still learning to plan, stay in their

---

Like it or not!   Nicole

I Like	I Don't Like
Rideing MY Bike.	Mosquitoe Bites.
I like swimming.	I don'T like
I like Ice skateing.	Bee sTing's. I don'T
I like roller skateing.	like going to Be!. I
I like jumpingrope.	don'T like geTTing
I like Ice cream.	Teased. I don'T
I like finger knitTing.	like getTing Hurt.
I like camping!	I don't like War.

Best of all: I like ChrisTmas.

The very worst thing is I don'T like Throwing up.

---

if   NICOLE

If I were a color, I would be Red.

If I were a job, I would be Model.

If I were a machine, I would be Soda Machine.

If I were a teacher, I would be nICe.

If I were a parent, I would be Caring

If I were ice cream, I would be Mud Pie.

If I were an insect, I would be A Cricket.

If I were a mood, I would be Happy.

If I were magic, I would be Magiccian.

If I were a word, I would be

Beautiful.

seats, keep their minds on their work, control their voices and work cooperatively.

Everyone will complete their self-portrait book. The books will to be read aloud, cherished in the class archives and shared with families. Everyone will have learned, or started to learn, the ways I expect them to work in my class. And we will all have learned more about each other. We know about Marsha's operation, Gerald's motorcycle ride and Danny's dislike of bees. We even know Tommy's middle name.

Moving on from stage two

Before I can concentrate on teaching new skills, concepts, and content during Stage Three, the class needs to be relatively proficient in the following skills:

1) Children work independently for structured periods of time. They should be able to:
    * Choose an appropriate task
    * Choose an appropriate workspace
    * Stay on task for most of the work period
    * Moderate voice and physical movement.
2) Children work in pairs or small peer-directed groups (e.g., play attribute game, rehearse poem together). They should be able to:
    * Choose an appropriate task
    * Choose an appropriate workspace
    * Stay on task (illustrating, not tickling)
    * Moderate voice and physical movements.
3) Children work in teacher-led groups. They should be able to:
    * Come prepared and on time with necessary materials
    * Follow directions, written or spoken
    * Attend to group-given information
    * Cooperate with peers by sharing space, materials, information
    * Cooperate with the teacher by listening, asking for help if needed, participating in activities.

Stage three: independence and responsibility

Stage Three lasts the rest of the year and stresses independence and responsibility. The children are ready for content groups which require undivided attention from a teacher and present new, challenging subject matter.

The goals for Stage Three are part of a continuous learning process. Depending on the nature of the classroom, you may expect students to be able to:

- Follow-through with a plan for an entire work period
- Make an appropriate choice
- Demonstrate voice and body controls
- Solve a problem without the teacher
- Set up, care for and clean up materials
- Be responsive (helpful and friendly) when working with a partner, in a small group or in the class as a whole
- Care for the rules of the classroom

When I am teaching a small math group on decimals, the rest of the class works independently. Some are busy with a piece of writing. Some are busy with weekly assignments. A few work on an art project or play a game together. They are purposeful and engaged, using quiet voices, but if they forget — which they will — there are always consequences (Ch. 4) or "time out" (Ch. 6).

I don't always stay in the back of the line or observe the progress of the children through the corridors. I no longer need to angle my chair and divide my attentions as I sit with a group. Most of the time, the rest of the class is industrious and responsible as most of the children internalize their responsibilities. The words that remind, reinforce and redirect (although never scarce) are more focused and particular.

If during the first six weeks we have patiently taught the children how to manage, we can refer back to those basics at any time during the year. (See Appendix F for some expectations for a social curriculum.) If children internalize the expectations established during Stages One and Two, we can generally rely on their behavior as they grow in knowledge, independence, and responsibility. (See Figure 2.2 for an overview of the stages, including some content and techniques discussed in this chapter and later in the book.)

Summary

This process of classroom management is based on the assumption that to feel safe, children need to be seen. Literally, we see children, observing how they do things, as well as what they do. But we also "see" more symbolically. To be "seen" is also to feel known. During these first six weeks, we get to know new children, or get reacquainted with "old" ones. We show them that we know them by seeing what they do and commenting on it in positive language. *The more children feel seen, and thus known, the less we need to watch them.* We can extend independence and responsibility, the goals of Stage Three.

A final caution: this "seeing" is dedicated to knowing children with affectionate interest. It needs to be distinguished from acting as "Big Brother," becoming a judgmental, watchful presence which is intrusive and antagonistic, and involves hovering, over-correcting and negative surveillance. The "knowing" that we employ in our classrooms is most powerful when it is used to encourage and inspire hope — hope in the ultimate

Figure 2.2

GENERAL STAGES OF THE SCHOOL YEAR

	Goals	*Some General Content*
Stage One: "I See You" and Group-Building (1st 6 weeks)	• Listen • Use kind language • Ask questions • Share solutions to problems • Put things away • Have fun and enjoy jokes (not teasing) • Get ready in an appropriate time • Know everyone's name • Follow the rules of the classroom • Carry out orderly transitions	• Care for the rules of the classroom • Information and general rules • Guided Discovery for materials (e.g., crayons, math manipulatives) • 3 R's — reinforcing, reminding, redirecting
Stage Two: Paradoxical Groups (1st 6 weeks)	• Work in small groups with the teacher • Work independently away from the teacher	• Small groups • Expectations for "Choice" periods • Guided Discovery for areas (e.g., block area, computer center) • Discussion and generation of logical consequences • Role-plays of time-out
Stage Three: Independence and Responsibility (the rest of the year)	• Follow through with a plan for an entire work period • Make an appropriate choice • Demonstrate voice and body controls • Solve a problem without the teacher • Set up, care for and clean up materials • Be helpful and friendly when working with a partner, in a small group or in the whole group	• Content areas with Clear Positives defined • Small group work • Independent work • "Choice" periods

Some Specific Activities

- Safety signal
- Routine for circling up
- Bathroom routine
- Transitions
- Morning meeting — discussion, role-playing
- Expectations for choosing a book, writing periods, etc.

Criteria For Moving On

- Group up quickly for meetings, story time, games, work periods, etc.
- Locate and replace materials in the room
- Listen and make relevant comments at meetings
- Stay with an activity for the expected, appropriate period of time (with some exceptions)
- Make simple choices

- "Self-Portraits"
- Use of written directions
- Use of materials and resources — dictionary, computer, blocks, etc.
- Practice independent work

Work independently, in pairs, and small, peer-directed groups by:
- Choosing an appropriate task and workspace
- Staying on task
- Moderating voice and physical movements

Work in teacher-led groups by:
- Coming prepared and on time with necessary materials
- Following written or spoken directions
- Attending to group-given information
- Cooperating with peers and the teacher

- Problem-solving meetings
- Application of logical consequences, including time-out
- "Pretzels" or "Center Circle"
- Critical contract
- Individual "jobs" contracts

creation of self-controls and community.

During Stages One and Two, which encompass the crucial first six weeks, the following techniques are used:

- The teacher's chair faces the classroom so that the classroom is observed at all times.
- The teacher sees what is going on, and comments on behavior using positive language:
  * Reinforcing
  * Reminding
  * Redirecting.
- Students learn and practice the expectations and valued behaviors of the classroom. There are social as well as academic expectations.

Stage One establishes expectations for whole class routines and group cohesion — meetings, "circling-up," "freeze," etc.

Stage Two focuses on small group work ("paradoxical groups") and independent work away from the teacher.

Stage Three lasts the rest of the year and stresses independence and responsibility as children take on new, challenging subject matter.

I spend the first six weeks of school teaching my children how to behave. It rarely takes less time, sometimes it takes more. It takes six weeks even when many of the students were in the same class last year, and have been in the same school for several years. I cannot presume that what was so clear last year is remembered and accepted this year. I start again.

I do not apologize for this use of time. It is not a waste, not a waystation along a more important course of educational mastery. It is the critical foundation of learning. I first must give children the security that I "see" them as individuals and as a group. Then I work to "see everything," to extend this positive sense of security beyond my line of sight. When children begin to internalize positive expectations, they are then free to learn in an atmosphere that fosters independence and responsibility.

3

The Rules

Recently, I asked a group of teachers how they defined the word "rules." In their school, the rules were uniformly posted and highly consistent. The children knew the rules, which is important. But the rules consisted of lengthy lists of "don't's:" "Don't push. Don't talk out. Don't run. DON'T . . . " Yet, the definition suggested by these teachers was that rules were "guidelines." In general, guidelines frame what we *do* want, and what we hope to achieve or become.

Creating rules *with* children is an important part of the work of Stages One and Two during the first six weeks. These rules help set the classroom tone for the year. I have found children are more apt to respect rules they help make, and that rules lead to greater growth if they are framed in the positive. *I know that classrooms are happier with a few rules that are honored than many rules that are forgotten.*

I do not want my rules to legislate every action. I want them to encourage reasoned thinking and discussion. I want rules that we "like," not because they give license or permission, but because they help us construct a community that is orderly and safe. And I want rules that have meaningful applications to concrete behaviors, which require not just passive submission but active participation. This chapter describes a number of different ways to formulate these types of rules *with* children.

Foundations in theory

Active, participatory rules take into account what we know about human

development. Jean Piaget, Erik Erikson, Lawrence Kohlberg and Carol Gilligan have conducted extensive studies on the development of ethical and moral thinking in children. They have observed children's capacity to resolve conflicts and abide by rules at different stages of growth. The following is a summary of my understanding of a few of their basic ideas.

One underlying idea of their work is that knowledge is actively constructed, rather than passively received. That means that children learn by creating a "schema" — beliefs based on their own experiences — as well as by internalizing the "correct" models that are presented to them. The schemata which children form are often wrong, since they are based on insufficient experience to build accurate models. By comparing their "wrong" ideas with the ideas of others — adults and peers — or by experiencing the inaccuracies, they progressively refine their conception of the world. When we allow children to encounter problems, and to say what they think they can do about them, we help them acquire knowledge by refining their conceptions.

A second underlying principle of developmental psychologists is that children grow through predictable and progressive stages. These stages affect the way children think about rules and make decisions in situations of conflict. These may be broken down into three basic stages.

In the earliest stage, children see rules as based on the all-knowing power of adults. Compliance comes from the desire to please and gain approval from these adults, or from fear of punishments — "It's wrong to take things because my teacher gets mad and then I'll have to go to time out."

Young children's thought is also characterized by their egocentric thinking and need for immediate gratification. Fear of punishment or wish for approval may mitigate their impulses. Still, rules are easily bent and twisted in the face of keen desires. Leah, age five, wanted to go and pick berries, but knew that the rule was to ask permission first. Anticipating an answer of "no," she went instead to the garden, well out of her father's range of hearing and called out, "Cabbages, can I pick berries?" She then dutifully returned to the house, telling her babysitter that it was OK if she picked the berries.

Daniel, age two, was told over and over not to pull out the books from the bookshelves. He was found one day in a mountain of books, extracting one after the other, saying aloud, "No, NO, Daniel!" The words and deeds were still an unwed pair.

"Well I want to . . . I need to . . . I felt like it . . . I just had to . . ." may begin the explanation of a lie, a grab, a push, a pocket full of objects belonging to others, or other misdeeds. The young child may solemnly tattle on a classmate, or righteously cheat his way through a game, explaining, "It wasn't fair, he was winning and I didn't want him to."

The early years of school are marked by children's struggles to gain control over their bodies and to achieve a sense of autonomy, while still earning the approval of their teachers and parents. Even at the height of a testing period, I see children yearning to be perceived as "good" in the eyes of the adult. A five-year-old wants to master the limits, then quickly wants to test the limits at six. A six-year-old's sense of adventure takes her into places she knows not to go. When confronted with misbehavior, broken rules, or loss of control, children may (according to Erikson) experience a sense of shame or guilt. When the confrontation is too harsh and severe, there is a danger of stifling the growth of initiative and autonomy.

If, on the other hand, there is a weak or passive response by teachers or parents to children's misbehavior, there is the danger that the children will not develop an interest in restraint or ethical conduct. During early stages of development, I stress regulation that does not use harsh threats or instill fear, but is inescapable.

In the next stage of development, rules are seen as based on social conventions rather than individual authority. Children become aware of the shared nature of norms and values which are necessary for the game or the group to work. They struggle for the uniformity and consistency of rules, often at the expense of anything else. They begin to see rules as existing outside of adults, as part of society and its conventions, which prompts children to consider other factors besides the calculated risks or rewards of their most immediate intentions. There is an interest in ethical matters, a concern for fairness and the well-being of others. They do not consistently or easily act on these concerns, especially if social claims tug them in another direction. But there is a growing capacity to travel both intellectually and morally — to see the legitimacy of a broader view that includes, but is not limited to, the needs of one's self. They are beginning to believe that rules are necessary for the game to work, for events to be fair, and for everyone to meet their obligations to the group.

If at five or six, children worry that their teachers will dislike them if they are "bad," at eight or older, children aren't as worried about these labels. There is at least equal concern for peer judgment, and a fear of public exposure and embarrassment. But — and it is a big "but" for these children — there is an important second judgment. "Is the teacher fair? Are the rules fair? Do I get my say? Am I treated right?" While children are developing their own judgment, adults need to help them implement their own best intentions. At twelve, Ricky announces that he doesn't like teachers who "let you get away with stuff," and Simon says that he likes that his teacher can "intimidate" him into doing his work.

In the third stage of development, children may want to help their classmates not just in order to earn stars or social status, but also out of a belief that it's best if people take care of each other. This is the beginning of autonomous thinking, the capacity to be governed by ethical ideas rather than social approval and disapproval. During the growth of autonomy, especially through the critical periods of adolescence, children need opportunities to make choices on the basis of principled thinking, rather than in submission to the authority of adults or peers.

These stages of development can be roughly translated into age ranges. The first stage is most typical of the ages five through seven, the second stage is likely to include ages seven through eleven, while the third stage may begin anytime during adolescence and continue through adulthood. These stages also represent a progression of social and moral thinking, which depends in part on development and in part on opportunity. Growth is, to some degree, a reflection of a child's experiences. If, and when, a child moves through these stages — from considering only her own needs to considering the needs of others, and then to deciding matters of right and wrong apart from external sanctions — partially depends on the child's opportunities for growth. Opportunities to help make rules in the classroom are important for children's development.

I also want to mention here the interesting and divergent work of Carol Gilligan in *In a Different Voice*, which focuses on the development of moral thinking in women. She has identified two different ways in which people characteristically think about moral conflicts. One she called "the ethic of justice" and the other the "ethic of care." In the ethic of justice, thinking is focused on issues of equality and reciprocity, everyone getting a fair share. In the ethic of care, concerns center on needs for connections with others; conflicts may involve such issues as being left out or abandoned by others, or acting in such a way that others will be hurt. Critical values involve obligations to relationships, to show care for others. In her findings, these two approaches or "voices" are frequently identified by gender. Boys have a greater concern for issues of justice, girls for issues of response and connection. From an educational viewpoint, the ideal would be to encourage both an ethic of care and an ethic of justice: to provide opportunities for girls, for example, to examine the merits of a situation, regardless of whether a best friend is involved; and for boys to face up to questions of attachment and care-taking.

Making the rules

"We are all workers in school," I tell the children. "What are the most important rules we need to help us in our work?" Discussions follow, discussions that help move children from the most narrow self-interest to collective ideas of fairness and consideration. We work on rules for our games and rules for our classroom. Setting up rules may involve a lengthy process of construction, with the children taking much of the responsibility. Or the teacher may simply suggest rules that the children amend or put into their own words. Both methods work if children are given a voice and an opportunity to explore the meaning of rules before they are adopted.

The Golden Rule

*As you go through the life cycle, every stage of life has to add
something to the possibility of being able to obey the Golden Rule...*
Erik Erikson
Interview, Boston Globe Magazine

In the Greenfield Center School, the "Golden Rule" provides a unifying school ethic or principle. We call it our "one rule." It is certainly our first rule. We ask parents to read a parable called "Horse" to their child before the first day of school (See Appendix A). It illustrates many faces of the Golden Rule. It tells how a big, strong horse, leader of the pack, is afraid to cross a bridge that the smaller creatures scamper across with ease. It shows Horse's false pride and others' false perceptions. Fear and mistrust grow from ignorance, but finally interdependence helps Horse to "cross his bridge."

The parable suggests many concepts: the cooperation of big and small, bold and timid, and the strength of combining talents and attributes; that the small often tend the big; that mistakes and false starts may lead to growth and movement. We read "Horse" in class on Day One. We enact, play and discuss the meaning of the story by asking questions: "Are we ever Horse? Are we ever afraid? Do we ever need to get care? Are we able to give care? How is it that we can care for each other in our classroom and our school?"

We explain that the Golden Rule is the ideal. It describes how we want to be with each other and how we want to be as a school. "The Golden Rule," Robby says, "means you gotta' treat others as you want to be treated back." It directs us toward ideas of caring, but these ideas need to be anchored in particular actions and events for children to understand them.

We ask children to give examples of what it means and how to use this "one rule." Over time, we make up dramas and "what-if" plays:

"What if I am trying to concentrate and you are talking to a friend and I ask you to please be quiet. What might you say, if you are using the Golden Rule?"

"What if I accidentally bump into you? Do I say, 'Hey, watch out!'?"

"What if you fall down and get hurt? What could I do?"

"What if I can't solve a math problem and it's hard for me, but it's easy for you. Do you say, 'You can't do that cinchy math?' "

"What if we disagree about something? Can you disagree and still use the Golden Rule? How would you do *that*?"

"What if you ask me to play and I don't feel like it? What might I do?"

"What if a teacher asks you to help with something and you don't feel like it?"

We draw on the situations and events that are common to each age group. For fives, we focus on sharing materials, taking turns, or taking care of one's own body. Sixes may have trouble playing by the rules, even coming to some mutual agreements about what they are. Being the boss of yourself and not everyone else often involves the Golden Rule. Self-critical sevens are apt to be competitive and critical of others, as well.

Protocols of friendliness are important for eights and older. "What if someone asks to join your game and that someone isn't your best friend? Do you ignore the question? Give an excuse? Grumble a 'yes'? What do you do?"

When children use the Golden Rule they show respect for differences in people and different ways of doing things. Gaby needs time to think about her answer. "Are you using the Golden Rule when you answer for her?" Lucas writes using a special pencil grip. "You may want him to explain how he does that, but you are forgetting the Golden Rule when you make silly comments or tease." You are not sure about some of Micky's drawing. "How will you ask him about it and use the Golden Rule?"

The Golden Rule is introduced and practiced during the first six weeks of school. Children put it into their own words, write it out, and post it in the room. It is a rule that governs by its repeated use, not by a single instance. When a group of girls (ages nine and ten) flee to the bathroom to "gossip," we invoke the Golden Rule. When there is a sudden problem with disappearing pens, followed by casual accusations, we recall the Golden Rule. We remind students of it when Dolores is off by herself day after day, carelessly ignored by the rest of the class; when Dino is obnoxious and mean and everyone else gangs up on him in righteous retaliation; when children are rude and disruptive with their lunch aide; when globs of paste or reams of paper are left for others to clean up.

The Golden Rule is posted with only the translated words, "Do to others, as you would have others do to you" or "Treat others as you would like others to treat you." Teachers may then construct, with children, the rules for particular areas of the program: Meeting Rules, Block Area Rules, Computer Rules, etc. A teacher from another school explained that she distinguishes ethical rules from other rules by calling the others "procedures."

◆

The Golden Rule does not provide direct solutions to problems of missing pens or left-out children. Its strength, I believe, is in this very fact. It provides an ethical or moral reference point, a place to begin the search for different ways to act. As we ask children to address problems themselves, we can begin by asking questions. "What do you think it feels like to have your things taken?" "What do you think it feels like to not have anyone talk to you all through lunch?" "Is it right to pass the ball only to the best players or do you think everyone should have a chance?" The Golden Rule can be applied to nearly every action of significance to children.

We desperately need to prepare children to examine questions of right and wrong for themselves and to see the consequences of their choices. Classroom life is rich in opportunities. There is no need for imaginary problems or situations. Discussions come directly from the classroom, playground or lunchroom, and children then have the chance to act on their choices. The Golden Rule can become a living standard, an operative rule in everyday life at school.

"People learn to be human by being involved with other people," noted Erikson in *Childhood and Society*. Children need to create inner rules that go beyond even the hawkish eye of the teacher. Here are my steps for using the Golden Rule:

1. The teacher introduces the Golden Rule by adapting or creating a parable or story to illustrate meaning. (An alternative would be to simply recite the Golden Rule and discuss it.)

2. The teacher very briefly and simply explains the Golden Rule: "It is our one rule. It is our most important rule. It belongs to all people. I didn't make it up. The principal of this school didn't make it up. But it is ours to use, if we take care of it." (It is important for children to have a sense of both its universal and personal importance.)

3. Teacher and students construct meanings that show specifically how we bring the Golden Rule to school. This needs to include modeling and role-playing, as well as verbal illustration. Asking children to act out situations and demonstrate alternative solutions makes it concrete and personal. With older children, ideas about how to use the Golden Rule may be recorded on a chart. (Examples may be reviewed over many days and weeks.)

4. Teacher and students discuss purpose, individual responsibility and cooperation. "Who's in charge of The Golden Rule? What makes it work? How will we know when it is working?" My goal is to create an ethical order, a sense of respect for self, others and environment. I explain that goal to children by saying that I want everyone to feel good in school. To feel good means to feel safe to do the work you need to do and to have friends. I explain that when we all struggle to use the Golden Rule, we make our school a place we want to be, a place that feels good. We can only accomplish that task together. Like the story of Horse, it takes our best efforts together to get across the logs.

5. Teacher and students discuss consequences. "What happens when people forget the rule?" (Ch.4)

A fifth-grade charter

I decided to construct a "constitution" with a fifth grade class to initiate a unit on the American Revolution, but it quickly expanded. It became much more important and useful than any single social studies unit.

"Tell me any rules you know," I began, although I might have gotten a truer response had I asked them to tell me all the rules they broke in a week's time! This was the "difficult class," not known for its rule-abiding citizenry. It took a moment for the responses to begin:

"You mean like no chewin' gum in school?" (His cheek puffed with a wad of gum pocketed in one side.)

"Yes. Like that."

"No running in the hallways."

"No fighting."

"No swears."

"No taking someone's money or stuff."

"Be nice."

"That's not a rule!" someone protested.

I wrote, "Be nice" on the chart headed "Rules."

I wrote down all the rules they said, which in the end numbered close to fifty and most began with "no." I told them to think about it and to add any more rules they remembered before the next day.

I copied the chart for the next day's meeting and I gave everyone a sheet. "Check the rules you like. Cross out the rules you don't like," were the instructions.

"Whattaya' mean?"

"Some of these rules you like. You might say to yourself, 'That's a good rule.' Some rules may seem silly or not important or even wrong. Cross those out or put an 'X' mark."

"Most rules are dumb cause nobody can make you do stuff," Roger stated.

"You mean if you don't follow a rule, it's a bad rule?"

"Yeah."

"OK, but for now imagine what rules you might make yourself follow if you could boss yourself."

Roger nodded.

After another pause, I decided to incorporate Roger's idea and suggested that we add a new notation. "If you like a rule, but think it's hard to follow put a star beside it."

When I collected their papers, I was struck with the clear patterns and common themes. Rules that related to safety were checked as "liked." Rules that had to do with personal styles (gum chewing, candy, dress codes, swearing) were often crossed out. Rules that had to do with ethics and "rights of others" (stealing, fighting, cheating, name-calling) were good rules but qualified by the stars — hard to follow. Rules that concerned classroom conduct were also starred — no talking, quiet voices, don't bother or interrupt, stay in your seat, etc. I found it interesting that there were more stars or checks than cross-outs, even from this band of rule-shakers! I planned to share the results of this first survey with the class.

For the next meeting, I returned their papers so that we could examine the results together. In this case, I assigned everyone in the class a job — to collect information, collate the responses, and report on the data. Children cut their rule-sheets into strips and passed them out before tallying their own slips. We gathered again when everyone had checked and rechecked their figures. In the meantime, considerable interest and investment in the survey were building. They were excited about discovering the group reactions and regarding themselves as researchers.

The group was quiet, almost solemn, as students presented their reports. One student entered the information on a master list. Sometimes I interrupted and asked for predictions, but mostly the children were intent on finding out, item by item. Towards the end, however, children were seeing patterns and spontaneously drawing conclusions. Despite the momentum, I postponed further discussion for the next day and gave out a second worksheet with questions to help them begin to organize and classify the information.

1) What are the most popular rules?
2) What rules were least liked by the class?
3) What kinds of rules did people like/not like?
4) What kinds of rules had stars?
5) What do you think would be the most important rule, if you could only choose one of these?

Immediately, students asked what I meant by "kinds of rules." I explained that I wanted them to think about how some of the rules were similar or different and might be grouped together. For example, "Are some rules easy, and that's why people liked them? Picking up trash is easy. Not fighting is hard. Do kids like easy rules and not like hard ones?" I pointed out they were now trying to understand and interpret the research they had gathered.

Throughout the day, I observed students puzzling and talking over their worksheets. They were eager and excited to begin the next day's discussion. I began with questions about methodology. How did they decide what was the most popular, or least liked? There was a clear agreement on counting the checks or X's. But controversy surrounded the starred items. "Be nice" — one girl pointed out — was the most popular, if you counted the checks and the stars.

Children also noted the popularity of categories that included ideas of safety, care, and fairness. Someone else had come up with two categories, "kid rules" and "teacher rules." Kid rules were rules that kids needed and teacher rules were the ones the teachers wanted. Roger had stayed with his enforcement concerns and divided rules according to how you might get caught, in which he raised issues of intrinsic moral conflicts as well as external sanctions. For example, "If you cheat and no one catches you . . . or if you fight outside of school . . ."

The most vigorous discussion centered on question five, the "most important rule," although just as we got into it, something else occurred. I stopped reminding and monitoring the interruptions, and the rule about raising hands in a meeting was quickly lost in the excitement. I had stopped "enforcement," as Roger would say. The tone of the meeting changed to a more competitive and edgy one.

"Hey, I was talking and you butted in."

"Yeah. But you've been saying and saying." Chuckles. Hand slaps.

"Teacher, don't people got to raise their hands?"

"Why?"

"It's a rule."

"So?"

"So, if it's a rule, people got to do it."

"But you listed over fifty rules and a lot of them you don't like, a lot are hard and many you don't even try to do. So what's a rule?"

Throughout the process, things were beginning to "click." There was a connection forming between needs and the concept of rules. Further discussion about priorities, or "one" rule, stretched their thinking further. Once again, I asked them to choose one rule that they thought would be most important for our classroom this year. I said that they could combine or reword the rules from our charts. I added one more thumbprint. I said that I didn't like rules that began with "no" and that they needed to state their rule in a "yes." "If we don't run, what do we do? If we don't fight, what do we do? If we don't interrupt, what do we do?" I reminded them that they had already figured a lot of this out. They liked rules that kept people safe; they liked rules that involved being nice to each other; they liked rules that had to do with fairness.

The aim was to have everyone contribute a rule he or she agreed was important to create our class charter. In order to avoid a long list, we combined and honed, until there were six rules:

1) We will treat each other fair.
2) We will keep quiet when others are working.
3) We will help teachers or classmates when they ask for help.
4) We will walk in the halls and in the classroom.
5) We will try to solve disagreements by talking it over ourselves. If we can't, we will ask the teacher to help.
6) We will use only the things we need and put the tops back on stuff.

Not all of these rules worked — or could work. Number one was vague, resulting in many discussions about the meaning of "fair." Is "fair" treating everyone alike or is it fair that some people get to work in the hall, while others have to stay at their desks? Number two, was often forgotten and needed frequent reminders from the teacher for a while. Number three was effective, although some kids could be "too helpful!" Number four was clear-cut, easy to monitor, but left out other issues of physical safety. Number five was a true ideal, of passionate interest to the children, but requiring teacher guidelines and limits — "Come back in five minutes and tell me what you have figured out about this problem." Number six was too narrow — not everything has a top!

It was a powerful beginning and instilled a sense of mutual responsibility. The interest of these students in ethical issues was keen and incontestable, even if there were moments when it was more to someone's advantage to exploit others than to be fair!

The charter, and the standards the students had helped to create, had weight. The continuing conversations which engaged everyone in issues of right and wrong, good and bad rules, fair and not fair, added to the importance and the vigor of the document. I am certain that the charter would have failed without this on-going commitment to dialogue. "Amendments," we called it!

"Cooperation leads to autonomy," wrote Piaget in *The Moral Judgment of the Child*. Cooperation is rooted in the kinds of discussions practiced by this fifth grade class, taking sides, arguing the rights and wrongs of their own issues, discussing whether it's right to hit back or mess up someone's paper that messed up your paper. It is cooperation, Piaget asserted, that allows children to perceive not just results of actions, but the intentions. Cooperation forces "the individual to be constantly occupied with the point of view of other people so as to compare it with his own."

Although discipline never becomes perfect, children clearly have a greater stake in rules if they are part of the process of constructing them. Eventually these fifth graders studied the United States Constitution. I recall Roger's brash pronouncement, "Hey, they did like us!"

◆

This experience started in the Fall and ended in June. There are many other ways to conduct rule-setting sessions with students. It is important to remember that the process is a collaboration. Teachers are not "turning-over" the task, nor do we lead students to foregone conclusions. We apply guidelines. I use these guidelines:

- Rules provide positive directions — what you do, not what you don't do.
- Rules serve a purpose. The purpose is to make our classrooms and school a good and safe place for teachers and children. For example, it's hard to do good work if you fear mistakes. So a good rule might be that people offer constructive comments about others' work and not laugh.
- Rules need to be meaningful to the workplace and the workers. This means specific and concrete — what Roger called "enforceable." We need to know when we are following a rule and when we are not.

- Few is better than many. Rules should be posted and easy to read.

Since I conducted my experiment, several wonderful programs have been developed for schools. There are peer-mediation programs, which train students (grades four through twelve) in mediation and conflict resolution. In schools where these programs have been instituted, there have been immediate effects on behavior in lunchrooms, playgrounds, and classrooms. There are also "Just Community" programs in several high schools, which involve students in governing the school, supporting self-discipline, and sponsoring "fairness groups" on a school-wide basis.[1] The research, so far, is overwhelmingly positive. The attitude of children towards themselves, each other and the school improves. Students are more apt to respect and practice what they have helped to create.

The class covenant: a sixth grade contract of binding rules

This is a different way to create rules with a class that adds an interesting research component, devised by a colleague. It was titled a "Covenant" in keeping with the class studies of King Arthur and medieval history. The task involved selecting four rules, representing four constituencies: teacher, students, parents and principal. Each group was asked to answer the same question: "What's the most important rule, in your opinion, that we need to help students do their work and take care of themselves in class and school?" The students interviewed each other, their principal and their parents.

The teacher went first, modeling her perspective. "As your teacher, I think that the most important rule for this year is that you use your self-controls to show independence and responsibility. That means you will manage yourselves well outside of the classroom, or with other adults in the classroom, and when you work on projects with each other."

The teacher's response reflected relevant expectations in relationship to the specific needs of the group and to their developmental potentials. They were a group that was devoted to their teacher, cooperative and responsible, as long as she was in charge. They were more difficult to manage during recess, and vigorously dispatched most substitutes. The teacher's choice of "most important rule" was meant to stretch these children and also to prepare them for the independence that they would need the following year, as they moved on to junior high school.

The students enjoyed preparing for the interviews with their parents and the principal. The "round table" (from King Arthur) discussions comparing parent responses and exchanging their own ideas were rich and extensive. The students worked to edit the parent responses, to synthesize and define the common objectives. They boiled down the responses to a single basic one, "Do good work." Then they expanded it, believing that parents wanted to get

---

1 See Bibliography for more information on mediation and Just Community programs.

examples of good work each week. The work would need to be neat, spelled correctly and in good handwriting on clean paper.

The principal chose as his most important rule, "decent behavior on the playground." The teacher asked that the students give at least three examples of "decent playground behavior." If they were to follow the principal's rule, what would they have to do? The children agreed that it involved taking care of the equipment, making fair teams, and solving conflicts without swears or fighting. They reviewed these points with the principal, who was willing to take time to set up routines and give them responsibility in each of these areas. In fact, this class took on the job of looking after the equipment and did so with pride and conscientious devotion throughout the year. It was harder to share authority over game selection and team captains, but there was certainly more interest in finding solutions to such conflicts.

The student rule (which was actually a request) was to have "free time to do things we want to do as long as it belongs in school." They argued forcefully that it was still a rule because it used rules. Eventually, it was edited by the teacher to be "choice time," when they had to be responsible, get things they needed, and behave.

The "platform" this class evolved helped them consider others' thoughts as well as their own. The set of rules they selected was purposeful, meaningful and brief. Papers did go home every week to their parents — almost without fail! The playground behavior improved, and if sometimes there was a fight, at least it wasn't a war. The growth of independence was significant, both in terms of the teacher's rule and the student's quest for "free time." It is important to remember that it is the struggle, not the achievement, that is the true measure of learning.

Rules for classroom workers

With the set of rules illustrated in Figure 3.1, teachers engage the class in discussion, example, and application, similar to the way the Golden Rule is introduced. These rules can inspire mutual responsibility through the concept

Figure 3.1

CLASS RULES

We are all workers in school.
We value our work and our work place.
Good workers need to take care of their tools.
Good workers need to keep their work site safe.
Good workers are helpful, friendly and respectful of one another.
Good workers *make mistakes.*
Good workers don't laugh at their own or others' mistakes.

of school as a workplace. Rules are needed to help everyone accomplish their jobs.

Note that these rules are stated in language that elicits strong, affirmative images — "good workers," valued work and workplace, care and respect. The rules are general enough to be inclusive and yet concrete enough to apply directly to experiences.

A third grade teacher, Debby Roth, used this approach in 1989. She described her experience in her classroom journal:

"We spent about two weeks discussing rules, writing down rules, revising our rules. The first day of school we discussed rules that the students had previously. I explained how we were going to write down our classroom rules for the year. For homework, the students had to write down one rule that they thought was important to have. We discussed positive and negative wording for rules. I modeled different ways of disciplining, using positive and negative wording. The students decided that they would rather have a list of positive rules to follow. The rule they brought in was to be a positive rule.

"The next day, I shared with them my list of rules. The students shared with me their rules. I listed them on chart paper. We compared the two lists of rules to see if all of their rules were covered. We worked on this every day until everyone was comfortable with a final list of rules. It was a long process, but I feel it was a worthwhile one. I think the rules will have more meaning to them since they were a part of them."

♦

All good workers will "forget" the rules sometimes. We honor and respect our rules by using consequences. It matters that rules are followed or not followed. What happens when children forget the rules — and they will — is the subject of the next chapter, "Logical Consequences."

Summary

- Rules provide positive directions — what you do, not what you don't do.
- Rules serve a purpose. The purpose is to make our classrooms and school a good and safe place for teachers and children.
- Rules need to be specific and concrete. We need to know when we are following a rule and when we are not.
- Few is better than many. Rules should be posted and easy to read.

I do not want rules to legislate every action. I want them to encourage reasoned thinking and discussion. I want rules that we "like," not because they give license or permission, but because they help us construct a community that is orderly and safe. And I want rules that have meaningful applications to concrete behaviors, which require not just passive submission but active participation.

4

Using Logical Consequences

*Where did we ever get the crazy idea that in order to make children
perform better, we must first make them feel worse?*
Jane Nelson
Positive Discipline

Now that we have created rules with the class and practiced the 3R's, we can
sit back and rest assured that everyone will behave. Yes?

No. Everyone will not behave. Children will break the rules, even rules they
cherish and respect, because they helped create them. The way we manage the
rule-breaking is critical to the development of discipline and community. The
next four chapters describe the application of consequences in the classroom.
In this chapter I will describe three kinds of logical consequences and their
relationship to specific classroom behavior. The next chapter discusses class
meetings to solve problems, and the next two focus on "time-out," since it is
the most frequent consequence used in many classrooms.

When we use a system of logical consequences with children, we seek to
instill responsibility for choices and actions. William Glasser and others found
that punishment does not increase student responsibility; rather, it increases
evasion and deception. Research suggests that consistent classroom dialogue
on real issues of consequence has a significant and lasting impact on the
development of moral thinking. Logical consequences are effective not
because they intimidate or deprive, and not because they offer rewards or
threaten punishment. If consequences work, it's because they reinforce the

internal requirements of self-control and commitment.

In the long run, the process can help children internalize the ethics of our community — respect for the values of justice and the rights of others — and a pride in membership. We want children to take part in a process that will encourage their own decision-making and participation in the classroom community. The goal is to invoke logical consequences in a way which helps students look more closely at their own behaviors and consider the results of their choices.

When children break the rules of their school and classroom, logical consequences are invoked in a reasonable way. Here are some guidelines for logical consequences:

- Logical consequences are respectful of the student and classroom. This is an essential criterion proposed by Dreikurs in *Maintaining Sanity in the Classroom*. It entails giving students input into possible consequences and including some choices about the specifics of the consequences. Logical consequences are *not* intended to humiliate or hurt.
- Logical consequences need to respond to choices and actions, not to character. The message is that misbehavior results from poor judgment or bad planning, not from poor character.
- Logical consequences need to be put into practice with both *empathy* and *structure*. Empathy shows our knowledge of children and our willingness to hear what they have to say; structure establishes our capacity to set limits and provide appropriate direction. Jane Nelson, in *Positive Discipline*, talks about the need to be both firm and kind. Kindness, she says, shows respect for the child; firmness shows respect for oneself.
- Logical consequences should be used to describe the demands of the situation, not the demands of the authority. This helps avoid power

struggles. "For our classroom to feel safe, you need to contribute in a more friendly and agreeable way. When you put down other people, it doesn't feel so safe anymore."

- Logical consequences should be used only after the teacher has assessed the situation. Misbehaviors may result from expectations that are not appropriate to the developmental needs of children, or from expectations incompatible with an individual's particular needs. The best alternative may be to restructure the environment and readjust the expectations. For example, sustained periods of quiet work take significant control for children even as old as ten or twelve. If they are then released to go to the bathroom, they can't be expected to stay in straight and silent lines. Instead, they release pent up energy; they tap dance, chatter, and tickle. Do these children need a consequence or do they need breaks and outlets for movement and social contact? By providing a fifteen-minute activity or social period, or relaxing the hallway rules, we may make the problem disappear.

    When Kyle copied from another student on his spelling test, he was compensating not for a lack of study (he had studied), but for an inability to memorize twenty new spelling words each week. He was a student with a specific visual memory weakness and the class expectations, despite his efforts, were not within his grasp. When he was given a portion of the list, and able to succeed, the cheating stopped. He needed the expectations restructured, rather than a consequence for cheating.

    Confronted with misbehavior, we first ask ourselves two questions:

    * Are my expectations appropriate to the age needs of the group?
    * Are my expectations appropriate to the individual needs and abilities of the student?

- "Stop and Think" before imposing logical consequences. Teachers often need time to think, not just react. Confronted with aggravating behavior, our first responses may not be the most logical! We may also need time to decide on a reasonable consequence. "Your rudeness is not acceptable. You need to go back to your desk and we will both need to think about this for a while. I will talk to you later" (or after lunch, or tomorrow morning). The message is that students may not go on when behavior is unacceptable. The next step will be decided when the teacher has time to think and respond appropriately.

- Logical consequences help to restore self-controls and self-respect, because self-respect demands not just words, but actions.

The remote control car

Gerard was frantic. The small remote-control car he just got from his uncle was missing, the car he so proudly brought to school to show people, the one everyone admired and wanted to hold. After a class search, the car was found in the trash, its batteries gone. Its disappearance was traced to another classmate, Richie, who was ashamed but also insistent about his right to retaliate. "He calls me names and tells kids not to let me play, and sometimes they don't."

In this situation, the teacher offered two responses: one attended to the issues of Richie's anger, the other to how Richie's anger was expressed. She was able to validate Richie's feelings, while also helping him find a different way to confront Gerard. The teacher also insisted that Richie replace Gerard's batteries and help him get the car working again. The next day, the two boys demonstrated the reclaimed car together, and the class applauded.

Replacing the batteries made Richie's apology more credible to Gerard and to himself. Helping children come to ethical judgments and responses, not just psychological explanations ("I felt angry"), suggests a more abiding respect.

◆

It is not always easy to wean children from becoming "excuse-junkies," or believing that everything is solved with a casual "sorry." On the other hand, we also want children to learn the healing process of amends and forgiveness. Grudge-holding and revenge — "I'll get you later" or "I never want to be your friend again" — creates intimidation, not cooperation.

Consequences vs. punishment

It is *how* we handle the rule-breaking that differentiates consequences from punishment. For example, either a consequence or a punishment may involve a "time-out." It is more apt to be perceived as a consequence if it seems a direct result of the child's "choice" to continue to whisper to her friends during meeting time, and if the manner of the teacher is firm, but respectful. The intent is for the child to regain controls so she can rejoin the group. The "time-out" will be seen as a punishment if the child is sent out of the group and the teacher's manner is sarcastic or derisive.

All logical consequences need to be implemented with both empathy and structure. Empathy preserves the dignity of the child. Structure preserves the dignity of the classroom. If we are too harsh, we risk discouragement or vengeful defiance. If we are too lenient or inconsistent, we risk neglect and self-indulgence, leaving children with a confused sense of their own power.

Our goal, when children break rules, is never to make them feel "bad" or defeated, although they may, in fact, feel bad. Our goal is first to help them recover self-control and self-respect. When I observe a child acting the part of the bully, or sneaking out of a job, or putting down a classmate or teacher, it is not a picture of self-control and self-respect. It is a sign of distress and a signal for help. Something needs to stop. The use of logical consequences urges respect for the rules and the people they are designed to guide.

Natural consequences

Sometimes consequences occur naturally, without adult input. A student who forgets his lunch may get hungry. A child who is a bad sport, may not get chosen to be on teams. A student who doesn't do her work, may get behind. I say "may," because often adults intercede to protect children from their own childish indiscretions. Mothers scurry into school with forgotten lunches. Teachers find a place on the team for the poor sport, with a mild warning. And we all needle and cajole children to complete their work, rather than allow them to fall behind. Our good intentions may insulate children from the instructional results of their own behaviors.

Yet it isn't satisfactory to sit idly by and do nothing. There are many occasions when natural consequences are not productive in the ways we might hope. The hungry child takes a classmate's lunch. The bad sport dominates the game. The non-worker becomes more and more discouraged and loses all motivation to participate. Clearly, a system of logical consequences requires active teaching to be effective. I've categorized three types of logical consequences and their relationship to broad areas of behavior. The categories and consequences are meant to illustrate, not to govern. I've provided just a few examples. You will quickly think of others.

Reparations:
"You broke it. You fix it."

Reparations give children opportunities to actively face mistakes, rather than to "weasel out" of responsibility. Here are some responses to consider if a student:

- Spills milk
  "I'll help you find a sponge so you can clean it up."
- Accidentally knocks over another child's block building
  "You need to ask if he wants you to help build it back up."
- Is inattentive and tears someone's drawing while reaching for something
  "You need to apologize and see if you can help him do it over or tape over the tear. You need to take better care, or you will have to work alone."
- Trips a classmate on the playground
  "Did you stop and see if they were all right or if they needed any help?"
- Puts down a classmate ("You don't know that?" one student boasts to another, "It's cinchy.")
  "You need to find a better way to speak to someone when they aren't sure of an answer. Show me a better way and think if you need to apologize."
- Knocks over someone's lunch in a playful scuffle, spilling the food onto the floor ("You dumb jerk," is the angered response. "Hey, it wasn't my fault," is the reply.)
  The teacher comes over and redirects the scufflers. "Chris, you start to clean up the floor before someone slips and gets hurt. Jed, Chris and Tony, figure out how you will share lunch today."

Groups may make reparations, too:

- A group is socializing and they don't finish their work
  "Your work isn't done because you have been chatting. You owe yourself a thirty-minute work time today. When will you make it up? It needs to be done before you go home."
- A group becomes argumentative and noisy while working on a map together, accomplishing very little work and disturbing the rest of the room
  "This group is disturbing our classroom and also getting very little accomplished. You need to quickly divide up the jobs and work alone. Do you want to do that right now or should I?"

Breach of contract and loss of trust:
"You must forfeit your rights."

The "contractual" agreement stresses a trust between teacher and student, and between students. We agree to tell the truth, honor our agreements, take care of property, and treat each other with respect, fairness and friendliness. A breach of that trust includes telling lies, disregard for others' rights or feelings, and disregard for materials in the room. Consider these types of responses if a student:

- Says her work is done, when it isn't, in order to play games or avoid a task
  "I won't be able to believe what you say, or trust you to follow routines for finished work. You will have to show me your finished work every day this week."

- Leaves the room to go to the bathroom, fools around in the bathroom and doesn't return in a reasonable period of time

    "You're not taking care of yourself in the bathroom, so I guess you won't be able to go by yourself for the next two days. You will have to wait until a teacher is free to go with you."
- Leaves the room on an errand and gets into a water-fight at the fountain in the hall

    "You're not taking care of yourself when you leave the classroom, therefore you will not have the privilege of leaving the room on your own for the rest of the day (or week), until you show me you are ready to follow rules in the classroom again."
- Cheats when playing games

    "When you cheat you make the game less fun for others. You will need to leave the game until you are willing to play by the rules." Students are encouraged to also stop a game if there is cheating and to say, "If you continue to cheat, I don't want to play with you."
- Is rude to a teacher, ignoring a request to not interrupt and then making a face

    "You ignore me when I speak to you, which tells me you don't care to be in my group. You are welcome to return when you are ready to show respect."
- Makes faces or sarcastic remarks to peers during an activity or group

    "I see you are not ready to work in a friendly way in this group. You will need to leave until you are ready to use kind words, or show you know how to respect the good ideas of others in our group."
- Leaves computer disks scattered on the table, after several reminders

    "You have been mishandling the computer center. You won't be able to use it by yourself until you show me that you are ready to follow all the procedures."
- Pushes to get a place in line

    "I see you push people to get in line. You'll have to get out of the line and wait in the back with me, until you show me that you know how to line up safely."
- Requests help from her teacher using a demanding and unpleasant voice

    "I don't like people talking to me in a rude voice. I do not talk to you in a rude voice. If you want me to answer your question or explain something you don't understand, you need to use a pleasant voice and nice words. Or I won't feel like helping you." (I walk away.)

Groups may forfeit their rights as well

- A group lesson becomes very noisy

    "There are a lot of people talking to each other instead of listening. I'll wait. I won't talk when you are. I do not plan to continue until people show they are ready to listen."
- Room clean-up is sloppy and difficult

    "You have not been cleaning up with care, so for the next few days the art, library and science centers are closed. You will have less clean-up to do. Then you can decide if you want the responsibility for these centers."

- The class is particularly rude and unruly with a substitute

    "Your conduct when I was absent was not acceptable. I know it's hard to have your teacher absent. Sometimes, I will need to be out when it's the only way I can take care of important business. I know that you know how to take care of your room and your work, even without my help. I will have to be away again, so I'll give you a choice. The choice is to remain in your classroom and follow the rules, or go to another room with a teacher you know. If you feel you can't manage with a substitute teacher, and will do better elsewhere, that's a good decision. If you choose to stay in this room, you are choosing to take care of your own selves. I will be angry if you choose to stay and then don't manage. The next time, I will not be able to believe you and I will make the decision. Think about it."

- There is a misuse of class supplies

    "This class has been using so much paper that we are almost out of a month's supply. Since you are not able to regulate it now, I've put out what I think is a reasonable quantity. When that is gone, there will be no more drawing paper for the week."

Time-outs:
"You must forfeit participation."

Time-out is discussed in detail in the next chapter. These types of responses may be appropriate when a student:

- Talks continually to a neighbor during a group activity

    "You are disturbing us; you need to stop or leave the group."

- Bangs his pencil and drums on the table

    "You are making it hard for others at your table to concentrate. You will need to stop or leave the group."

- Takes extra turns or pays no attention when it isn't her turn

    "You have to pay attention to the game or not play."

- Makes negative and sarcastic comments

    "You need to contribute helpful comments, or leave the group."

- Repeatedly comes to a group with work not done

    "You haven't done your assignment, so you're not ready to be here. Leave the group and come back when your work is ready."

- Refuses to work with a partner or participate in a shared project unless she gets her way

    "Time-Out. I want you to think about one thing that is important for you to work on and one thing that your partner wants to work on. Come back when you have figured that out and when you are ready to cooperate."

Groups may forfeit participation as well:

- Class noise level is high, after a warning

   "You are still not remembering to use quiet voices. Now there is no talking at all."

- Children come to their math lesson unprepared

   "I see that many of you do not have your work done or do not have the things you need for this lesson. I will go do other things. When you are really ready, let me know. I am sorry you will miss some of your valuable math time." (The teacher actually takes a "time-out.")

- Class transition is shoddy

   "This room is not ready to go to recess. I'll be at the table working. Let me know when you think you're ready." (Again, the teacher actually takes a "time-out.")

- Group is not able to cooperate

   "I hear a lot of bickering from this foursome. It sounds like you haven't figured out how to work together on this project. Take a time-out and think what you might do to make it work better. When you come back, I will hear one solution from each of you."

Summary:
Steps for implementing logical consequences

To ensure that I use logical consequences in a reasonable way, I try follow these steps each time:

1) Stop and think

To present reasoned and reasonable consequences to children, we often have to get past our first reactions, which may be anything from a desire to cry to a desire to strangle. "I don't like what I see here. I need to take time to stop and think. So do you. Go to your seats and sit there quietly. We will talk about it — in ten minutes (at the end of the day, tomorrow)."

2) Evaluate the options

I ask myself questions:
   * Do I need to restructure the environment?
   * Do I need to restructure individual expectations?
   * Do I consider this a problem that requires reparation? If so, how will the student fix it?
   * Is it a problem that involves a breach of our contract? Is it a breach of trust, respect, or care for others in the community?
   * Is the student disruptive or unpleasant in a group, and needs "time out?"

3) Provide a workable, realistic, specific action as a consequence

A workable consequence is specific and related to the problem — leaving the group is related to being disruptive in a group; missing recess isn't. Realistic means possible for the child and teacher. Children can clean-up, wash off graffiti, provide a service, give up a privilege, help rebuild or mend, or find nicer ways to say things. Teachers also need to think about what is practical — if a child has to stay until a piece of work is complete, then the teacher must be prepared to stay with her or arrange for supervision.

4) Provide a time limit

It's important to restore privileges quickly so that children are able to resume their responsibilities and try again. A child who is not managing in the block area loses the privilege of working there for the rest of the day, but tomorrow, "I expect to see you show me that you can follow the rules." We can repeat consequences and extend the times, but generally there is an assurance of another chance. (In some cases, of course, a consequence is not effective with a particular child. *Nothing* works all the time with children.)

5) Emphasize the language of "choice" and "privilege"

"If you wish to remain in this group, you choose to follow the rules." "You may come with us and follow the rules, or stay back. Your choice." "If you want to benefit from my teaching, you need to do the assignments."

6) Use empathy and structure

Empathy shows faith in the student's ability to improve, and reaffirms that I like the person, even if I don't like the behavior. Structure sets limits and provides a way for children to follow through. Explain what needs to happen, without apology or negotiation.

5

Problem-Solving Class Meetings

- Children rapidly increase their teasing and picking on one another.
- Cliques and secret clubs begin, excluding others.
- Money disappears from coat pockets.
- Nasty messages circulate and graffiti appear on desks.
- Transitions become chaotic and take too long.
- A child is afraid to ride the bus because he has been taunted and teased about everything from his curly hair to his sibilant speech.
- Independent assignments are messy, careless, and filled with mistakes, although the children insist they have checked them over before turning them in.

Every one of these problems occurred in the course of last year and, plus or minus others, each year that I have been a teacher. Yet I am convinced that these problems provide a context for developing moral and ethical thinking. I do not mean that we sit children down and rant and rave, telling them what will happen if such and such happens again. And I do not mean that we enlist the "do-gooders" to identify and expose the "do-badders." If our goal is to give children the courage to think about the problems they experience and to search for ways to act that reflect moral thinking, then we need a very different approach.

Years ago, William Glasser wrote in *Schools Without Failure*, "Given little help, children tend to evade problems, to lie their way out of situations, to depend upon others to solve their problems or just to give up." Without our help, children will "solve" a problem by manufacturing an excuse, blaming someone else, or providing an empty promise to the teacher so she will

shut up. But children will become involved in problem-solving if we give them help in dealing with what matters most in their lives. The episodes of the playground, the bus and the classroom have deep and immediate meanings compared to contrived work sheets, or abstractions children gather from soap operas and older siblings.

Specifically, we can involve the whole class in problem-solving through meetings. It is one technique for dealing with the nasty messages, the taunting on the bus, the missing money, or the careless work. I use a problem-solving class meeting format taken largely from the work of William Glasser and Rudolf Dreikurs, combined with other approaches I have tried and found successful.

Purpose of class meetings

"The two main purposes of class meetings are to help each other and to solve problems," writes Jane Nelson in *Positive Discipline*. William Glasser (*Schools Without Failure*) describes class meetings as a time when "the teacher leads a whole class in a non-judgmental discussion," and children learn that "they can use their brains individually and as a group to solve the problems of living in their school world."

The first goal of class meetings is to generate honest discussion among children. We must give permission for children to say what they really think, not what they think we want to hear. A non-judgmental tone is essential for honest and open discussion.

The second goal is to develop children's capacity to solve problems. In a class meeting, it is the students who must propose and choose the solutions that they think will work, not the teacher. The solutions often work because there is an investment in them working, not because they are so brilliant. Other times, solutions will fail, and must fail. But a failure can produce an even greater educational dividend — the process of revising and learning from mistakes. "I worry that there isn't time for failure," one teacher cried. And that may be one of the greatest failures of our schools — the lack of time we give children to learn from necessary mistakes.

There are a few things that do *not* belong in any class meetings. *Do not:*
- Allow children to blame or accuse others
- Enlist other children to detect and identify wrong-doers
- Punish the whole class for the behavior of a few individuals

These tactics build resentment and suspicion, not cooperation. To involve the class in finding a just solution is to enlist cooperative and collective enterprise. "What do we need to do right now to keep our classroom safe?" is a good question to initiate a meeting. "Who did it?" is not.

Rules for class meetings

These were developed by Franklin Mediation Center at the University of Massachusetts (see Bibliography). Students agree to:
- Try to solve problems
- Not use any put-downs — physical or verbal
- Listen to each other and not interrupt

I present these to the class as the three important ground rules for class meetings, but ask if they think we need others to help solve problems and speak honestly. Sometimes children suggest the added rule of confidentiality, for example.

Each rule needs to be discussed, as well. For example, it is useful to talk about the possibility that solving problems as a group may mean giving up your own ideas when you think others are better. I have often modeled this, because children can get into a contest over the owner of an idea. "Suppose I have a solution and Terry has a solution. How should I decide what solution to use?"

I also role-play put-downs, like making faces, rolling eyes, exchanging glances with a friend, or showing indifference with body posture. In class meetings, children also learn to exercise vital social skills. It is important to be aware of these skills, and to remember that they depend on a developmental progression which involves maturation as well as experience.

Skills for class meetings

Children are learning to share by exchanging ideas and views. An important aspect of participation is learning to use the "I voice," rather than the "you voice." We help children communicate their own feelings or attitudes, rather than criticize and blame others for the problem. Is it just the fault of the lunch aide that bedlam breaks out? Can this class of eleven-year-olds move from saying, "She can't control us" to "What can we do to better control ourselves?"

When another group begins to discuss a problem they have raised about too much noise, they initially say, "Some kids start arguing and talking as soon as the teacher leaves." If the question is redirected — "If I like to talk, what can I do about it so that it doesn't become too noisy?" — it exposes the genuine need to have a time to talk in school. Then the problem becomes personal and the "I voice" is used. If we focus on the personal, immediate questions, we sow the seeds of genuine participation.

Active listening is another necessary but difficult skill. It involves attention to the meanings and intentions of what someone is saying. It includes the ability to paraphrase or repeat back the main points someone else is making. We use it when we teach children to have writing and peer conferences. We call it "receiving the piece," which means that you have attended to the meaning and message another communicates, and told what you heard or understood.

In a class meeting, we are teaching (as well as exercising) vital skills in cooperation and problem-solving. We will need to be patient and encouraging. Figure 5.1 provides an abbreviated list of social skills, adapted from *The Developmental Acquisition of Skills* by Sarah Pirtle, which I use as a guide to assess children's growth. I compare results from before a program of class meetings with those after six months. These skills have a developmental base. As children mature, they are better able to reflect, consider multiple view points, anticipate the outcome of various solutions, and even control the impulse to speak out of turn (although even as adults we interrupt too regularly).

Class meetings — and the skills they require — take practice. Teachers need practice in creating a comfortable and secure atmosphere. It's usually best to start with morning meetings, or circle times, which focus on group sharing and lively group interactions like games, singing, and personal sharing. Next, work on developing cooperative skills and team work in academic or artistic enterprises, in small or large groups. Teachers and children build familiarity and trust gradually, through many group activities. Once you've established some common ground as a class, problem-solving meetings can deal with the tougher issues, and result in deeper bonds.

Class meeting procedures

- Meet once a week at a regular time
  Meeting once a week gives children time to digest and reflect, and makes the procedure special.
- Keep time

Thirty minutes for 3–5th grade, forty-five minutes for 6th–8th grade is the maximum. There is a tendency to prolong a meeting when the discussion is going well, or to finish up an issue. But long meetings are difficult for many children, so they begin to dislike them. It is better to come back to the issue next week, with a fresh and renewed interest.

- Meet in a circle, not at desks
  I prefer to have older children sit in chairs for this meeting, rather than on the floor.
- Set up a weekly agenda
  Teachers and children may put issues on the agenda.
- The teacher takes the role of "gatekeeper"
  She sets the tone, begins and ends the meeting, keeps the group focused on the topic and on the meeting rules. This includes selecting and presenting

Figure 5.1

BASIC SKILLS FOR PROBLEM SOLVING

K–3rd Grade
At these ages, children can:
- Describe problems or give information without using put-downs or blame
- Give their own opinions in a group
- Express their own views and thoughts (using the "I voice")
- Listen while another shares ideas or opinions
- Maintain eye contact
- Wait rather than interrupt
- Say something affirming about the ideas or solutions of others
- Accept more than one possible solution to a problem
- Choose the most "workable" solution to the problem and then stick to it

4th–6th Grade
At these ages, children can:
- Develop more than one solution to a problem
- Explore different points of view
- Anticipate different outcomes of proposed solutions
- Evaluate the advantages and disadvantages of solutions and give logical reasons
- Use active listening to paraphrase and recall the ideas of other students
- Listen and respond to others empathically
- Agree to consequences and abide by them

---

topics. Teachers need to have final say over whether a topic is appropriate for class discussion and problem-solving.

- Assign other roles to students once they become familiar and comfortable with class meetings

  The class may want a note-taker to record and summarize, or a person to read the agenda. Some teachers suggest a student "affirmer," who gives encouraging feedback during the meetings.

Steps for problem-solving meetings

1. Introduce the problem and review the rules
2. Gather information
3. Begin discussion — "What do you need in order to . . .?"
4. Propose solutions
5. Choose a solution
6. Choose a consequence
7. Close the meeting

Tattling and picking on each other

1. Introduce the problem and review the rules

"I have noticed that there has been a lot of tattling and picking on one another lately. I hear complaints about name-calling and see that some people are feeling bad. I don't think this makes our classroom a good place to work. I want to talk about it in our meeting today. Does everyone agree to try to work on solving this problem, with no put-downs and listening to each other?"

I go around the circle. Everyone nods. If I know that some students have a hard time with meetings, I emphasize the decision and choice to attend. "Are there people who feel they may have difficulty with these rules and would rather not participate today?" Sometimes, a student leaves, but usually returns the next week with much better behavior.

In initial meetings I may select problems from a list "brainstormed" by the class. I want to make sure that the content of the meeting matters — it should be immediate, real, and solvable. I tackle easy-to-solve problems to build success and confidence.

2. Gather information

Begin by asking a specific question so that everyone has a chance to respond. It needs to be a question which focuses on personal observations and feelings, but does not make (or ask children to make) moral judgements. I do not want to ask if it's wrong to pick on others, partly because the answer is so obvious and partly because children continue to do it, despite everyone's agreement that it is wrong. If I begin with the wrong question, the discussion can only become accusatory or defensive, depending on whether you are a "picker" or a "pickee." Instead, I want to phrase an open question:

"We all probably pick on people some times or deliberately tattle. Sometimes if I'm in a bad mood, I might begin to pick on someone, or I remember tattling on my brother, if I wanted to get him in trouble. I wonder if you could remember a time this week when you picked on someone or tattled. Gerry, will you begin, please? Were you a tattler or a picker?"

At this moment the class chuckles a bit, but they are involved. As I go around the circle, I find that most of the children quickly describe their place:

"I pick on people."

"I get picked on," another adds.

"Both," a number reply. The nods of others in the group seem to confirm the personal testimonies. The honesty is striking.

"What makes you feel like picking on someone," I ask next. Or, if a child seems uncomfortable, "What's your guess, why do you think some kids might want to pick on other kids?" When a child is reticent, I might say, "Would you like more time to think? I'll come back to you if you raise your hand when you are ready." A few children will hold back in the early meetings or have difficulty expressing their own feelings, but may take part in finding solutions.

As you gather information, it is important to give *everyone* a chance to have a say. This is a time for only brief comments, not conversation. In the beginning, teachers will often need to redirect and reinforce expectations:

"See, Billy is always bothering me and he don't listen when I tell him to stop, so then I tell the teacher," says James.

"So, when you are bothered and the person doesn't stop you feel like you have to tell the teacher." (Here I just rephrase the statement, eliminating Billy's name).

"I stop but . . ." begins Billy.

"Billy, let's wait on discussion. Molly, you're next."

To encourage information gathering:

- Go around the circle
- Make questions specific
- Narrow or refocus a question if a child seems unsure
- Encourage short responses but not conversation

At the end of the information gathering, the teacher sums up what she heard, and models active listening.

"I heard many of you say that sometimes you pick on someone else and sometimes you feel picked on. A lot of you said that it's a way to be funny and a way to be cool, especially between boys and girls. I heard some people say that they like making people laugh, but I also heard someone say that they think it's funny to get people mad. I also heard that mostly you tattled when you ask others to stop and they didn't. So you weren't listening to each other. It sounds like it's hard to know when picking on people is just 'dumb' or when it gets 'mean.' And I still think that most people don't always feel good about it when it gets mean, although a few think it's not a problem, just 'comedy.' Did anyone hear anything else?"

I try to discern attitudes about the issues and to find the common themes. In this case, it seemed that much of the taunting was a way to get attention and make contact, particularly with the opposite sex. In only a few instances was there an undercurrent of actual hostility, and that seemed restricted to one or two children. The taunting and the tattling both resulted from problems with social skills.

3. Begin discussion

"It sounds like people in this class like each other pretty well and want to be friendly. What do you think you would *need* in order to be more friendly and stop picking on people?"

I frequently begin discussion by asking the students what they think they might need in order to work on the problem. It is often an unusual question to consider — what do I need in order to stop picking on people, or stop tattling, or whatever the issue might be. I do not expect children to automatically know the answer. Questions give focus, point in a certain direction, and stimulate a particular type of discussion.

The discussion that followed (in a group of eleven-year-olds) focused on the nature of the joking in the group.

"No one should be joking about someone else's mother."

"Nobody should be calling you fat or ugly or stuff."

"Like if someone says your clothes look like you got 'em in the dog pound or something, you feel like you want to say something bad back, but you should be able to just not mind and not say nothin' back."

The first two comments reveal concerns with the language they used to joke, probably a crude imitation of the "ranking" they observed with older children, but lacking subtlety. The last comment goes a bit further, and considers the ethics of retaliation. It contrasts what the person feels like doing ("say something bad back") with what a person should do ("not mind"). However, none of the statements were phrased to answer the "What do I need" question. When I rephrased the statements, there was some discomfort.

"You mean I, Joseph, need to stop making jokes about people's hair or ways of dressing? Try saying it that way," I asked. Reluctantly Joseph did.

"Sometimes we know we should do things differently but we feel like doing them anyway. Why is that?" I asked. "Why do you feel a little like making these kinds of jokes?"

Again, it was a relief for the children to be allowed to talk about the reality of their joking. Many agreed that it made them feel smart, or cool, or powerful.

"You know, Miss Charney, if you put somebody down good and everyone laughs, then you feel, well, important."

About tattling, there were numerous statements about children not listening to each other. "I tell her to stop but she don't listen to me. She only listens to the teacher."

"Can you think of some times when children do listen to each other?" I asked.

"At meeting."

"In groups with the teacher or sometimes when we do something like a project."

"I notice how well you listen during those times. Would you like to be able to listen even when the teacher isn't there? How would that make you feel?"

There was general acknowledgement that it would feel good. "Would you feel important like Joseph was saying?" I asked. Most nodded. At that point, the group was ready to "brainstorm" solutions to the two problems which I stated as the "bad jokes" and "kids not listening to kids."

"How do we start to have good jokes, and how do we get kids to listen to kids?" The meeting had taken forty minutes and it was time to stop. I asked if they would agree to think about solutions and bring them to next week's class meeting. I went around the circle, receiving a "yes" from everyone. I closed the meeting by affirming the way I saw them use the three rules. "I really liked your interest in solving this problem. It felt good that you were able to share honest thoughts. I noticed good listening and there were no put-downs. Excellent meeting, class."

4. Propose solutions

In the next meeting (or as part of the same meeting), I want children to brainstorm solutions. Real solutions have to come from discoveries about their needs. When we rush to solutions, or skip over the question of personal needs, we usually end up with "we should" solutions, which tell us what is supposed to happen, but do not bring us any closer to acting differently.

"We should all be nice to each other," one child says. "We should ignore it when someone says something mean." But what will really happen? It's important to help children look for real solutions resulting from a true explanation of the problem. That often means prodding or questioning. "Give me an explanation of how you could be nice to people, even people you don't like a lot." Sometimes it means framing a question so that children confront the contradictions of *wants* and *shoulds:*

"You *should* ignore it, but you *want* to hurt back."

"You *should* be quiet, but you *want* to talk."

"You *should* be nice, but you *want* to ignore someone."

I find that when children are able to explore these contradictions honestly, they also begin to recognize possible solutions.

When the class is ready to seek solutions, the aim is to explore as many ideas as possible and to suggest things without a critical response. I try to set an experimental and playful tone, rather than a sense that every idea must be serious. Good brainstorming needs a sense of release and ease. I ask children to say whatever ideas "pop" into their heads and assure them that they will not be "married" to the ideas. I write each idea on a chart. This is also kept *short* and *lively*, about ten minutes. If the brainstorming is successful, I move on to a serious consideration of the solutions. If not, I may decide we need more time to consider ideas and either go back to more discussion or postpone it for a week.

In this example of picking and tattling, the children's solutions involved creating taxonomies of jokes — what was OK to joke about and what wasn't. It got very complicated and I feared it would be unwieldy, but thinking about what was funny or hurtful was very useful, and endlessly controversial.

It is very tempting for teachers to offer solutions, but we must try hard to resist. As soon as we give in, the children stop working. The teacher becomes the solution-finder. We send the message that there is only one good solution, one which is deposited in the teacher's head for them dig out. For children to learn to solve problems, we must provide the structure and focus, but keep our good advice to ourselves. If there is only one solution, and it is ours, the problem is not a subject for a class meeting. It is simply a teacher mandate, and must be presented as such.

5. Choose a solution

I present two criteria for solutions. They must be:
- Workable and realistic
- In accordance with school rules

I begin by going down the chart and eliminating suggestions. When we do this as a group, the criteria are clarified. If there is disagreement, the solution remains on the active list, which often boils down to no more than three or four suggestions. I will then give children a few minutes of quiet time to think about the advantages and disadvantages of all the potential solutions. I point out that often no single solution is perfect, but that they should try to choose one. I ask them to think of at least two good reasons for supporting their choice (rather than reasons for negating the others). After they've thought for a few minutes, I ask someone to tell what solution they picked and their reasons for choosing it. I stay with that solution and ask if anyone else thought of other advantages.

I then move to disadvantages, modelling ways to disagree without insult. These include "I think" or "It seems to me" sentences:
- "I don't think it would work because . . . " instead of "That's stupid."
- "I agree with the part about _____, but I don't agree about _____."

It's best to avoid linking children's names with ideas. It's not George's idea but "an idea," which helps to establish some objectivity. If I feel that the children are choosing on the merits of George, not the merits of his idea, I will intervene.

After a period of discussion, the class may take a vote. If the solution is to be binding, it needs a consensus or a unanimous decision. "We need a solution that everyone feels comfortable accepting, even if it isn't your most preferred one." An advantage to seeking a unanimous decision is that it gives more weight to a minority opinion, since one lone voice can hold up the decision. I find that children generally take this seriously, but if I believe that it is merely a power struggle, I will invoke "majority rule" or speak privately to the student.

In this case, the children decided on this tattling solution:

"You would only tell the teacher if you had told someone to stop three times and they didn't. But if someone says to stop you gotta' try to stop whatever you are doing wrong to them."

It's of primary importance to specify how we will know if the solution is working. We agreed that our solution was working if:

- There is less picking on each other and tattling
- There is more friendly conversation and activity
- There would be jokes, but no jokes about bodies or family or clothing

To judge our progress, we designed a self-rating check list and a class rating checklist to be filled out weekly (See Figure 5.2).

6. Choose a consequence

What happens if the solution doesn't work, if people don't keep to the agreement?

"What if people don't stop and you tell them and then they're still picking on you?" someone asked.

"There should be a consequence," someone else suggested.

At this point, it was important not to entertain endless "what-if's." It was more important to close the meeting — to sum up the decisions that were made, to remind children of their solution, and to suggest that the agenda for next week was open.

In the weeks that followed, the class behavior was not perfect, but there was visible effort and improvement. The children seemed proud of their work on the problem and anxious for their solutions to work. The cooperative spirit of the meeting also spilled over, and the tone of the room improved. I also began to introduce other types of jokes and joke books into morning meeting and other parts of the curriculum. They especially liked finding out about puns and doodles.

7. Close the meeting

At the end of the meeting, the teacher compliments the class. This reinforces the positive efforts of the children to follow the rules, to listen, to respond, to show respect. If the rules do break down during the meeting, there is one reminder. If after that the rules still aren't working, the meeting should be stopped prematurely. I might say, "I see that it's hard for you to keep to your agreement right now to try to solve a problem; therefore, we need to stop. We will see if this problem is on the agenda for next week." I find that children are far more likely to come back to class meeting in a positive way if the meeting is stopped rather than allowed to deteriorate. The teacher also has time to think about whether the children were having difficulty with the subject or whether it was merely the pre-spring blues. Often the problem is with the subject.

Appropriate topics

Teachers need to translate some topics so they are appropriate for discussion. One common issue is cliques and exclusions. For example, a teacher observed that eight-year-old Kevin was trying hard to find a place with the boys in the

Figure 5.2

INDIVIDUAL AND CLASS SELF-RATING CHECK LIST

Name: _____   Date: __

--- This week I picked on people
 □ not at all   □ Some times   □ alot

--- This week I was picked on
 □ not at all   □ Some times   □ alot

Class Tally for Week of —

Picked on	Tally Marks	Class Totals
□ Not at all		
□ Some times		
□ alot		
Picked on others		
□ Not at all		
□ Some times		
□ alot		
Conclusions:		

room. He had generally played with one other boy, but now he wanted more friends. He was struggling for an "in" by doing favors or clowning for attention. Still, he was left out. In a class meeting, the teacher raised the topic of acceptance. "I see a problem in this class," he said. "Some people seem to be accepted and some people seem not to be. What makes people feel accepted and how do you show that you accept others?" he asked. The children were very specific. He then asked if classmates should be accepted even if sometimes they act like "jerks?" This question grew into an animated discussion of ways we might all sometimes act "jerky" and things to do about it without leaving someone out.

The topic of study habits and work is also fruitful. "How do you decide what is good work? What makes you want to do your best work or what makes you turn in work you know is not very good? What do you need in order to feel good about your work in this class?"

In general, material that is drawn from exposure to the media or older siblings, does not usually make for productive dialogues — drugs, scandals, or teenage pregnancies, for example. The children need to work from their own experiences rather than vicarious ones. They also need to work on problems that are appropriate to their skills and conceptual development, not ones that call for adult expertise.

But it may be possible to take these larger issues and redirect them into meaningful topics. For example, when a class began talking about parents and teenagers who smoke, I translated it into a discussion of "ways you take care of yourself and ways you might not." We were no longer talking about what others did, but why they ate candy or watched scary TV programs. By redirecting some questions, I have encouraged rich discussions about fears and what kinds of things kids do when they feel worried or afraid.

Regardless of my intentions and skills, there are times when I become frustrated and discouraged. I am determined not to have one more meeting. How many more times can I discuss work habits or room clean-up? There are times when I resort to more direct control:

"No one goes home until the math is done beautifully and accurately."

"The next time I hear a complaining voice, there will be no talking for the rest of the day in this room."

But I am still convinced that in the long run, my efforts to engage and involve children in dialogues about the rules and the consequences of breaking them are essential to developing their potentials for ethical behavior — especially when the teacher isn't watching.

Fighting in school

"I'll get you after school."

"I'll see you later . . ."

"Wait till you try to walk home . . ."

The issue of fighting seems worthy of a separate discussion. The hint, suspicion, threat or outbreak of violence is disruptive to the order and safety of school life. Responding to it as an issue, rather than reacting to particular fights, may involve a problem-solving class meeting or a broader, school-wide approach. Punishment is the most prevalent and traditional response, but it is not an effective deterrent to school fighting. Detentions and suspensions are more apt to produce defiance than submission, and fighting may even increase. A student returns to the playground angrier, more isolated and more responsive to taunts from peers. A student returns from a suspension even further behind in school, more vulnerable to academic failures and feelings of inadequacy. Rebellion is more likely than cooperation.

I walked by a fist-fight, outside of my school, just after three o'clock, one day during my second year of teaching. I was in a hurry to get to the subway and get home, so I ignored the fight. Truthfully, I was afraid of the fighting children — they were almost as tall as I was, and perhaps as strong.

For the next five blocks, an elderly man followed, accusing the teachers of not caring about the children. "You call yourself teachers?" he jeered. The voice echoes still. It was one of the hardest things I had to learn — to stop the fights, barging into the circles of riled children and sending them all home. Then, I could do it with kindness, putting an arm around a fighter, clucking about the wrinkled clothes and mussed hair. Even now, when street fights are more unpredictable and laced with the fever of drugs, most children are only mildly resistant to interruption. There is tacit permission to fight if we ignore the threats we overhear, or allow fighting to go on outside the school yard. "I'll get you," mumbled by some fifth grader, within hearing of her teacher, is a communication to the teacher as well as to the enemy.

We can use logical consequences to cope with fighting. The whole system should be discussed, put in writing and agreed upon. The more the student body has a say in deciding the system, particularly for fighting, the more likely they are to follow it. Peer-mediators, systematically trained in mediation techniques, have been very effective in settling disputes and decreasing fights during lunchtime and recess (see Bibliography). Lunch and playground aides would benefit from mediation training also, not only so that they wouldn't have to wait for teachers to return from breaks, but because we need to empower all school personnel to make the community's standards consistent and effective.

It is possible for the faculty to draw up a series of steps they are comfortable with and then to submit their proposal to students for suggestions and ratification. It is essential that students agree to follow these steps beforehand. For example, to agree that if a fight starts, they will have to take a time out and then accept mediation. The contract may be written and signed by all students and parents at any point during the school year.

Systems have many variations, but should probably include the following steps:

1. Declare a time-out

   Students are separated and removed from the scene so they can recover their controls and take time to stop and think. It is important that children are accompanied and monitored, not just sent out into a hall or off, by themselves, to another place in the school.

2. Mediate

   Allow them to say what happened and explain what they need to get along better. Use both empathy and structure. Be willing to listen and hear what each student has to say, but also be prepared to set limits and preserve the rules of conduct the class or school agreed upon.

3. Help with a plan

   Both sides need to compromise and agree. After students say what they need, and hear what the other person needs in order to get along, each agrees to try to work on it by doing one thing that the other needs. A successful solution is where both sides get one thing they want.

4. Make an agreement

   It should be both verbal and written. Both students need to sign it.

5. Agree on a consequence

   If the agreement is broken, the consequence should be clear and unambiguous.

   This type of a system will not stop all fights. But I believe it will decrease fights and the fires that fuel them, rather than escalate them. This process may help children choose the tools of bargaining over the practice of knocking heads!

"Pretzels"

I invented "Pretzels," many years ago, to develop stronger social skills in a first grade class I was teaching. This class was particularly feisty and reckless. A day didn't pass without tears, tattling and teasing. And, in addition, a special threesome intimidated and bullied classmates out of lunch treats, playground balls, and small change. The idea of "Pretzels" was actually inspired by observing the keen bartering powers of some of the children ("Give me that and I'll pick you for my team") and by reading the book *Reality Therapy* by William Glasser. The technique proved effective for this class and on other occasions when I have used it for group building.

Goals:

- Help children identify and name positive social interactions
- Create, model and reinforce friendly and kind interactions, in order to build group trust and cooperation
- Provide a safe and concrete form of reparation when children hurt each other
- Provide a safe and concrete form of appreciation when children help each other

Procedure:
1. Class circles up one time a week for thirty minutes.
2. Teacher passes out ten pretzels sticks to every student in the circle.
3. Going around the circle, each student may make two statements, each accompanied by an appropriate gesture;
   - The first thanks someone for helping or for a special kindness that week. The student then offers a pretzel as a thank-you or token of appreciation.
   - The second tells about a hurt or upset caused by someone in the class. The child making the statement then collects a pretzel as a token of apology or reparation.

Rules:
- Everyone needs to take time to stop and think in order to recall a special kindness or hurt.
- We may only talk about what happened during this week.
- We may only talk about things that happen to ourselves.
- We use a "tagger's choice" rule. If someone thinks that you bothered them, it is what they feel, so you pay. You do not argue.
- "Pretzels" is confidential. That means that you do not talk about what happens in the Pretzels activity with other students in different classes. "Will you say to your cousin in the fifth grade," I ask, "'Guess what happened in Pretzels today!'?"
- "Pretzels" is over when everyone has taken their turn and the teacher announces "Pretzels is closed." Discussions are finished.
- When children had difficulty keeping to the rules at first, I exempted them from the group, allowing them to observe but not to participate. In some cases I set up a "pretzel bank," which accepted and paid pretzels on behalf of non-attending children. In all instances, after one or two times, students asked to return to the group and acted appropriately.

Using "Pretzels"

My introduction of Pretzels to the class emphasizes my positive goals for the class.

"We are going to begin a new activity, which has a kind of funny name but is really for a serious purpose. It's called 'Pretzels' and pretty soon you will find out why it has such a funny name. Pretzels is a way for us to learn to be friendlier and kinder to one another in school, which I think is very serious. I believe that in order for us to do our best work, we all need to feel safe and good in school, and teachers can't make that happen alone. Only when we do it all together do we make it safe and good. That is what I want us to learn and that is why we are going to try this serious activity with the funny name."

"First, I see people act in friendly and kind ways in our class. I see people help others open a thermos that is too tight. I see people help someone to spell a hard word. I see people say nice things like, 'I like your drawing of the house.' Who else has noticed nice and friendly comments or actions?"

The children respond and the teacher records responses on a chart, with the heading, "Ways We Are Helpful and Friendly:"

"Sometimes Sheila shares her jump rope with me when I ask."

"Glenda asks me to play a game with her sometimes."

"John lets me hold his markers."

"Robert gives me some of his cookies."

"People help you when you don't know some things and they tell you stuff."

After brainstorming helpful, friendly behavior, the teacher continues on to identify the negative interactions. "Sometimes, I also notice ways that you hurt each other physically or with your words. I see people push in line. I hear name-calling and teasing. I notice tattling and bossiness. What do you notice that we do in this classroom that hurts other people and isn't kind or friendly?" I do not want to get lists of accusations! I list on a chart, under the heading "Ways We Hurt Each Other" key words, such as "unfair," "teasing," "put-downs," "bossing," "bullying," and a few examples for each.

"Sometimes people say they hold seats and you can't hold seats."

"Kids pick their friends to be on teams."

"Kids say bad things about your mother."

"Kids take your stuff and don't ask."

"Kids say you're stupid if you don't know how to do something right."

We read over the charts, reviewing "Ways We Are Helpful and Friendly" and the "Ways We Hurt Each Other."

"My goal is to help, not hurt" I say emphatically. "What is *your* goal? What do you think makes us all feel good and like to be in school? What do *you* think?" I ask different children directly.

Eventually, everyone responds unanimously, "Our goal is to help and be friendly."

I then teach the children the steps in Pretzels. The children quickly proposed a modification, which involved how many pretzels were given out. They felt that if someone was very hurtful, they should pay more. So we set up a scale — three pretzels for hitting or calling bad names, but just one if a person is joking when they tease, or something was an accident.

When I first started Pretzels, I felt that it was a risk. I wasn't sure what would happen when children were singled out consistently for hurtful behavior. I wasn't sure if there would be an increase in resentments and retaliation. I also wasn't sure if children would be too intimidated by the bullying to be able to confront it. Mostly, I worried that there would be far more complaints than compliments and thank-you's, and that Pretzels would turn into endless gripe sessions, with little affirmative relief.

In fact, with the aid of teacher modeling and reinforcement, children came to love noticing the kind and friendly contributions of their peers. They enjoyed passing over the pretzels, and often volunteered extras, "'cause she really made me feel good when I was crying." They were highly observant and able to be very specific in their comments. Clearly, they enjoyed the role of giving praise and seemed motivated to receive it from others.

My fear that some children would be singled out was accurate. Martin, for example, went into "deficit-pretzels," if there was such a thing. Robert and Elise learned about negative numbers, as well, since the other children weren't hesitant to identify their behavior. Strikingly, Robert, Martin and Elise quickly paid up, till empty-handed of all pretzels. It was also evident that hostilities were decreasing rather than increasing. The class seemed more appeased and Martin, for example, appeared to be generally less aggressive.

Pretzels marked changes for me, as well as for the class. I recall paying Martin a pretzel one week for helping me clean and set up the paints. Other children followed suit, so that Martin received a number of pretzels for helping others out. Some time later, he exclaimed, with obvious pride, "Look, Miss Charney I got six pretzels this week." And then he did a funny thing. He went over to another child and handed over his pretzel stash. "Here, you can have these. I don't like pretzels," he said.

◆

In Chapter 10, I describe another group process, "Center Circle," in which children identify and name social interactions in a format that is safe and supportive. Other gestures replace the exchange of pretzels. But for this first grade class, the pretzels were both gift and payment, a logical consequence of one's own choices and actions.

Summary

I use logical consequences based on two assumptions. The first is that this approach is valid for all children and will work for all children. It is not restricted to the highly verbal, high-achieving or socially adept populations. It may take more time with children who are more impulsive, or by history more troubled, but it preserves the integrity of the child. Their direct and essential involvement in solving problems is as central to the process of growth and healing as sun and exercise.

Second, it is not a process that occurs in a vacuum. It depends on a responsive collaboration of teachers and students. Teachers work to set boundaries and limits, give structure and responsibility. Students plan their actions and think about their choices. It is a process in which both students and teachers make mistakes and, ideally, grow because of them.

6

Small Things — Time-Out

"Why do you think kids go to time-out?"
"Cause, like you aren't following the rules . . . and I pushed somebody."
Seth, age 6

"What's time-out feel like?"
"Like you've been bad. And you wanna' be good."
Anne, age 7

"Should you have time-out in your classroom?"
"Yes. If you didn't, everybody would be out of control and doing
whatever they wanted. They'd just wrestle all day."
Jamaal, age 8

"What's the worst thing about time-out?"
"You gotta sit, sit, sit."
Steven, age 5 1/2

"Time-out" is one part of a system of logical consequences. All children, in the natural course of things, explore limits, test boundaries, lose control, act out, defy authority and "forget" the very rules that they uttered just five minutes ago. Used correctly, in combination with other techniques, time-out can help them to make mistakes and test the limits well within the guardrails of adult controls. It is a system which is protective, and at the same time allows the

93

child's own struggle for autonomous control. Time-outs can establish the safety nets and boundaries of rules, while promoting the incentive and dignity of self-control.

Marty pokes her neighbor during a meeting. "Marty — time-out!"

Rachel interrupts . . . again. "Rachel — time-out!"

Billy tumbles backward off his already tilted chair.

Tyrone shoves ahead of the line to get out *first*.

Janie continues to draw after the signal.

Maggie tells Paul, "Shut up, stupid."

Simmie and David are pencil-dueling during math lesson.

"Why should I?" whines Corky, when you ask her to pick up her things.

The teacher responds each time.

"Corky, Simmie and David, Billie, Tyrone, Janie, Maggie — time-out!"

Guidelines for a time-out program

The following ten points are suggested as ways to implement an effective time-out program in the classroom. They are based on my own experience and the work of other teachers, particularly in the Greenfield Center School, where time-out has been used in grades K through 6. Each will be discussed in depth.

1. There is a familiar, predictable and consistent procedure for classroom time-outs.
2. "Small Things — Time-Out." The key is to pay attention to the minor disturbances, rather than waiting for the work of the classroom or the controls of the child to deteriorate.

3. Time-outs affirm the integrity of the school rules, the work of the group and the disruptive student.
4. Time-out is a direction, *not* a negotiation. The appropriate times for explanations are before and after the consequence, *never during*.
5. "I like you. I don't like that behavior." Time-outs focus on the behavior, not the character of the student. Teachers need to reassure children of acceptance even when rules are broken.
6. Time-outs emphasize choice and faith. Children *choose* to follow or not follow the rules. When they lose controls or make poor choices, time-outs help them recover their controls, and make another decision. Teachers express *faith* in the ability of students to return and follow the rules again — and again.
7. Time-outs are democratic. They are for the sneaky and rude activity as well as the loud and rowdy. *Everyone* gets a chance at time-out, because everyone breaks a rule some time — from the boys wrestling on the math rug to the girls whispering in the corner!
8. Time-outs may be carried out in another classroom. This is best if:
    * The distractions continue while in the time-out chair
    * The stimulation of the room continues to overwhelm or agitate the student
    * The teacher needs a time-out from the student
9. Teachers need to show empathy for their rule-breakers.
10. Time-outs do *not* work for *all* children, especially when children are already out of control or willfully engaged in power-struggles. Teachers may need to continue time-outs, to protect the work of the group, while also seeking other strategies.

1. A familiar, consistent, predictable procedure

Marty gets up from her seat and goes to the time-out chair, located in a visible (not central) area of the classroom. She sits for five minutes, or until she receives a gesture from her teacher to return to her group. Signaled by her teacher's nod, Marty quietly returns to her place. There has been no explanation, no discussion. The unstated message is, "You know the rules. You know you are disturbing the meeting. You will be able to recover your controls and return as a member of the group."

The time-out chair

Time-out is a designated chair, located in a visible place in the classroom, away from a door or busy aisles and activity centers. It is not adjacent to the easel or blocks, and never in the hall or a dark corner. One teacher of eights used a time-out pillow instead of a chair. Children liked the idea of being less conspicuous and more comfortable.

A standard time

Time-outs are generally two to three minutes for fives, and five minutes for ages six and older.

A standard way to be released

Children may be released from time-out in several ways. It's best to be consistent once you choose a way.

- With fives, the teacher tends to release the child using her voice, "Laura, you may come back now and remember your quiet voice." She names the expectation and appropriate behavior.
- With sixes, sevens, and eights, a signal from the teacher is preferred — a nod or hand gesture. There is still a brief contact between the teacher and student, a recognition and confirmation that the student is ready to return, which assures the student as well as the teacher.
- With older students, nines through twelves, familiar with time-out, my preference is for a procedure which shares decision and responsibility. "Return when you know you are ready to follow the rules" or more specifically, "Return when you know you are ready to make helpful comments to your math partner." Even with older students the responsibility is shared, not turned-over. If I see a student return and resume the misbehavior, then I will determine the readiness next time.
- Some teachers like to use timers, such as sand timers, which are quiet and don't attract attention. Often children like the timer, which gives them a sense of control, although it must also be understood that the task is not merely to bide time, but to recover controls.

Time-out is carefully introduced

Teachers introduce time-out to the class during the first week of school as part of the process of establishing rules and consequences. I present time-out as a way that grown-ups help children to get back in control. Children can also teach themselves to get back their controls and remember their rules. I stress that time-out is a job; it is work to recover your controls.

I also explain that other people have a job to do when someone is in time-out — to help a person concentrate by not disturbing or making fun of the person. Over and over, I remind children that time-out doesn't mean teachers don't like you. Time-out is a way for the teacher to help you teach yourself to recover your controls.

"Everyone forgets their controls sometimes and everyone forgets the rules sometime. Children forget the rules, so do teachers and parents. Our rules make it safe and good for everyone in school. Not just me, not just Betsy — everyone. So, it's very important that we respect the rules and use them. When we do forget or choose not to use a rule, we need to remember. We need a time-out. Time out is a special time to think, to think about the rules we need to keep our classroom safe and good and to gather our own controls. Then we are ready to come back and join the group."

Role-playing

From ages five through eight, students love to role-play and practice the steps of time-out. Students rehearse how to go to time-out, "think" and return to the group showing the appropriate behavior. It is also important for the other students to rehearse their "jobs" when a classmate is in time-out.

I act the part of a student who sits in the time-out chair and bangs her feet and chants provocatively. "Is this the way to be in time-out?" I ask. Students respond with a no. "And why not?" I will continue. I want to make sure that my class understands the purpose of time-out.

"You're not supposed to make noise, " one student replies.

"Why not?" I want to reinforce the idea that time-out is for "thinking." "If I see you singing I'm not sure that you are really thinking and remembering your controls," I might say. "Now, who can show us the right way to sit and think in time-out?"

Another time, I might play the part of a student and read the sign that says to take two crackers for snack. I look around to see if anyone is watching me and gobble up six crackers. Another student, acting the part of the teacher, says, "Time-out." I start to argue and fuss. "Is this what to do when the teacher says 'Time-out?' Who can show us what to do?" We will also go over what to do if you want to talk to the teacher. "If you have special reasons for taking extra snack, when may you tell the teacher?"

Later, Margie acts out going to time-out and I act out the part of another pestering classmate. "Whattaya' doin', Margie?" I whisper, and start to play with her. "Am I doing my job now?" I ask the class. I reinforce that the job of classmates and friends is to help the person in time-out to concentrate. "How do we help our friends when they are in time-out?" I will ask. Eventually the answers come:

"Let them think."

"Let them concentrate."

"Let them be alone."

It is critical to remind children that they can be helpful after a time-out, not hurtful. "You can welcome friends back to the group, after a time-out. You can show them what the group is doing. You can give them a friendly pat on the back."

Share feelings about time-out

It's important for children to talk about how time-out feels. Most often it feels bad, although that is not the objective. Five-year-olds tend to feel bad because they strongly want the approval of teacher. Sixes are more apt to experience

Noah may not call Mark "Fatty," even if he claims he's joking.

"Time-out, Noah."

pangs of guilt, stemming from confused desires to do good and also to do bad. With sevens, the children are vulnerable to self-criticism and criticism from adults, and sometimes an exaggerated fear of disapproval. At eight, peer visibility and the resulting embarrassment surfaces. Issues of fairness and justice (particularly the teacher's) appear by ten and eleven, and students regularly take sides or make judgments about their own and others' time-outs. They are more apt to be angry, at the teacher or at classmates.

Here are some examples of typical feelings:

"You feel bad in time-out cause you wish you were good." (Age 5)

"The worst thing about time-out is you get sent away from everybody and you can't talk." (Age 6)

"Time-out feels angry. I'm angry at myself for doing what I did, like punching." (Age 7)

"I'm embarrassed because the whole class was there." (Age 8)

"You feel embarrassed and that you've done the worst thing in the world! Especially if the teacher yells at you and then everyone stares." (Age 9)

"Time-out feels bad, because it takes time out of your day with friends or important things that you have to do." (Age 10)

"It's a quiet place if I know what I did to get there. It's an angry place if I don't know what I did." (Age 11)

"Sometimes time-out is OK. I mean I feel bad when it happens, like when I'm hyper and I have to go to time-out. But sometimes I think there should be other things too, cause kids don't really learn that much from time-out when they get older, anyway." (Age 12)

2. Small things — time-out

The key to using a time-out system effectively is to pay attention to the small disruptions, the minor infractions and misbehaviors. If we use time-out correctly, children do not take the step from control to out-of-control. We take action before the lesson is in ruins, before self-controls deteriorate — the student's and our own. When we wait for things to get worse, we are rarely disappointed.

We don't allow the minor drumming on the desk to reach a crescendo. The nagging and nuisance-behavior does not go on until finally all our "buttons" are pushed. The background whispers and snide teasing are not ignored until fists fly or tears pour.

When we wait for an explosion, we risk ugly confrontations. It can be very difficult for children to reenter their group and recover a sense of good will after making a scene. The eruptions tend to be frightening and isolate the child from peers. They may also threaten the relationship of the teacher to her class. I recall once, in a rage, yanking a child (who had just hurled scissors at someone) out of the room. A little later, at a drawing and writing time, another child showed me her picture. It depicted a large lady with a terrible frown holding a smaller person with tears. The caption said, "Miss Charney taking Michael outside." It was a scary picture.

The hope is that we will be able to intercept Michael before he throws things and before our patience is gone. We must deal with the small things so they don't grow. We try to deal with the rude remark rather than the physical fight, the distracting gesture rather than the outburst that stops a lesson, the whispered secrets rather than established cliques.

A pattern of casual "shut-ups" is not allowed to grow into one of constant insults. Noah may not call Mark "Fatty," even if he claims he's joking. Kevin may not use his superior size to push others aside, take a pencil or reserve first place in line. The group lesson might be stalled if I say, "Martin, the blackboard is this way!" for the fiftieth time between clenched teeth instead of saying, "Martin, time-out." The small side-shows will not devastate the lesson, or the temper of the teacher. But, unless they are confronted, these "small disturbances" add up to constant noise and interruptions which drain and divert the best intentions. Often they are the very things we pretend not to notice.

Every teacher could make an endless list — during class meeting Eddie spaces-out, Margie fiddles with her shoes (loudly ripping the Velcro straps), Darryl waves his hand while someone else is talking, Jeannie smiles and winks in secret collusion with her friend Sara. Alex regularly careens around the room — his idea of walking is full-speed-ahead. He's a large boy, and he frequently bumps into the furniture, other children and even largish teachers. He's quick to say "sorry" and express genuine regret, but if he slowed down he would hardly crash at all and no one would get hurt. Why make a fuss? He's only ten — he can't help it. But the fact is that he *can* help it! He can move slowly and with planning — or not move at all.

It is important that children understand that they can help it. Minor disturbances are within their control. Eddie is able to listen; Margie to disregard her shoe straps; and Darryl to put his hand down while someone else is talking. We know that at age two the ability to inhibit behavior is lacking. At age four, wishes may still dictate over reality. But at age ten, Alex can tell himself not to run, and he can follow his own directions. If we focus on "small things," the poke does not turn into a punch, and the poking child is still very much in control of his own body. With help, he is able to "pull himself together," recover his controls. When we intervene before the behavior escalates, we increase the chance for self-regulation and we protect the child from outbursts which threaten self-respect.

3. Time-outs protect the integrity of the school rules, and the work of the group and student

Donny

Sherill is speaking. She is telling the group about a week-long visit from her cousin. She confesses that it wasn't so easy to have to share her room, her possessions, her parents. She further admits that she wouldn't let her cousin ride her bike and her father made her. "That was just so unfair. I had a terrible weekend." Donny meanwhile is fidgeting with an eraser, which he has balled-up so that it rolls. He begins to roll it, making an inclined plane with his leg. He watches with rapt attention as the eraser-ball travels one leg, then another. He is so intent on his own activity, Sherill and the group have momentarily ceased to exist. As the ball gathers momentum, he looks around catching the eye of another classmate, a giddy grin spreading across his face. "Time-out, Donny." I say quietly.

Donny gets up and leaves the group. He looks back, making a face. The group stays riveted on Sherill. The few initial displays from Donny, as he settles into the time-out chair, are ignored. After several minutes, he appears to relax, tension subsiding. His attention — he is still within earshot of the circle — returns to the meeting. A nod lets him know that he can return. He takes his seat. The group is still questioning Sherill.

"What did your father do when you grabbed your bike away from your cousin?" the class wants to know.

Donny raises his hand. "Did your cousin get mad at you, too?" he questions. Donny has rejoined the class.

◆

Several things have happened. The teacher has preserved Sherill's turn to speak. She has followed through on the expectation that children respect each

Translation:

They are bad to their
friends. They hurt
people's feelings.

Kids can learn how to
control themselves.

You can't talk.

Name: Erin

Group: _____ Age: 6

1) Why do you think kids go to time-out?

tery Bod [to friends]
teny hyret Pre)Pi's   Fiei)ngs

2) What's good about time-out?

Y   kids   can
    Lren   how +0
   Canteri   teme Scveds

3) What's the worst thing about time-out?

Yo y   Can't
take

other's "turn" by actively listening to one another. She has also intercepted Donny before he receded further from the meeting or became disruptive. The short time-out allowed Donny to redirect his energy and take charge of himself, making it possible for him to reinvest in the group. The brief exchange between teacher and child did not distract from Sherill's story or divert attention from the sharing to the misbehavior. The time-out ritual is not intrusive and leaves Donny's action as inconspicuous as possible. There is no need to admonish or scold. The objectives — to safeguard the group and ensure individual conduct — were met. Donny's behavior did not progress to the point where it upset Sherill, the teacher or Donny because the teacher reacted to "small things."

4. Time-out is a direction, not a negotiation

In the immediate enforcement of time-out, lengthy verbal explanations and negotiations are strictly avoided. Imagine if instead of the directive, "Time-out," the teacher had said, "Donny you need to go to time-out, because you are rolling a ball and not listening to Sherill." Would Donny, now the center of attention, be more apt to agree or to argue, "I *was so* listening . . ." An argument might lead next to a confrontation, and Sherill's sharing would quickly take second place to the duel between teacher and student.

If the teacher had just reached over and taken the ball from Donny, called his name or nudged him gently back into the activity, with no mention of time-out, wouldn't that be as effective and easier? My experience is that while reminders work occasionally, small disturbances usually keep erupting like popcorn — one after another that take the attention of the teacher and group. Time-out sends the message that you are *truly* expected to follow the rules.

There is a strong urge in teachers and parents to justify and defend their enforcement of the rules each time an incident occurs. We want to be clear and want to be sure children understand, and we also want them to agree. This may promote a form of child "blackmail." Children will use whatever language is effective, such as "You're a bad teacher. You're not nice." or even the "H" word, "I hate you, Teacher. You're mean." When we hasten to convince children that the rules are right, fair, and necessary, we shift attention from the misbehavior. It is vitally important that children understand what is right, fair and necessary about the rules, but they don't usually understand those concepts at the moment a rule is invoked. In a meeting circle, my students brilliantly explain and defend the Golden Rule, but when caught shoving someone on the playground, it's usually the other person's fault, the referee "stinks," and the rules are "stupid."

Gabrielle

Gabrielle was an eleven-year-old student who had developed negotiation to an art, but also to her own detriment. A fifth grade student when I met her, she came to work with me on her reading, which was delayed for her age. At age eleven, she was presented to me as a difficult but appealing child. "She has tantrums," I was told kindly by the principal and former resource room teacher. I could expect at least one tantrum a week, which showed progress because they had once been more frequent.

Along with the usual tears and blubbering, Gabrielle hurled selected insults, which revealed a knack for the precise words that might hurt and offend her teachers. To the kind, mild-mannered principal, she yelled, "Child-molester." To her stern, but fair-minded classroom teacher, she yelled, "You're picking on me. You pick on me 'cause I'm not your pet." And to another, warm and affectionate teacher, she charged, "You think everyone likes you, but they don't."

Usually, in the din of comforting this wailing child, in quieting her accusations and offering reassurance — "Of course I like you" — no one remembered what had started the tantrum in the first place. It was always the same. Gabrielle was asked for some piece of work, work that she couldn't — or wouldn't — do. The tears and stomping stopped the minute the threat of the work was removed. She was hardly out-of-control. She was using her controls effectively to manipulate teachers and hide her real deficits and fears. The vulnerability of the adults helped to establish this pattern of behavior. Gabrielle was skilled at creating a sense of doubt and loss of clarity. It was easy to over-explain and reassure her with affection. In the end, she was not asked to come through with her work or required to use self-controls like other children. Always, her academic program was modified and reduced in hopes that another tantrum might be averted.

"You have two minutes," I told her the first time. "Get yourself back together, go back to your work or you go home." Sobs, tears, loud cries, insults. I counted. I pointed to the timer. Two minutes. Through the blanket of red eyes and writhing motions, she watched me. At the two-minute buzzer, the principal entered, according to our prearranged plan, and took her crying and cursing to the office. Her mother was called immediately, according to the second part of the plan, and she went home. Gabrielle returned the next day, cheerful and composed. The day went fine, the week passed without event. The second week she told me the work was too hard and began to whimper.

"No whimpering, Gaby."

"You're supposed to understand," she said puckering her mouth, jutting out her lips in disdain. "You're supposed to help us kids, and not be so mean."

"Time-out," I replied. "Two minutes"

I was very prepared for this student. I had school and parent support. I knew her history, her deflated self-esteem. I'd seen her bluff and fake. I knew the many counts against her — family problems, reading disabilities, dark skin in a light-skinned community. I struggled with my own controls, to appear calm and to keep my mouth shut. I would not say, "Yes, I am understanding. No I'm not mean. I do this for your own good." I would not try to convince her that she could do her work, or try to explain, reason or argue her into compliance. It is not a disgrace that this young, willful girl could create such a rush of anxiety and doubt in the minds and purposes of adults. Certainty is seldom found in teaching. With Gabrielle, it took a while to put the pieces of the puzzle together.

It is not remarkable that this girl never went home again, that she returned after one and a half minutes to her work, mindful of the timer. She looked grim and wary. She snarled and glowered, but she sat back at the table, beginning a long journey through syllables and vowel utterances and Judy Blume's captivating stories to achieve some degree of reading success. The next couple of years were good for Gabrielle with all her teachers, although the onset of adolescence and new social pressures again took their toll.

Gabrielle helped me realize my obligation as a teacher to insist that children draw on their own controls — and not to apologize. She was not the ordinary student, testing and experimenting with the boundaries of the world. She was erecting a shield for what she saw as failures and inadequacies. Time-out helps create self-controls for the majority of children who do not have a misdirected need to manipulate and control others. But it is not the time for negotiations and explanations.

◆

There are key times for explanations — before the time-out process begins or after it is completed. Children must be reassured that there is meaning to what they are doing. I believe that meaning creates trust. Rules grow from a social contract which enhances everyone's well-being. We work together to secure the contract and establish rules with children which assert meaning and value. We need to consistently refer to this framework. Why is it wrong to call names? Why do I feel angry that you lied to me about your work? Because they are actions which break our contract, which work against our best attempts to create trust, friendship, justice, and a community where everyone — adults and children — wants to work each day.

At the right moment, explanation and discussion help students construct meaning and take responsibility. At the wrong times, explanation creates evasion. My hunch is that discussions which involve students in constructing rules, or occur some time *after* a "time-out," foster responsibility. Discussions which occur when a rule is being enforced will stimulate evasion.

After time-out, a short conference with a student may be productive. With younger children, teachers may want to end time-out by reiterating the expectations:

"You can go back now and use your quiet voice."

"You look ready to go back to the blocks and remember to be a safe builder."

"You may come back and show me that you remember how to use the meeting rules."

The teacher reinforces the appropriate behavior and reiterates her faith in the child's ability to use the appropriate behavior.

With older children, no additional explanation is usually necessary. Later in the day, the teacher might ask, "Do you know why you were sent to time-out this morning?" or "Tell me why you think you had a time-out today." If time-outs have been repetitive, I might start a *short* conversation by saying, "I notice that you have been in time-out several times this week. You seem to have trouble taking care of yourself during writing period. What's up?"

This is the time when I am willing to listen, to hear the other side and even to negotiate — "What do you think might help you during writing time?" or "What do you think might help you avoid quarreling with Maggie?" After time-outs may be the best time to reassure children of the next guideline as well.

5. "I like you, but I don't like that behavior"

"I like you but I don't like it when you hurt other people."

"I don't like it when you don't listen to directions, but I do like you."

"I like that you have so much to say, but I don't like it when you keep interrupting."

These statements preserve the knowledge of the teacher's ongoing approval and secure the child's own sense of inner approval. I've done something "bad" but my teacher still likes me — and I can still like myself. If either statement is lacking, children may become utterly discouraged.

These statements are not made every time a child is sent to time-out. I introduce the concept at the start of the year and periodically repeat it. I also reassure children when I see that time-outs are frequent, or hard, or if I feel angry. Angry or intense feelings, calculated or not, are best dealt with *after*, not during, time-out.

"When I sent you to time-out yesterday, I was feeling angry at you. It makes me angry to see you act silly at every meeting. And I think it makes you feel bad when I get angry. Is that true?" (Student nods) "I get angry because I want your good contributions at meeting and I want to see, not the silly behavior, but the smart behavior I know you have." I acknowledge my anger and the student's response to it, often a combination of anger and upset. I also want to convey the idea that my anger comes from positive expectations. The aim is to affirm, by recognizing and naming the strengths that we see in students, while holding them to the limits.

Children are particularly vulnerable to criticism and to consequences at certain ages. At seven, I have seen some severe reactions to time-out, and teacher disapproval of any kind. The reactions often grow from the fear of not being liked and a need for immediate reassurance. I don't eliminate time-outs from the classroom, but I do make a concerted effort to use a mild manner and to provide many assurances, often at the end of the day. A positive comment is better than a reminder of the time-out. "I see you really made the block shelf look beautiful."

Children entering adolescence also tend to be highly vulnerable. Adult rebukes become easily exaggerated, as do many other things, particularly when children are in the throes of finding everything from their hair to their parents unacceptable. While there is often a surface disclaimer, such as "Who cares," I am convinced that most children care deeply and need repeated reassurances. I find that they need to hear that they are liked and that they are likable, in specific and realistic terms.

There are some children, at any age, because of their make-up or temperament who find time-outs especially painful. They are sometimes our most difficult children, yet they must be protected from becoming unlikable to themselves, their peers and their teachers. My approaches to these children are detailed in Ch. 7.

Time-outs work best when there is a reliable message, in words and body language, that teachers accept and like their students even when they don't like some of their behavior.

6. Time-outs emphasize choice and faith

When I say, "Time-out," I am still implying choice, but a choice that the student has already made. The child has chosen not to cooperate — this time. Next time the choice may be different. The choice is either to follow meeting rules or to go to time-out. It is a true decision. When I remind a child who has started to whisper to her friend instead of listening, I restate that choice. Sometimes the child decides to stop whispering and plugs-in to the meeting. Sometimes she doesn't, and a time-out is enforced. The vocabulary of time-out establishes over and over the choices, and importantly, the consequences of those choices. "You can choose to speak quietly to your partner while you're working together, or you can choose to keep yelling and go to time-out. You have to choose."

When we state the choices for children, and stress their essential role as the choice-maker, we state our faith in their ability to achieve self-controls. One eight-year-old boy made daily rampages to be first in line. He pushed, he ran, he calculated his timing to the second so he could always to be first. Finally, after several time-outs, he was told, "You can continue to try to be first in line, and to shove or push and then go to time-out. Or you can decide that being first isn't always so important and probably then you won't go to time-out. It's your choice."

After a few days, there was a noticeable shift in his behavior, as if he were testing out a new mode. A few more days after that, he quietly confided to his teacher that he didn't think he had to be first every day anymore. It really wasn't *so* important, but he still wanted to be first once in awhile.

It was important that the teacher did not attempt to argue the objective importance of being first in line with him. The teacher could and did establish the boundaries, but she could not establish the essential meaning of being first in line for this child. That was his choice. He was allowed to come to a meaningful decision and then to take charge of that decision for himself, even though it meant giving up something he cared about. That, I feel, is a perfect example of self-control.

When there is not a real choice, I will modify the expectations until there is a choice. For example, when I feel that a child cannot choose to sit and attend for a thirty minute period, I might say, "You can sit and pay attention for ten minutes." This affirms the controls that exist in all children and our faith that each of them can make the choices to use those controls.

7. Time-outs are democratic

"I think that kids go to time-out for foolin' around. Well, that's boys. Girls go cause they're talking when they're not supposed to," said Peter, age 11. "I guess you could say that girls are loudmouths and boys act goofy."

Time-out needs to applied equally to the chronic troublemakers and the victims of the occasional mishap. Everyone has an opportunity to misbehave. It applies to the boys who are most likely to tumble from chairs, wriggle instead of paying attention, and flick the pattern blocks across the floor. It applies to the girls who may be more apt to tell secrets and make snide remarks. It applies to the sneaky, as well as the obvious, misdemeanors. It applies to Gretchen who loves to sit next to Seth, who is so easy to engage. Given a little poke or tickle, Seth flops and writhes flamboyantly, quickly catching the teacher's eye and often a seat in the time-out chair. But when the teacher notices Gretchen's provocation, she must say, "Gretchen, time-out."

While some children struggle more with their controls, and thus receive more time-outs, most children forget the rules at some time, if we pay attention to the provocations as well as what Peter called "goofy" behavior. Time-outs need to be there for Gabrielle's outbursts, for Alex when he bumps a path through the classroom and for Dinah, who is usually a model student.

Dinah was cheerful, serious about her work, adored her teacher, got along with her fifth-grade classmates. She was a class leader and an ardent contributor to each and every project. She loved to play and she loved to work. She was tearful when her best friends left her out and tried to be a better friend when she was the "leaver-outer." She put in overtime as a school tutor, enjoying her role as a young teacher and counselor for smaller peers. It was something of a surprise, a year later, to see Dinah in the time-out chair in her sixth grade classroom. Dinah?

"I went to time-out today!" she announced with a twinge of boast in her voice. "What a jerk," she added, speaking of her current teacher. For the first time, Dinah had risked a challenge to authority. It was in part a function of her age and development. Unquestioned devotion to teachers was a thing of the past. Usually by age eleven, children are anxious to try out a small act of defiance, to question and judge the fairness of elders.

"She blamed Angela and Angela didn't do a thing," Dinah stated righteously.

"So what did you do?"

"I told her she was a jerk. Well, she was!"

It would have been simple for her current teacher to dismiss Dinah's behavior, to pretend she hadn't heard. But, it was important that Dinah got sent to time-out because it demonstrated the teacher's self-respect, "I don't insist that you like me or agree with me. I do insist that you show respect." Time-out provides a safe way for children to test the limits, while still maintaining the structure and order of the classroom. It is the "deed," not the character of the child that is the issue. Time-out is there for all children.

8. Time-outs may be completed in another classroom

Children go to time-out in another classroom when:
- The distraction continues while in time-out
- The stimulation of the room continues to overwhelm or agitate the student
- The teacher needs a time-out from the student

All three conditions should be anticipated during the course of a year. Some children may try to use time-out as an attention-getter. Others may initially test the process by leaving time-out or refusing to leave it. Sometimes a child is already too aroused or overloaded to recover and continues to call out, cry or carry-on while in time-out. Last, but not least, a child may have stripped the patience of the teacher by flicking the paint one too many times or making one too many insolent remarks. Before losing her control, the teacher sends the student for a time-out in another classroom. To minimize the chance of escalating a conflict, these steps are suggested:

- A child is sent to get another teacher, according to a prearranged "buddy system." That teacher will leave her own class temporarily to come and get a child who needs the time-out. Such a request is treated as a priority.

- When the "buddy teacher" enters the room, the classroom teacher says, "Marty, you need to go with Ms. Clayton now." Marty leaves, escorted by Ms. Clayton, but without conversation. Ms. Clayton does not ask Marty what happened or scold in any way. The student is ushered to a quiet area of the new room for a time-out, which is visible to the teacher and is not by the door. Marty's controls may be borderline at this point. It is important that he or she is not left alone, in an empty room or hallway, or out of eyesight of the teacher.

- The usual period of a time-out in another room is fifteen minutes, although in some cases an entire morning or afternoon may be the anticipated consequence. One child observed, "The worst thing about time-out is that sometimes teachers forget about you!"

We certainly do "forget," when suddenly there is peace in our classroom and relief from an obvious strain. I think there are times when memory is jostled only after we have properly recovered our own controls. The demands that certain children place on teachers and the class are not to be minimized. If a half-hour break allows everyone to "regroup" and rejuvenate, it's a useful and effective procedure.

"You're right, I did forget, " I admit to Peter, who had sat dutifully in another classroom for forty-five minutes. "Suddenly I noticed that it was too quiet in the room, no one was arguing, and I realized we were missing Peter!" I added. Peter grinned. I grinned.

- The teacher comes to get her student, releasing the child from time-out. She is able to assess whether the child is ready to return and can help him or her reenter the group gracefully.

"Do you think you are ready to return and follow the rules of the room?" If the child simply agrees, then teacher and student return to the classroom.

If the child starts to cry or attack the teacher, the teacher might say, "It looks like you need more time to gather your controls so you can choose to return to our room."

There are two cautions. First, don't try to process the incident with the child at this point. Generally, children are ready to return before they are ready to discuss. Returning to work allows the child time to settle down and the anger or upset to subside, so there can be a productive dialogue later. We may soothe or hold a child shortly after an incident, but a quick hug, pat on the back, or appointment to talk later usually facilitates recovery better than discussion. Both student and teacher may need some distance to think through a problem. (With younger children, "distance" may be only five minutes.) If necessary, I have children wash their face and straighten themselves out so they can return to the classroom collected and composed.

Second, teachers must monitor the response of other children during time-outs and establish a respectful tone, not a shameful one. This is done by introducing and reinforcing time-out as a serious task, and by modelling a quiet and considerate manner. Children in both classrooms must do their job. Their job is to let the person in time-out concentrate and then to receive him or her back into the group.

- When children are sent out of the room for time-out, it is best to have a discussion later that day or the next morning. The goals of the conference are to try to work together to find a way to prevent the problem from reoccurring, and to reestablish a friendly flow between teacher and student. (See Ch.8 for a detailed discussion of teacher-student conferences.) In these meetings, there is an exchange of views and an exchange of ideas. It is not necessary for teacher and student to figure out exactly what happened or to reach absolute agreement. It is less important to try to figure out causes and cures than to listen, to try to understand the other's perspective, and to come up with a realistic alternative acceptable to both. The teacher must offer to help the child manage better and to show that she is an advocate, not an adversary.
- I usually call parents when children need to be sent out of the classroom. Sometimes I will anticipate, and alert a parent that this step may be necessary, or I may inform parents afterwards. This helps avoid misunderstandings and encourages a united effort to help deal with the issues. Generally, parents are supportive, and concerned about their children missing classroom work. The effectiveness of time-out can be greatly increased with parental approval; parental disapproval often makes the system counter-productive. Indeed, *nothing* works if the parents aren't working with you.

9. Teachers need to show empathy for their rule-breakers

One thirteen-year-old defined, for me, an empathic response to children when he explained why he liked his teacher, why all the kids did. "'Cause he doesn't let you get away with stuff, like not doing your work, but if it's raining and he knows you're restless, he'll let you run around awhile."

I do not equate empathy with pity or excuse-making. Instead we try to understand the *child's* experience, in the way that he or she experiences it. It is a way of listening to what the child is saying, even when we do not sanction the behavior. We may not sanction a child's lie, but we identify its humanness.

We show empathy for our rule-breakers when we welcome them back to the group, express faith in their capacity to improve, show that we "see" their strengths, as well as their weakness. Empathy cements the bonds between teachers and children and allows them to learn, not in opposition, but in trust.

10. Time-outs do not work for all children

Most often they do not work when children are engaged in power-struggles, which are discussed in depth in Ch.7. Teachers may need to continue to use time-out to protect the work of the group, while seeking other strategies. Generally, we need to question the effectiveness of time-outs if we see mounting or lingering signs of resentment, withdrawal or insecurity. In some cases we may want to reevaluate our program or individual expectations. If time-out doesn't reflect an appropriate choice and a realistic expectation, it will discourage, not encourage, discipline.

Sometimes children come to school or back from recess already upset — fists clenched, bodies aggressively in motion. A teacher described one of her five-year-olds who began the day kicking, punching, and knocking over anything or anyone in his path. These children need a "time-in" rather than a time-out. They need comfort and holding, a time to build up a sense of self which is prior to self-controls.

Summary

You may want to review the ten guidelines for an effective time-out program listed on pages 94–95. This approach accepts the fact that many children do not come to school with self-controls intact, no more than they come ready to take full charge of their learning. Not all can sit still, use materials creatively, or speak up to say something nice. Some will throw the books rather than read them. Some will wander and dawdle over their assignments. Some will exploit and bully their classmates; some will just retreat into limited use of their potentials.

Most children take looking after. By using time-out for small things, I find a way to do some of that looking after. It is a system that is sometimes faulted as too punitive, and other times as too lenient. It is clear to me that time-out works, even when parents fear its harshness or fear it will not be harsh enough. It works in classes where a firm hand is needed to start the year so that a looser one can emerge as the year progresses. It is one technique which can be used to establish and affirm the values of self-determination and self-control.

7

Power Struggles

Time-out is part of a process which begins where children are and takes them in the direction of self-control. But time-out doesn't work for all children. It may need to be modified or abandoned for children who continue to find time-out fearful and punishing because of their temperaments. Rather than gain insight from time-outs, they develop an aversion towards school. And time-out does not work for children engaged in "power struggles." They show a deliberate desire to challenge the teacher with defiance and insurgence, rather than an unwitting provocation or imperfect impulse controls. An increasing number of children lock into power struggles, and lock us into that struggle with them — with serious consequences for the well-being of the classroom. This chapter includes two variations on the time-out strategy which may help us deal with our more obstinate scrappers. They are called "The Time-Out Place" and "Bargaining."

Power struggles

Katy is deliberate and artful in her provocations. Asked to hurry, she dawdles. She is the last to come to line, or circle-up, slowing down her preparations in response to the readiness of the group. Asked to use a quiet voice, she makes airplane landing noises. Asked to wait a turn, she shoves ahead. Rather than appear oblivious or in a daydream, she defies with a gaze riveted on the teacher. If her first gestures are ignored, she does it again — and again. A smile crosses her face, when her teacher finally bursts

with impatience.

Twice the teacher has asked Eric, age 8, to carry, not shove or toss the blocks. Eric takes hold of another block, looks boldly at the teacher, and shoves it spinning across the floor. He gives a glance of smug satisfaction and then framed innocence, as he is sent to time-out. "Me? What did I do?" He will later complain to his parents that the teacher picks on him.

Lester spends most of his energy on a steady pattern of evasion and trickery with teachers and classmates. He tells his teacher that his reading assignment is done, which is why he is so busy drawing rocket ships now. Asked to produce the finished work, he pretends first to hunt for it, slowly and deliberately fumbling through his bin, his eye still on the teacher. Then he appears to forget that he is searching for something and wanders off in a different direction. He believes his absent-minded teacher will also forget. When the ruse fails, he protests wildly, "You didn't tell me. You only said to do a picture. You made us clean up, so I didn't have time."

Lester, whose work is often missing or hurried or unfinished, is quick to comment on the insufficiencies of others' work. "You only did that much?" he guffaws, looking over at someone's paper. He is always ready with a snide comment, or an assertion that he has a bigger computer, went on a better trip and knows a harder fact. He has to be boss of every game and never loses. He seeks constant teacher attention, but mostly to show or announce, rarely to receive a reply. Mostly, Lester wants to play. The games he wants to play are, in fantasy and in fact, games of power. Lester is 7 1/2.

◆

Katy, Eric and Lester are all engaging their teachers in a power struggle. Sent to time-out, they are hapless victims of their teacher's disfavor. At the same time, if their misbehaviors are ignored or overlooked, they increase the pitch until the teacher or fellow students become *their* victims. The prize, in either case, is a disturbance and disruption, usually at the expense of the intended agendas of work and play.

Time-out will not improve the behavior of Lester, Katy or Eric. They have no rules to remember because it was "the teacher's fault" or "unfair." Lester will go home and tell his parents that he spent all day in time-out because his teacher is "so mean." Katy will cry and carry on, refusing to come to school the next day. Her mother will complain that time-out "humiliates" her. Eric swears he didn't do anything and never got even one reminder. His parents are opposed to time-out and tell the teacher that. A home-school conflict is added to the stress.

Still, while time-out may not improve Lester's behavior or attitude, it may be necessary to secure the well-being of the group and prevent Lester from flicking the paint in people's hair, browbeating other children, or continually occupying the attention of the teacher. It is important that other children and teachers not be permitted to get so angry and fed up with Lester (or Katy or Eric) that they start to dislike him. It is important to rescue these children from the ingenuity of their own alienation. But, because Lester perceives the time-outs as "unfair," more evidence that his teacher or classmates or the school "picks on" him, he will disturb the class again, and again. Time-outs are not creating self-controls.

Is it possible in a school setting to help Lester or Katy or Eric develop self-controls rather than to control others? Or should we be satisfied with a patient and consistent use of external structures and sanctions? The answer to both questions is important and yet somewhat paradoxical. I find that children such as Lester or Katy respond, in the short-run, if we impose stiffer sanctions — when they lose the power struggle and the authority appears to gain the upper hand.

However, a defeated or discouraged child is not transformed into a productive one. It is more likely that the battling will continue, even through an eventual suspension or another school dropout. So somehow we need to alter the terms, to refuse to win a power struggle, to decline the war. And this in itself is a slow, arduous and protracted struggle. It takes inspiration and stamina and outside support, most importantly from the family. When the family only pretends to cooperate, privately agreeing with the child that the school and the teacher are terrible, *they* have to be turned around before the child can be turned around.

One aspect of changing the terms is to try to relocate a legitimate source of power. Often the children I see trying to boss me, their parents, their peers or the rest of the world are most at a loss for a sense of place — what Dreikurs calls "a sense of significance" in *Maintaining Sanity in the Classroom*. They are not children who seem to solve problems, overcome frustrations or fears. They are often the first to quit when something is a little hard or doesn't come swiftly and easily. Despite many mental or physical resources, they give-up right away. Children who have high self-esteem associated with power show a sense of persistence in the face of a hard problem, some inner conviction that they can jump a hurdle. We need to help children who persist in power struggles to rediscover a constructive use for their power, or learn to conquer their own fears and insecurities.

The time-out place

Katy and Lester are not sent to the time-out chair. Instead they go to a time-out place they have selected. It is a place they choose in the room where they can be quiet and peaceful, a place where they can recover their controls. They can return from their time-out place when they are ready to cooperate.

Katy lies down on the floor during circle time, strumming her fingers on the floor, humming lightly while Maggie attempts to read the chart.

"Katy," the teacher says, "you are showing me that you are choosing not to cooperate. You may either join the circle or go to your time-out place."

Katy bangs her foot and scowls at the teacher.

"I see you are choosing to go to your time-out place."

At this point, Katy removes herself from the circle and goes over to a table, taking with her a specially designated bin with prearranged work. She goes grudgingly, she pouts along the way, but she goes. She takes out the booklets that contain a maze or dot-to-dot and slowly begins to draw. She stops to glance at the teacher or catch the eye of a classmate; unsuccessful, she returns to her own tasks. But after a time, the tasks engage her, and her body appears to relax. She will soon be done, returning for the very end of the morning circle time, silently resuming her place in the circle, as if she had never left.

When Katy was presented with the plan, emphasis was placed on Katy's own choice to cooperate or not to cooperate. If she decided not to cooperate, the teacher explained, she would go to a time-out place. It was up to Katy to pick the time-out place, a place in the classroom where she liked to be. She would need to be quiet and alone in her place, but she could select some special work to do there that would help her relax and feel peaceful. Katy chose a table that was fairly central, often used as a work space for drawing or looking at books. It was understood that when Katy was in her time-out place, it was hers alone. At other times it could be used by classmates. Katy could leave her time-out place when she was ready to return, which she would show by cooperating with her teacher and classmates.

It was also understood that if she chose not to cooperate, she would go to her time-out place by herself, and in an appropriate manner. If she did not, she went home. In this case, the parent was supportive, willing to work with the teacher to improve Katy's behavior. During the first week of the plan, the parent was available and expecting a phone call. It came, and Katy went home. She did not go home for further punishment, although she did not go home to television and treats either. The message was that she showed she wanted to be in school by cooperating and by using her time-out place when she didn't choose to cooperate. Otherwise, she was showing her teacher and her mother that she wanted to be home. So, home it was. Katy, despite her negativity, her outbursts and defiance, went home only twice for the rest of the year. The need for the time-out place diminished, although there were sporadic upheavals. Her willingness to embrace school improved measurably.

Lester also had a time-out place. When he was presented with the decisions of place and time, and the language of choice, his sense of control increased. The timely involvement of his parents (when he needed to go home or when they checked in weekly) also developed a visible web of communication for Lester. The lies and attempts to manipulate were intercepted, which was a key for his adjustment. Like Katy, his behavior and acceptance of school improved markedly.

In some cases, children are not sent home but to the principal's office or to another classroom. If parents are unable to leave work but are supportive and will meet with the teacher at their earliest convenience, this has been an effective procedure. Without parental support, the procedure is less effective. As much as possible, we need to enlist our parents as allies, not against the child, but as part of a team working toward the child's happy and productive school life. Without strong parental participation — or even with it — we may need to move to the next alternative, which I call "Bargaining."

Bargaining

I often combine a time-out place with an approach I call "Bargaining." It is an attempt to try to enlist cooperation, or establish a "negotiated peace." The notion of bargaining is taken here from my Grandmother. As a child, I used to go along on my Grandmother's grocery expeditions, first to the butcher, then the bakery and finally the grocer. The best was the butcher. The butcher saw her coming. Here my grandmother became the seasoned haggler to get the freshest cut, the most tender piece, the good price. She left only when she was convinced of her shrewd buy. In all her years, she would never buy her meat any other way, never cellophaned, pre-packaged, or pre-priced. Bargains were everything. I have never enjoyed negotiating my marketing, but Grandma's training turned up in my teaching. I use it to avoid a power struggle. In order to bargain, it's important to remember Grandma's skills:

- Be clear — know what you want
- Be specific about a bottom line — know what you won't accept
- Establish a good mood & use a sense of humor

♦

Grandma says, "So, what's good today Louie? Don't tell me everything cause your stories don't interest me today. I want we should have some nice lamb chops, but some you can *see*, fat ones, Louie, thick like your head! Yes? You got?"

Louie replies, "For you I got."

Steps in a bargaining conference

1. Naming — stating the problem with specific examples
2. Emphasizing the student's choice — "I can help you, but I can't make you . . . It's your choice."
3. Bargaining — setting a friendly tone and establishing a "fair deal"
4. Sealing the bargain — a contract with clear expectations and consequences

1. Naming

"Louie, what you sold me yesterday, you call that tender? You could break your jaw it was so tough. What do you think we are, tigers for such chewing?"

♦

In a private meeting, I tell the student what I have noticed. For example:

"When I ask people to come quickly to group, I notice that you go in slow motion."

"When I ask for your work, you tell me that it is lost."

"When I need your help to get the room in order, I see you whiz around with the broom stirring up noise, not dust."

"I leave the room and when I come back I find you fooling around."

"I hear you call people mean names like 'fatty' and 'retard.' "

"I notice that you make faces and whisper to friends when some people are presenting in the group. It seems unfriendly."

These are my rules of thumb for naming:

- Examples are real and specific. Don't use generalizations such as, "I notice that you lie (or bully, or never do your work)." They may be true, but they overwhelm the child and tend to elicit rebuttals and more power struggles. Usually I will only cite one behavior and a few examples of that behavior.
- Use "I" statements. "I notice that . . ." or "I see that . . ."
- Use a manner and voice that is as objective and businesslike as possible — not angry and blameful, or cozy and cuddlesome.
- Be brief. This is not a lecture. If I use specifics, children tune-in. If not, they are expert non-listeners.

2. Emphasizing the student's choice

"Louie, I know you got some extra good meat special for my son-in-law. You take a good look before you show me something, yes?"

♦

Here, I try to withdraw from a power struggle by pointing out the choices and responsibilities that belong to the student. My responsibility, as teacher, is to state clear expectations (and limits). The student's responsibility is to choose how they can work on them. Some examples:

"I want you to enjoy being in the group, but I can't force you to do that."

"You are the one with the power to 'push the right buttons' so you can use kind words or take care of your work."

"I want to help you, but you are the boss of your own self so you have to decide, 'Yes, I want to contribute to my class.'"

"I'm not so strong that I can make you want to do your best stuff. Only you are that strong over your own self."

"I know you have a lot you might share with us and could contribute a lot to our class, but that's your decision to make. However, I won't let you hurt others."

3. Bargaining

"You know me for all these years, Louie, and you still think to say such a price? You know I pay a fair price — but that much, never! Tell me a dollar less."

♦

I try to set up the lively spirit, humor and savvy of bargaining. I want to use specific terms and language which reinforce mutual effort. It is "our problem" or "our good deal"; "We need to figure out a fair deal," or "I'll trade you this for that."

Beginning bargaining

When you begin bargaining, remember that it is the butcher's meat, not the butcher, which is sometimes tough:
- Avoid analyzing and explanations.
- State clearly what you want from the student:
  * "Be on time for groups."
  * "Have your work done and in your notebook."
  * "Contribute good ideas or nice comments."
- Be prepared with a specific, definite and concrete demand. Again, choose one behavior and give two or three examples:
  * "I want to see more independent work in class. That means you know your own assignments, get your work done without several reminders and check your own completions for accuracy and neatness."
  * "I want to see you use your serious thinking in class. That means you ask good questions in math group, you write full-page compositions during writing, and you help solve problems during class work."
  * "I want to see the friendly Sheila come to school. That means you say 'yes' when someone asks to join your game; you offer nice comments and make positive suggestions about the work of your classmates; you share your own good work without bragging."

Helping students bargain

"I might consider those chops you're holding if they didn't cost the Brooklyn Bridge. How much, Louie? Remember you're not talking to the Rockefellers here."

◆

"This is what I want," says the teacher. "What do you want to trade me?" We need to be prepared to help the student bargain, to figure out what they want, and how to put it into words. To help children understand the concept, I sometimes use the story "Jack and the Beanstalk" and use symbolic objects — a toy cow and beans. I have the beans. The child has the cow. I want to get the cow. The actual trade of the cow for the beans provides a role-play and drama which is both fun and meaningful, even with older children.

To help students figure out what they want I often use the "could it be" questions from *Maintaining Sanity in the Classroom* (Dreikurs):

"Could it be that you would like extra time to read or work on the computer?"

"Could it be that you would like a special time to work on an art project?"

"Could it be that you would like an extra reminder or signal when you start to get silly?"

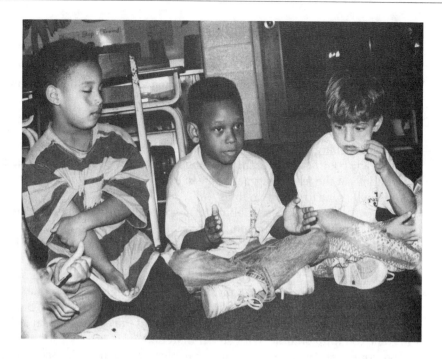

"Could it be that you need a special time to relax and listen to music on your Walkman?"

"Could it be that you would like us to know that you are an expert on motorcycles? How might I help you share that with the class?"

To help children "deal," I use my knowledge of their interests, skills and needs. The "bargain" validates one of the child's strengths and satisfies a child's preference, in return for enduring a "hardship." Bargaining (not bribing) sets up an exchange which allows children to *accept* what is given and then to *give* in return.

Jon, who regularly disrupted school assemblies, bargained to skip one of the two meetings each week and to manage the other. Interestingly, after about a month, he attended all of them and no further incidents were reported. Tammy decreased her incidents of aggressive behavior because she bargained to retreat into her Walkman. Marcy was permitted to do a morning job, instead of joining the meeting circle before she felt ready. Lester chose to help the teachers with class reading, which reinforced his excellent reading skills and "helped" his teachers. Lenny took charge of stapler repairs and Verna became a "class curator," arranging a bulletin board to make *our* room more beautiful. Mary Beth learned to play jacks and will soon be ready to teach others how to play. She has to practice, not just picking up two's and three's, but how to be a "nice" teacher, especially when someone "goofs-up"!

4. Sealing the bargain

When Grandma nodded her head once and began to open her pocketbook, the deal was done. Neither Louie nor Grandma would consider changing it once they had agreed.

◆

The classroom bargain is sealed with a handshake, a smile or a written, signed contract. The contract restates the agreement — what the student agrees to try to do and what the teacher agrees to try to do:

• Katie will come to group on time.
• Katie will have the special job of taping stories for our listening center instead of morning meeting on Wednesdays.

It's important that the contract is worded in specific language. Does Katie have to show her good faith by coming to group on time three days in a row, before beginning her special job? And, what does "on time" mean? Is she on time when she is sitting in the right place, but has to get up to get her book and pencil? If the contract isn't specific, children will say (rightly), "But you didn't tell me that!" It may be necessary to amend the contract to say "Katie will come to group on time, with all her materials."

Consequences need to be an integral part of the bargain because the expectation is that there will be improvement, not perfection. The bargain will not always be kept.

Lester does his work without arguing every question or losing every assignment now. But during art group, he flicks his paint off the brush into someone's hair chortling, "Rain painting."

"Time-out Lester."

Consequences may need to include a time-out. Lester will help clean up his friend's hair and the sprayed paint. He will also lose the privilege of painting for that day. We continue to set limits, even as we extend a special bargain.

The contract is signed by the student, the teacher and parents. Again, without parental support, the success of your new rapport and "deal" will be weakened. Parents need to be enlisted to support the arrangements of the contract and the consequences.

Some teachers worry that striking a bargain which gives a child a special option (such as listening to a Walkman) reinforces the misbehavers or is unfair to the rest of the class. "Why does she get to listen and we don't?" a child asks.

"Janey needs to listen to the Walkman to relax. You don't." Differing needs, interests and skills are admissible facts of school life. They are valued and respected. "This is a way we can help someone in our class feel good," I point out. "When you need a special consideration, then I will help you too." In this definition of fair, we extend opportunities to children to help them get what they need the most in order to work and feel good in school. Children understand.

There is one more small group of children for whom time-outs are not an effective tool. They seem less at odds with their teacher, or authority, or with the rules, and more with school itself. They try, they mean well, they may even be cheerful, but they just don't adjust to school and don't seem to fit its schedules or routines.

Shelley

Earlier that day, Shelley (age 6) had to be sent to another classroom for a time-out. She had pushed her teacher's buttons too many times. Now she was back in her room happily engaged in the work she had so resisted earlier in the day.

"Gee, Shelley, what a nice job you are doing now. If you had just done this in the first place, you would not have needed to go to time-out," observed her teacher.

"Oh, I know that. But you're so much easier to mind when it's just you and me."

"Yes. But that's not school, Shelley."

◆

Many of these children are easily restless, hanker for the out-of-doors, and have large appetites for physical motion. They do not like to read, have little patience for detailed work, and avoid discussions. The children I have in mind are at their best on field trips or when given a serious custodial responsibility. But hammering and hiking are marginal school activities. For much of their time in school they seem out of place and out of sorts. They get into mischief, or generate mayhem out of boredom or in search of exercise and relief from the morning assignments. Time-out discourages, even sorrows, these children but little changes.

There are no ready solutions I see to this dilemma. In some ways, we need to flex the walls of school, to make it more responsive to human differences and potentials. The studies of Gardner on multiple intelligences in *Frames of Mind* and the schools that are seeking to tap a broader spectrum of intelligence may help us reach more children. In the meantime, we need to look toward expanding schooling, as well as expanding the behavior of students.

Summary

We must resist the temptation to win the power struggles which some children seek. If we win them because of our superior strength, the child may feel discouraged and temporarily defeated, but will probably be even more dedicated to creating and winning the next one.

For these children, we have to change the rules of the game, to let them "win" by choosing a positive alternative and following through with it. By using a consistent approach and enlisting parental support whenever possible, we can avoid the power struggles which threaten the community we are trying so hard to build.

II

Voices of Teaching

However important the thing you say, what's the good of it if not heard, or being heard, not felt?

Sylvia Ashton-Warner
Teacher

Introduction

The hockey game

The group of about twenty twelve- and thirteen-year-olds is bursting at the seams, full of excitement and dread in anticipation of the first hockey game of the year. Some sit in stony, pale silence, while others are constantly moving at a feverish pace. The desire to do well in this practice game is palpable as they make their way into the locker room. There is bustle and expectation, last-minute fix-ups, final arrangements, a review of tactics.

"Gene, I want you to watch that mouth," the coach warns. "There'll be no tripping. Hold positions. Everyone ready?"

The team stumbles out of the lockers, gear still trailing behind, and on to their rink-side stations. Just as they are about to begin, the coach raises one hand, for one last word.

"What is it I expect you all to do when you get out there? The most important thing you have to remember?"

There is a hush as the children wait. The grown-ups wait too, poised to hear this last directive, the final word, the most essential tactic.

"No fighting?" blunders one naive player, unaware this is not a question to be answered blindly. The hush continues for a moment more until the coach shouts out for all the stadium to notice, "LISTEN. LISTEN. I expect you to listen."

◆

Generations of coaches, parents and teachers add their voice to this injunction — it is the most important advice, the most necessary of all tactics. Generations asking, reminding, demanding that their children *listen*. This section is about listening, although it is also about talking. First, it concerns the ways that teachers listen and talk in the classroom. There is a vital relationship between the ways that teachers listen and talk, and the ways their children listen and talk. In both cases, we want to cultivate active listening, the action of hearing what others have to say, and showing that we hear and are trying to understand the intended meanings. Listening then becomes a willful *act* of respect and interest, rather than a passive stance of obedience.

125

Cultivating the best habits of listening is inseparable from the task of building respect. Rightfully, teachers expect respect, but they also must teach respect. This section focuses on methods and techniques which encourage mutual listening and mutual respect.

The central tool for this instruction in listening and respect is the tool of language — the way that we talk and listen. The teacher is the model and initiator of conversations based on the idea of "attentive love," a concept which belongs at the heart of teacher/student interaction. According to Simone Weil (quoted in *Maternal Thinking*), attention consists of two attributes, both "knowing" and "loving."

The act of knowing comes from seeing children as they *really are* in real situations. We see children throw food to get attention, cry because a game is lost, make snotty faces when they're crossed. We see children disregard their work, tell foolish lies, and be mean to the frailest one in the group; we observe also their struggles to do "good." We "know" real children as they really are in the world, not fictional children or false, sentimental projections. We "love" these real children when we see them through a lens of acceptance and compassion, rather than denial.

Weil describes attentive love as saying to someone, "How are you?" and truly caring to know the answer. Picture the teacher, at the door each morning, greeting her children and truly listening to their morning tales of adventure and mishaps, noticing and recording their trophies, new hats and small Bandaids. Attentive love withstands the frailty and limitations of human nature. It is an affection that allows us to look at children as more than beings to shape according to our own ideals and images. They are independent beings who may just as well resist and refuse our best attempts to shape them at all. Our use of language strives to communicate "attentive love," to give children the dual sense that they are both known and cared for.

"Teachers should be strict sometimes but they should also know when you need a break. They want you to come through with your work, but also like you're in a bad mood one day, they should know you may need to talk to your friends," explained Tara, age 13.

When children talk about respecting a teacher, they mention a number of interesting things: challenging assignments, self-confidence, " . . . not letting kids get away with a lot of stupid stuff," a teacher who is strict but also nice. But like Tara, they often express a wish that teachers know them and recognize their needs.

"They listen to you."

"They know things about you, not just like if you do your work."

"They greet you," one eleven-year-old said. She went on to explain that she knew a teacher didn't like her because, "when I see him in the hall, he never even says hello or anything."

"Maybe he's tired," reasoned a friend.

"He could just say hello."

Our words matter. The theme of this section is language, an essential component and tool of teaching. What we say and how we say it often takes thought, practice, even rehearsal. Over the years, I have learned to speak more effectively in the classroom, much as someone acquires public debating skills. We can make the most effective use of the tool of language when we learn to be more direct and specific, to simplify and encourage, to choose the right times for open-ended and narrow questions.

It is often necessary to speak less and listen more — to learn economy of speech as well as active listening. Our natural temptation is to repeat and repeat, to become a persistent "voice-over" like those deep-throated announcers in cleaning commercials. Some studies have shown that more than 70% of what teachers say to children is in the form of commands and directives. (I certainly recognize those days when almost every word from my mouth is of the "do/don't do" variety, and the times when I hear showers of words and realize they are all mine, choking out the voices of children.) Other studies show that less than four seconds are allowed to elapse between question and answer, too little time even to think. When teachers simply expand the time allowed for answers, children's responsiveness improves substantially.

The four chapters in this section describe different ways to use language in teaching:

- Chapter 8, "Teachers As Mirrors: Using Social Conferences," suggests a way to approach problem-solving with individuals and groups based on a teacher's ability to notice and reflect.
- Chapter 9, "Empowering Language: Say What You Mean & Mean What You Say," explores the powerful link between words and actions.
- Chapter 10, "Stress the Deed, Not the Doer," covers the use of specific language by children and teachers. It also explains "Center Circle," a group activity which permits children to express positive and negative feelings with specific language, while keeping individuals and the group safe.
- Chapter 11, "The Changing Voices of Authority," explains different ways that teachers can invoke authority: the Golden Rule, rules for safety and order, and personal rules.

8

Teachers as Mirrors: Using Social Conferences

*Children communicate with us through their eyes, the
quality of their voice, their body postures, their gestures,
their mannerisms, their smiles, their jumping up and down,
their listlessness. They show us, by the way they do things
as well as what they do, what is going on inside them.
When we have come to see children's behavior through
the eyes of its meaning to them, from the inside out,
we shall be well on the way to understanding them.*

*Only by learning to see children as they are,
and especially as they see themselves, will we get
our clues. It is not as simple as it sounds.*

Dorothy Cohen
Observing and Recording the Behavior of Young Children

Children continually seek attention and guidance from their teachers — for
protection and justice, direction and understanding. Sometimes, they express
their concerns verbally and sometimes they act them out. As teachers, we often
feel better prepared to explain fractions than fractious behavior. Yet, the
continual signs and signals for help don't go away. We need appropriate
strategies and techniques to help us respond, not as surrogate parents or ad
hoc therapists, but as teachers.

"Teachers As Mirrors" is a technique that begins with the basic skill and habit of "noticing" — both good things and "bad." We can then move on to a "social conference" which allows us to *help* children work on social problems in a non-judgmental way.

The importance of noticing

Good teaching depends on being keenly aware of our individual students and their interactions. I call this skill "noticing." If we aren't aware of what is going on, we have no basis for making accurate appraisals or informed decisions.

Noticing children is ingrained in the practice of teaching. We watch how children assemble, we notice their moods and dispositions, we clock their pace and assess their attitudes. We skillfully interpret the quiet and take the pulse of the noise. When we use the technique "Teachers as Mirrors," we use this skill to "see" and then to reflect what we see without judgment or interpretation.

When a child is having a hard day, I might say, "Boy, I notice that you had a hard day today." Or when another sticks with a tough project, "I noticed how long you worked to draw that map." When Mitchell, my baseball fan, shuffles into class late, "It looks like you had a long night at the baseball game!" Our greetings or casual comments pay notice on a daily basis.

"Good morning Derek. How's your puppy doing?"

"Good morning Cath'. How was the birthday party?"

"Good morning Maurice. I see you remembered your lunch today!" When we reflect, we communicate to children that we know them. Children need to feel that we, their teachers, know them. One way that we show what we know is by noticing. And we pay attention to *how* they do, as well as to *what* they do. Leon's report, though still containing spelling errors and a few scrambled sentences, represents hours of diligence. We notice that and are proud of his results. Margie sat in her place and raised her hand during meeting today, no flopping, no calling out. "Good job at meeting, Margie. I see you really tried today." When we reflect, we are careful to notice the kindnesses, the excitements, discoveries, and improvements along with the hard moments.

But there are times when it is important to try to understand what is causing the discomfort or disruption. We often do that by asking children the leading question, "Why?"

"Why are you having so many fights in the playground?"

"Why can't you get along better in your group?"

"Why are you getting in trouble in the lunchroom?"

"Why," I asked Brian, "did you write only a paragraph, when I assigned a story?"

"I don't know," Brian replied, looking puzzled and confused.

"I dunno'," answers another, "I just do."

The children most at odds with their classroom or classmates, are frequently at odds with themselves, too. Sometimes, children do know and don't want to tell, fearing censure or exposure. But more often, when children say, "I don't know," they mean it. They truly don't know.

We are not therapists. We are not trained to look for hidden or unconscious dynamics. It is not our job to help children with analysis or self-disclosure. We are, however, trained to "notice" children, to observe them as they really are in the context of school. Our capacity as child-watchers is the foundation for a powerful technique which helps children explore and cope with events and feelings in school. Our skill in noticing initiates a social conference where student and teacher can work on solving problems.

The social conference

A social conference builds a responsive relationship on two elements: behavioral boundaries and autonomy. The first draws on external discipline; the second, on internal discipline. Both are acknowledged as part of the responsive exchange. Teachers set behavioral boundaries by providing structure and appropriate alternatives. They also provide opportunities for autonomous thinking and self-discipline by giving children a voice in their own problem-solving and suggesting reasoned alternatives for their choices. "I notice this," says the teacher, providing the structure that comes from information and description. "What do you notice," she asks, giving the student a voice. The teacher does not give the student the unreasonable choice to continue to disrupt the group, but suggests several ways to contribute something positive. She describes the problem in a way that helps frame workable alternatives. "When you disturb the group, you prevent others from learning. You may simply choose to stop, or decide on your own that it's a problem we need to work on together. What do you think?"

The main objective of the social conference is to solve an immediate problem. However, the outcomes are often broader. When teachers notice and urge children to notice, they teach the discipline of self-awareness, and self-esteem. Child psychologist Sheila Kelly, speaking to a group of parents, noted, "It's what children say to themselves about themselves that constitutes and builds self-esteem."

I borrow the term "conference" from the dynamic "writing process" approach. In a writing conference, we talk to children individually about their writing work. We start with the text, but we are concerned with "teaching the writer, not the writing." Lucy Calkins, an advocate of writing process, also suggests in *The Art of Teaching Writing* that a significant variable in the development of competent writers is a connection with the teacher. The interest of the teacher in the life-subjects of the student builds confidence and voice.

In the same way, the interest of the teacher in the *social* life of the students also seeks to build confidence and voice. We often talk about social issues occurring in our classrooms, playgrounds or hallways. We apply words to the actions, which helps children to hold them up to scrutiny. We also attempt to uncover connections between observed behavior and the thoughts, feelings and attitudes of our children. Above all, we seek an authentic conversation, in which both the teacher and student play an active role.

There are several basic steps in solving problems through social conferences, illustrated in Figure 8.1. The steps are intended as flexible guidelines to be adjusted to differing needs and situations. Some conferences take five minutes; others spread out over several days. Some lead to immediate solutions and others will have to be reviewed and repeated. Some conferences

Figure 8.1

STEPS IN A SOCIAL CONFERENCE

1. Establishing What Teachers and Students Notice

Teachers and students notice specific events, actions, feelings, or expressions. This step always includes:
  * Noticing positive things
  * Noticing things that don't work
  * Asking what students notice

2. Naming the Problem and the Need to Solve It

Teachers and students "receive" and acknowledge a problem — something that interferes with caring for yourself or others in school.

3. Understanding the Problem

Teacher uses "Could it be?" questions to help the student understand the possible relationship between an action and a cause.

4. Generating Alternatives

Teacher and student (if possible) suggest two or three strategies which might make a difference. These may include a way for the teacher to do something differently (e.g., give the student a reminder or signal). Student decides which alternative — "strategy" — to try.

5. Establishing an Agreement to Try

Teacher and student agree to try one of the strategies. Agreement may be in writing or consist of a hand shake, and includes a time to evaluate progress together and a way to know if the strategy is working.
In general:
  · Use a kind, but businesslike manner
  · Speak to the student in private
  · Be prepared to propose some options, and to accept options from the student (but don't depend on the student for direction)
  · Be prepared to end the conference at any point if the student becomes defensive or resistant
  · Leave options open for teacher and student
  · Keep conferences as short as possible
  · Avoid lectures and sermons
  · Focus on solving immediate problems

---

take only the first step, while others need them all. It's always important to understand the developmental levels of children — how they think, what they know and are prepared to accomplish.

1. Establishing what teachers and students notice

This step follows a logical progression as well, beginning with a positive foundation, then building on it to acknowledge problem behaviors and children's perceptions in a non-judgmental atmosphere. I break this step down into three parts:
- Noticing positive things
- Noticing things that don't work
- Asking what children notice

Noticing positive things

I begin a social conference by establishing positive things that I notice. When I let children know that I see their efforts, likes, interests and goings-on, I provide a sense of belonging. I refer to observable and verifiable behaviors: the smiles and frowns, the concentrated efforts and frustrating attempts, the gestures and manners, the signs and sighs of comfort or distress. I notice the "what," not the "why" of behaviors:

"I notice that you really worked hard on making the outline for your map and added careful labeling."

"I noticed that you practiced your spelling words with a partner."

"I noticed that you were helping others in your group with the assignment."

"I noticed that you asked new people to be partners this week."

"I notice that you really like to do art."

I recall one teacher commenting how good she felt when a colleague, on a particularly dreary morning, brought her a cup of coffee — milk, no sugar. Her tastes were recalled, her needs felt. A sense of belonging permeated the day. I think that we provide that "cup of coffee" for children through our noticings. Julie likes art, especially painting. Martin loves baseball and plays first base. Jackie has an older brother in the tech school who tells him a lot about cars. Michelle has a young sister who can be a pest. "How's your little sister doing?" I ask. "Any new tricks?" Michelle laughs and happily tells me another tale.

Of course, children are not always direct and forthcoming. I recall one eight-year-old, Willie, who began the school term by bringing in several computer disks each day. He never used the disks, or talked about them, and took them home at the end of each day. Finally, one day I told him that I had noticed he was bringing the computer disks to school. He showed me the disks and we talked about his mom's new computer and how he would learn to use it one day when she had time. I asked him to let me know what he found out, especially about math programs and games we could use at school. After our short conversation, he didn't bring the disks back to school. Apparently, they had served their purpose.

Children wish to be noticed whether they show it subtly or more directly. When we notice their disks, baseball cards, or new puppy, we establish a foundation for a relationship and a supportive connection. It's essential to establish that we care enough to notice before moving on to behavior that doesn't work for them or the class.

Noticing things that don't work

When teachers act like mirrors for behaviors that don't work, they also focus on specific, observable behaviors. They do not call names, make judgments or interpret. I do not label what I see. I simply describe:

"I notice that every time we have outdoor games, you have a stomachache."

"I notice that when you get frustrated or angry, you swear, sometimes at yourself and sometimes at others."

"I notice that you can't find your things a lot."

"I notice that you cheat playing cards if you're not winning the game."

"I notice that you won't sit next to certain people in our class."

"I notice that you don't seem to want to share at circle times."

"I notice that you ignore some people when they ask you to play."

"I notice that you have a hard time sitting still and paying attention to your work."

"I notice that some of the kids in our class avoid playing with you and that you always want to be in charge of the games."

"I notice that when I have to leave the room you get silly. You leave your seat and run around. You start talking in a loud voice. What do you notice?"

Eva is acting "off the wall" this week, probably because her parents are away and she is staying with Grandma. I am careful to say, "I see you are having a hard time," rather than "Your parents are away so you're having a bad time this week." By starting with what I notice (not an interpretation), I validate the clues that children give, and invite them to enter the conversation and notice as well. If Eva agrees that she has been having a hard time, or Martin agrees that he acts foolish when the teacher isn't looking, we have the beginnings of shared perceptions. When children notice, they are more likely to take responsibility for their behavior.

Establishing what the teacher notices sets up three things:

- A concrete, here-and-now focus. She does not talk about opinions, judgments or interpretations.

- A straightforward and matter-of-fact tone. She tries to name the "deeds" openly and accurately, without blame or severity.
- Fact-finding as a method of thinking. She models an approach that requires information-gathering before conclusions are drawn and solutions considered.

Asking what children notice

After I share what I notice, I ask the child, "And what do you notice?" When we ask children to notice we:
- Encourage them to examine their own behavior
- Name that behavior without finding fault, blaming or judging

"Robbie and Mark, every time you play a game together this week, one of you quits or gets mad. It doesn't look like you are having much fun with your games. What do you notice?"

"Sean, I notice that you are upset about not getting your work done this week. I see that you get out your math book, but then it takes you a while to settle down to work. You get up a lot, hunt for pencils, talk with friends, search for pages. What do you notice?"

"Christie and Maggie, I hear you call each other names. I see whispering and tears. I see you make up quickly, but it must be hard to fight with your good friends. What do you notice?"

Maria (age eight) starts her new class in a quiet manner and after several weeks becomes more withdrawn and detached. The year before, she was generally outgoing and chatty with teachers and peers. The teacher approaches her one morning, saying that she would like to have a "conference" with her, asking if this is a good time. She nods assent.

"I notice that you have been quiet in your new class. I see you by yourself a lot. In the morning when you come into school, you look at books by yourself or draw pictures. At choice time I also notice you do things alone. What do you notice?"

"I'm just quiet."

"Last year, I used to see you talking to your friends. And you always said such a cheerful 'good morning' to everyone. I saw lots of smiles."

"I'm feeling like a quiet person this year."

Maria has not contradicted the teacher's perceptions. She is quiet. She is by herself. If Maria had objected or denied being quiet, the teacher might have said, "Well, I notice that you are quiet and by yourself a lot. You notice that you join in with others and are having lots of nice conversations. Perhaps we should both notice things for the next few days. How shall we do that?" And she would make a plan with Maria.

But most often, children do notice and name, either a general trait ("Yeah, I get restless at meeting") or a specific ("I shove sometimes").

Children generally do notice, and if given permission, readily acknowledge and take interest in their own behaviors. However, their perceptions do not always match our observations. At times, the perceptions are reasonably convergent. I notice that the child is slow to get to his work; he notices that he has trouble finding his book. I notice that another acts bossy with friends; she notices that she likes to tell her ideas.

At other times, there is a wider gulf. I notice that Amy didn't study for her test; Amy notices that she practiced every day. I notice that Seth teases; he notices that he tells jokes. In these cases, I may suggest more "fact finding," possibly collecting our observations as a shared record of our attention. Usually, faulty perceptions need to be examined before we can begin to solve problems.

Lisa and Darlene

Lisa and Darlene were both upset with the results of their math test. Both felt they had done poorly. The teacher knew that both had faulty perceptions, but of entirely different types. Darlene's faulty perception is that she is "dumb" because she practiced a lot and still got a "B" instead of an "A" like others in the class. Lisa, on the other hand, thought she had practiced, when what she did was to glance over the material for short spells, which didn't allow her to learn anything. Some of her "study" consisted of taking out her book and talking to her neighbor. Lisa complains that she didn't have enough time to finish and blames the teacher for rushing her. A conference with each has totally different goals.

By comparing herself to others, Darlene loses sight of her own achievement. Her performance showed real progress, as well as considerable effort, which she is unable to appreciate. Because her goals are often unrealistic, she suffers bouts of disappointment and hopelessness. She shifts frequently from "That's easy and I know that!" to "I'm stupid."

The conversation with Darlene began with a validation of her practice. "I noticed that you worked hard studying. I saw you practice with flash cards that you made yourself. That was a good idea."

"Yeah. But I still didn't get them all right."

"That's true. But you got a lot more right on this test than you did last week. I consider that significant progress. Do you know which ones you knew today that you missed last week?" (The teacher attempts to redirect Darlene to "see" her own progress and not just measure failures. Although she is quick to make the selections, she is not satisfied.) "I also noticed that when you practiced, you flashed all the cards each time. Is that right?"

Darlene agrees. The teacher then suggests a different strategy so that she could review the harder material more frequently. She shows her how to make three piles: sure facts, "iffy" facts and trouble-facts. They talk about how to move a fact from one pile to the next and how to concentrate her efforts. "I bet you'll have most of them by next week."

"Maybe it's just hopeless," she retorts with a smile and goes back to sorting her cards. In this dialogue, the teacher did not confront Darlene about her attitude. Primarily she wants to encourage and redirect her attention away from comparisons with others — to "see" that the pile of cards representing what she knew was much thicker than the pile she didn't.

Lisa had difficulty focusing on her work independently. She confused the appearance of study with the practice of it. In order to help Lisa, we needed to develop habits of independent study.

"I know you like math. I also notice that you aren't so pleased with how you did on your test today. Is that right?" Lisa nods. "I wonder if it has something to do with the way you practiced. I noticed that when you were studying your times tables, you were also talking to Cindy. It's hard to memorize facts and also do other things. What did you notice?"

"I did 'em at home, too."

"That's a good idea to practice at home. I wonder if you found a quiet corner at home or sat in front of a TV. Somehow I picture you with the TV or radio . . . sort of like what I see in school." Lisa nods and giggles. "I wonder if you could tell me where you would study right now if you had to? Show me, where's the best place in the classroom?" The teacher begins to engage Lisa in instructional role play — finding a work space, organizing her task, and using a study technique. She lets Lisa experiment with a study task by suggesting that she try to memorize ten examples that she missed.

Sometimes the best way to get children to "see" is to enact positive behaviors rather than focus on mistakes. It might be hard for Lisa to recognize or "admit" her lack of focus, since it's probably not a clear image for her. But her response was enough to engage her support and cooperation. We could then work together on solving the problem.

Stephen

Sometimes children give such mixed messages that teachers, as well as children, are unable to notice what is really happening. Stephen complained that his reading group was "boring. It's too easy." His teacher, noting his frequent complaints and stammering over the page, and his surly manner towards a lot of things lately, continued with the reading group. But, in fact, Stephen had progressed in his reading and the level of instruction was lower than necessary. Finally, in a conference the teacher reflected, "I notice that you are unhappy with your reading group. You say that it's boring for you. Sometimes boring means it's too easy and sometimes boring means you don't like to do it — maybe because you're not so comfortable with reading. What do you notice?"

Stephen was adamant that the reading was easy and demonstrated his proficiency on a one-to-one basis. He was very pleased when he received more difficult reading material, although he continued to struggle in a new group. He had other anxieties about reading, as well. Still, for the time being he felt "heard" and his general attitude about school improved.

Kim

Sometimes, there is no noticing on the part of the child. This social conference was initiated by the parent. Kim, age 7, didn't want to come to school this morning, her mother explained, trying to understate Kim's early morning dramatics. Asked why, the usual response was given, "I dunno'." Asked what she didn't like about school, she didn't know. Asked what she didn't like yesterday in school, she still didn't know. "Yesterday was an OK day." But this morning there were stomachaches, headaches and tantrums.

Sevens often experience fears that are diffuse, as well as intense. I could also tell that this child's slowness in coming to reading and writing created special worries and fears inside of her, and that she needed help setting realistic goals for herself.

I suggested to her that kids often have two main worries about school: "can't-do's" and "don't-want-to-do's." She could be a detective and see if her bad feelings about school were "can't-do's" or "don't-want-to-do's." She agreed. I equipped her with a "detecting pad" and sent her off into the classroom to notice. For several weeks, she carried her pad and made her lists, jotting down things in her own spellings and partial phrases. Once, but only once, she showed me the list. Her "can'ts" included spelling and writing. Her "don't wants" included being quiet, having certain partners and "I dont wont to hav mi dane [brain] not do stuf rit." The tantrums disappeared, and the lists disappeared once she had "discovered" and named her own fears. She would continue to express anxiety at times and have hard moments, but then we could refer back to "her brain" and agree that together we could "teach her brain to do stuff right."

◆

When the teacher notices, she shows children the strength and value of attention. When she urges them to notice, she begins teaching the discipline of self-awareness. When a child is able to say, "I see. I am making faces . . . I am acting bossy . . . I am afraid that writing is too hard for me," the faces may stop, the boss may decide (by himself) that someone else would make a better captain, and the writing may not be so blocked. Acting as mirrors, teachers make it possible for children to look more steadily at themselves. It is a reflection that is clear, but also loving.

2. Naming the problem and the need to solve it

Some conferences may include only the first step — establishing what teachers and students notice:

"Is that something you can change or do you think you need some help?"

"I think I can do it myself," the child replies.

"Fine." And the conference is over.

Or, there may need to be more stages in order to progress to problem-solving. With Darlene and Lisa the noticing led directly to alternatives. But more often, it's important to go slowly and help children uncover a connection between their current behavior and what they think is needed in order to make a change. Solutions are more realistic when they grow out of a child's awareness of a need — and they work better if they are not imposed by the teacher.

First, we need to establish that the "noticed" behaviors pose a problem. I define problems as those things that interfere with students' abilities to care for themselves or others in school. These might include issues of self-respect, making and keeping friends, pride in school work, friendliness towards others, and physical care of oneself and the school environment.

Second, we must establish that it is a problem we want to try to solve together. In general, I use this type of statement: "When teachers (I) see children looking (acting) angry (upset, frustrated, not doing their work, not getting along), they feel that there is a problem. Something is not working for their students (you). Teachers (I) would like to figure out a way to help you feel good about your work (friends, place in the group). What do you think? Would you like to work on that problem with me?"

For example, I might say:

To Jeffrey (age 6), who has been struggling with his behavior at group meeting time: "When I see you have so much trouble being at circle time, making silly noises, bothering and poking, I think 'Where is Jeffrey's good listening and sharing?' Then I think that meeting isn't working very well for you. And that's a problem for you and for us. What do you think?"

To Kyle (age 7), who has been highly aggressive with peers: "When teachers notice someone grabbing, shoving and swearing, they worry that the person won't have friends, or have a good time with friends. That seems like a problem we should work on. What do you think?"

To Emily (age 12), who is often seeking a teacher's or parent's assistance with friendship conflicts: "When I notice you need to come to me or your parents so often when you are mad or hurt or upset with friends, I worry that you don't feel you can speak up for yourself. That seems like a problem to me. What do you think?"

To the entire class, after a dismal math lesson, with a new problem to solve: "I noticed that many of you found this a hard math problem. I saw some people give up; I notice some people get angry and only a few tried different ways to find an answer. I know the problem was hard and new. If you all knew it before hand, it wouldn't be a problem. I want you to find out that you can be problem-solvers. When I see so many of you get frustrated and give up quickly, I worry that you don't know that you can be problem-solvers. What do you think?"[1]

Keep these guidelines in mind:

- The behavior, observed by teacher and student, is the problem — not the child. There is no reference to personality or character. The problem is associated with the deed, not the doer.
- Be sure to express positive motive and intent. I want for my students to get along with others, have friends, enjoy and take pride in their work, feel good about their efforts, etc.
- Emphasize that the teacher and student are a "problem-solving team." "Something isn't working. Let's see what we can figure out together." The teacher cannot solve the problem by herself. It must be a collaboration.
- To truly collaborate, children must be permitted to do their own work. As with a writing process approach, it's not enough to tell children what to revise. They must also decide, with input, what is clear or not clear, what works or doesn't work. We want to encourage a concept of "revision" that views change as a way to extend and expand, rather than to make an ordeal of correction.
- Set realistic goals. When children revise a piece of writing, they do not see every possible change or make every possible correction. Student (and adult) writers may get tired and pronounce it done while there is still more to do. The writing revisions have improved our story and we are pleased. Our social revisions improve our conduct. In helping children improve their social skills or conduct, we revise in stages, setting up drafts, asking one or two key questions, making one or two gratifying steps towards change.

I would like to add one caution. Sometimes when we ask a child if she wants to work with us on the problem, we get what Dreikurs calls, "a recognition response" (*Maintaining Sanity in the Classroom*). The child replies with only a slight gesture or nod of agreement — which is fine. We go ahead. Other times, a child is quite vocal, "No. I don't need help!" or "No I don't think it's a problem." It doesn't work to then just go ahead with the steps in the conference.

If a child doesn't want help or doesn't see a problem, I might offer to help if she changes her mind. Or, if I feel strongly, I might say, "I see that it's hard to discuss this right now. I'd like to help. Let me know when is a better time for us to meet."

---

1 Sometimes I will use the more general term of "Teachers," other times I speak with the "I voice." The general gives more distance and sometimes safety. "Teachers and parents often think that . . ." offers a more "hypothetical" approach, which puts the child more at ease. "What do children think . . ." also allows the child to respond in a safer, hypothetical manner. I rely more on the "I voice" when I feel children will respond to intimacy and the personal concern of the teacher without feeling threatened. It's possible to switch midstream, if I think the child is becoming defensive or, alternatively, needs a more personal approach.

3. Understanding the problem

Even if children can name the problem and the need to solve it, they can't always take the next step. Asked why they do something, they feel confused and uncertain. "I dunno'. I just do," is a common reply. At this point, I try to help children locate a source by suggesting possible explanations. These possible explanations are guided by an understanding of children's needs for acceptance and significance in the classroom.

The possible explanations are phrased as questions. We suggest reasonable hypotheses while maintaining the participation of the child in a search for understanding. I often use Dreikurs' "Could it be?" questions to initiate the discussion. I also may use a general, hypothetical question, such as "Teachers think that when children have trouble listening, it may be because . . ." Or we can identify with the situation: "When I get angry with myself, I sometimes . . ." We want to guide children's understanding by suggesting a relationship between a particular way of acting and a possible purpose for the action.

Even when the connections are very clear between behavior and cause, we *ask* rather than assert. If I am sure that Marcy is "off the wall" this week because her mother is in the hospital, I don't say, "You must really be upset because your mother is in the hospital." Instead, I give the child the responsibility to name her own behavior, to name her motives. "When I am worried about someone special, I sometimes act funny and have trouble paying attention to my work. Could it be that you are worried about your Mom?"

Marcy nods. Yes, she is worried about her mom. "She's in the hospital. She has to have an operation."

"It's scary to think about your Mom's operation. And it's hard to do your school work today. When you have scary feelings, what do you think might help you feel better?" Together we decide on some strategies. Marcy will make pictures for her Mom. Marcy will come sit near me when she is worried. Marcy will sometimes get a hug. There is an understanding that it is OK when you are upset to get hugs, to draw pictures and have a special seating arrangement, even if it isn't OK to tear books or hit or run around the room. We are not denying the feelings or their importance, but simply looking for acceptable ways to express them in the classroom.

Maria

The teacher had suggested a conference after noticing that Maria was particularly quiet and often by herself in the classroom (see page 136).

"When teachers see one of their students quiet and alone, not sharing any time or thoughts with their friends or teachers, they are concerned. They think that maybe that student isn't feeling very good in school and they want to help. What do you think Maria? Do you think maybe we could figure out a way to make school feel better — not always so quiet and alone?"

Maria shrugged. "Maybe" she concedes.

"Sometimes when kids are very quiet, it's because they are afraid that they won't find a special friend in school this year. And sometimes it's because they feel unsure of some of the new routines or work. And sometimes when children are very quiet in the beginning of school, it's because they miss their old class. Could it be any of these things for you?"

Maria was quiet for a while and then said, her eyes clouding with tears, "I miss my teacher."

Maria missed last year's teacher. It was too soon for her to have formed a bond with the new teacher, still an important source of security for many "young" eights. The connecting link with the teacher continues to be critical for some children even as they move towards more peer involvement. The teacher had imagined that the issue concerned peers, but that assumption was wrong. With some prompting, Maria had recognized and named the feelings inside herself.

"Mrs. Clayton was a special teacher for you, wasn't she?"

"Yes."

"And you really liked seeing her every day and talking to her . . ."

"Yeah, and she helped me a lot with my writing."

"You like to write, don't you."

"Yeah. I like writing stories and reading them to Mrs. Clayton."

"Well, I have an idea. Have you ever written a letter to anyone?"

"I write to my Grandma sometimes."

"Do you think you might write a letter to Mrs. Clayton? Maybe telling her some things about your new class?"

"Maybe."

"You might even invite her to come to see you sometime — that is when you both have time. You'd have to both figure out your schedules . . ."

"Yeah. We could do that. I could start today."

"Why don't you get some paper and let's see what you know about letter-writing."

Several things were accomplished in this conference. Maria was able to name and share feelings, and take a concrete action. She found a way to push forward, rather than stepping back. She could affirm her need for a connection by using the skills that Mrs. Clayton had carefully helped her acquire. We quickly moved to the next step in a social conference by generating alternatives. The idea of the letters grew out of the conversation with Maria. Would she have been as receptive if the teacher had started by telling her she missed her teacher and therefore should write her a letter?

◆

Even at our most diplomatic or subtle, we only gain the confidence of children when we invite them to participate in the conversations. This confidence grows, not because teachers have brilliantly solved the mystery, but because the child was part of the process.

Derek, my bathroom writer

"I notice that every writing time you have to go to the bathroom. What do you notice?"

"I guess so. I just have to go to the bathroom a lot."

"So, you also notice that writing has become a bathroom time for you? Do you also notice that by the time you get back, you have to hurry up and often you've only gotten about a sentence written?"

"Yeah. There's not enough time."

"So your story hasn't gotten very far."

"Nah'. I only have the first page."

"When I see kids go to the bathroom at a particular time like that every day, I think that they want to avoid something they don't like or find hard — math or writing . . . So I wonder if maybe writing seems like a problem for you this year?"

Derek grins and loosens his vise-like grip on the pencil he is twiddling. "Sort of. It's sort of hard."

"There are several reasons that writing could be hard for someone. I wonder if any of these make sense for you? Could it be that writing is hard because you have trouble thinking of ideas and what you want to say? Or, could it be that you know your main ideas, but you get confused about what you want to say next, or what words you will need to use? Sometimes writers start to worry about the spelling or the handwriting and as you think about how to spell a word, you forget your good ideas?"

"I'm not so sure. Could you tell me the choices again?"

"Sure." (I decide to write them on a paper for Derek to look at as I say them.)

"I don't think it's Number 1. 'Cause I have a pretty good idea about the time this truck broke down and I helped my Dad fix it."

"Yes. That seems right. You told me about your story. I thought you were pretty excited about telling that story."

"Sometimes I forget what I want to write next. I can't think of the words I want, like in this one (points to Number 3). So it's sorta' both things."

"It helps that you have figured out what may be the problem with your writing. Do you think we could also think of some ways to help you plan or remember words you need? I have some ideas. Would you like to try out some strategies and see if any of them will help?"

Here we moved to the next step by generating alternatives or "strategies." I deliberately use the word "strategy" because children like it — it conjures up a tactic used in sports by a coach. Derek agrees to try-out a "strategy." In this case I will help with a strategy to access and organize ideas. We may try "brainstorming" lists of words. We may try some "mapping" exercises. I don't know what will release his best potentials. To find acceptable alternatives, it will be important to experiment. But the rightness of the technique may be less significant than the attitude of searching for solutions — solutions which are tested and explored by Derek.

4. Generating alternatives

The more I can involve children in distinguishing an alternative strategy that works for them, the more they become problem-solvers. They no longer think "I can't write" or "I hate writing," but rather "I have trouble with a first sentence" or "It's hard for me to choose a topic." These are problems that can be solved, not "global" aversions. The key is to narrow and redefine the issues.

"I hate school," becomes a search. "Let's see if we can discover one thing you like to do in school."

"I hate writing," turns into a joint survey of forms or functions. "What kinds of writing are most fun? Least fun? What part of writing is hard? Is it the thinking part or the copying over?"

The best strategies or alternatives grow out of specifics, not generalities. In order to complete an independent math assignment or be a better speller, or a nicer friend, what needs to happen?

"What will you need to be able to concentrate more effectively?"

"What do you think you will you need to do to get along with each other?"

"What will you need in order to be able to manage a quiet talking period?"

It often helps to list several alternatives, rather than to focus on finding just one solution. A thoughtful and experimental attitude makes the problem less personal. "What might kids do when they want to make friends?" "What are some ways students can get attention and not get in trouble?" In the spirit of brainstorming, both teacher and student present ideas. Then I ask the student to choose one and give reasons for why he thinks it will work. If it doesn't work, we can learn from the experience. When we return to the list for another try, a better selection can be made. We are revising.

In the end, it's important that students feel they are selecting an alternative that *they* believe will work, not one that just pleases the teacher. Most research indicates that solutions chosen by students because they believe they will solve the problem are more effective than those provided by teachers.

In general, alternatives seek to repair some loss of belonging or significance. They seek to find a more constructive avenue for children to meet their needs — for acceptance (from peers as well as teachers), for work towards beautiful completions, for recognition and membership in the school community. William Glasser, in *Schools without Failure,* also identified other needs which he felt must be met for children to participate fully in school. These include the needs to "gain power, to be free and to have fun." Children need times in school that are relaxed and comfortable — they need to have fun! They are much more apt to invest in work which may not be fun if there are wonderful art projects, plays to put on, rowdy games outdoors, or chances to tell jokes and laugh. Sometimes finding an alternative means helping a child find that fun.

The strength of this approach is in its openness and responsiveness. We try to see children as they really are, "from the inside out," listening and exploring with them to find what they need to be able to feel better about their lives in school. We will try one way and if that doesn't work, we can try another. The best hope of the social conference is to increase children's capacity to deal with disappointments, setbacks and sorrows. A connection to a listening and responsive adult can provide faith and comfort — crucial to the struggle for growth.

5. Establishing an agreement to try

The conference concludes with an oral or written agreement to try one of the alternatives. The agreement may be reached after a few minutes or over several days. The agreement is to *try* — and includes the teacher as well as the student. Both agree to try alternatives, to do something different so that the classroom will work better.

The following example illustrates a more volatile problem. It was actually one of the first times I learned to "mirror and reflect," and realized the essential importance of an agreement to try. Although clumsy at the start, the approach helped me to teach a troubled student. I do not want to minimize the task of trying to help children who bear terrible scars and the open sores of poverty and neglect. I also do not want to minimize the importance of the teacher.

Charles

At 11, Charles was a charming, good natured and generous fifth grader at a school whose children came from families living in economic poverty. He loved to help everyone, and encourage others in their efforts. He was a natural athlete and team leader, giving tender assistance to even the clumsy and inept players on his teams. When it came to his own studies, however, he was anything but confident or patient. He bluffed, cheated, evaded and faked. He did very little of his own work in school; he kept busy sharpening pencils, repairing the pencil sharpener, emptying trash, finding a friend's missing book, opening the window for the teacher. When pressed, he found endless excuses. He did it, but left it home. He did it, but left it at his grandma's. He would have done it but the teacher didn't tell him the right page, so he did the wrong page . . . .

When pressed further, made to stay in from recess to do the forgotten work, kept after school, or seated next to the teacher, the agreeable and likable manners disappeared. Charles became sullen, threatening, and destructive. Punishments had not altered the pattern. Additional help with his work was refused. He didn't need help, he claimed. Besides, the work was "babyish," "too easy," "dumb," and he hated this "stupid junk."

To his grandmother, his primary guardian, Charles was an "easy child who didn't like to be crossed." She worried about "that temper" but he was always helpful to her and good with the little ones. She had her hands full. Charles got further and further behind in his school work. He had been held back once and was functioning two years below grade expectation when he started fifth grade. His ultimate recourse, when confronted, was to skip school. Charles was on his way to becoming a dropout. After about two months of getting to know Charles, enjoying his humor, cheerful nature, and small gifts and avoiding any serious challenge, I assigned a book report. He sputtered and argued; finally I agreed that he could give it orally.

His oral book report was short and ingenious; however, with the exception of character names and chapter captions, it bore no resemblance to the book.

"You didn't read the book," I charged.

"It's a stupid book and you're a fuckin' jerk," he yelled and then stormed out of the room, ending up down in the principal's office, where I went to redeem him. I felt furious and guilty at the same time — angry at this boy for denouncing me, humiliated by the provocation of his profanity, guilty for confronting him so publicly. In the principal's office, Charles stated that he'd rather be suspended than have to go back to my classroom. He wanted his old teacher back. I was a bad teacher. He wouldn't come to school if he had to be in my class.

Charles was effectively playing several parts. He was victim and he was rebel. It was a clever power struggle — "I did read the book/You didn't read the book." He was in command of the terms, issuing warnings and threats if he didn't get his way. I could yield or I could lose the student — a miserable choice for any teacher.

It was also clear, even as he appeared angry and insolent, that Charles was also miserable — his decisions weren't working and he needed help. I understood that. What I didn't know was whether I knew how to help him. But, I made a decision to try. I started with an acknowledgement of my mistake. I explained that it was my mistake to challenge him about the book in front of the class. I realized that my mistake made him angry, although I didn't like being cursed at even when people are angry. I asked him if he thought it was still possible to work things out, even after my mistake. I liked him and would like to continue to be his teacher, I said. Would he be willing to try to work things out with me?

Surprised or perhaps mollified by my conciliatory tone, he agreed. I told him that I was going to write down some things that I noticed in the classroom and some things that I would like to see change. I told him he could do the same. If we could agree on some changes, he would come back to class. If we couldn't agree, maybe the principal would place him in a different class. He seemed pleased with that option. It was decided that we would share our lists right after school and in the meantime he remained in the office.

I presented Charles with a list of about eight things that I noticed that

included both positive and negative behavior:
  * Always remembered to say hello to kids and teachers in the morning
  * Took out books but didn't read them
  * Did only one or two problems on a page of math
  * Made mistakes, but didn't fix them
  * Helped others find things or open containers
  * Got angry if a teacher tried to help him do his work
  * Handed in only two papers, but wanted to hang up one of the stories on the wall
  * Told jokes and made other people smile and feel good

They were all straight-forward, true and simply stated.

"Just to make sure you can read my writing," I said, "I'll read them to you." I asked him to check any of the things he thought might be true. I explained that I wasn't angry at him for these things, but that I did observe all these behaviors. Did he notice anything different?

Interestingly, Charles checked them all, no questions, no defiance.

"Is there anything else that you notice?"

"I swear and I shouldn't."

"Yes."

The differences between "You didn't read the book" and "Here are some things I noticed" created distinct outcomes. The first was confrontational and accusatory, and led to insult and rebellion. The second allowed Charles to remain in control and to name himself, which led to discussion. At the same time, I didn't feel like I was yielding to the destructive environment created by this boy. I was able to be honest and direct. Giving Charles the choice to work on the problem was the key to his participation.

I do not recall the exact words or sequence of events that followed but I can construct a rough script. I do know that it involved naming the problem and working together to propose possible solutions.

"When I see kids want to help others, but not help themselves, I worry that they don't feel very good about themselves as learners. I think that's a problem, because then you can get stuck and not go on learning. I might be able to help you with that problem, if you want to work on it with me."

"I dunno' . . . I don't really need help. If I want to do things, I do."

"OK. But sometimes I find that kids have other reasons they don't do work. Like you said, one reason is that they don't want to do things. Could it also be that the work is not hard, but confusing? Maybe it's confusing because they got behind or didn't keep up practice. Maybe it's confusing because they need some special ways to learn. Like, remember the way you showed Ronnie to tie the knot. You showed him a different way to do it so it would hold tight. It didn't work the first way. But it worked the second way. Then Ronnie could do it. You helped him. Maybe there are different ways to do reading or math also. What do you think?"

"Well . . ."

"Suppose I write these down for you and you think about it overnight. You may decide it's that you are confused and want to try some different ways with reading, writing and math. I think that if you decide that you want to work on it, I can help you. I suspect that you can do hard things. What do you think?"

"Well, yeah, I do some hard things."

"Yes. You mind your little cousins every day and shop for your Grandma. She says you always have the right change, too. That's hard for lots of kids."

"Yeah. It's not hard for me."

"Charles, you do need to work on your studies. Really work. If you don't think you want to work with me, maybe you want to think about another teacher."

Charles did come back the next day ready to return to his class and, he said, to "work on hard things." He did say that he thought he got confused when he missed some school and was left back. He was still defensive and afraid to be seen as behind or not able. When I showed him a book which he could read, but at a lower level, he dismissed it as "babyish." He also was reluctant to do math that looked different from his peers. He needed to learn in secret.

I was, for that year, able to find a tutor and to devise a "cover" that satisfied his image to explain Charles's absence from the class. He continued to do "fake" work or busy work for much of the time. The tutor, an enthusiastic and inventive intern, was slowly able to find ways to link him back to the classroom. Charles brought in models and directions he had read. He brought in stories he had written. He taught kids how to play Twenty-One, a card game that involved swift calculations. He used new cursive skills and a calligraphy pen from his tutor to make beautiful signs for our room. He would proudly demonstrate a new spelling proficiency.

Finally, he worked very hard preparing a book report during the spring about Willie Mays, his hero, but refused to read it aloud, saying that the book was "babyish." He slipped me the report in private. "Don't show nobody," he said.

"I found out a lot of interesting things about Willie Mays so I notice that you really read the book this time," I said. "I bet we could shake hands on it and not even have a little fight." So we shook.

I felt that Charles had come a distance. Clearly the gains were shaky and there was much more to do. Would Charles continue to work with his sixth grade teacher? Would he get another tutor? Would he take on more of the classroom program? Was he ready? There are a huge number of variables when we are dealing with children, and many that we don't control. But a link between teacher and child, child and teacher, which is established through a social conference can make an essential change in a child's approach to school and learning.[2]

---

2 See Appendix B for more details on "Holding a Social Conference," with more examples of some of the basic problems teachers encounter.

Summary

In a recent workshop, a teacher from Maine voiced a familiar worry. "Many of the kids now are coming in with such baggage from home. You find out that the child is upset because he tells you that his parents were fighting so hard he couldn't sleep and had the pillow over his head, and was very scared. As a result he was very inattentive the next day. His behavior isn't appropriate, but it's not as a result of what's happening in the class. And it's hard. It's hard to see it, and it happens more and more. And it's even harder to find time to address all these things."

The facts show that she's right. Recent surveys indicate that one in five children live in poverty. "Particularly devastating to the nation's youth have been sharp increases in the numbers of children and teen-agers who are abused, who live in poverty and who commit suicide."[3]

More of our children will bring awful baggage to school — baggage which will seriously impair or compromise their capacity to learn and to be with others. Another teacher in a neighboring school told me, "I know a four-year-old who has no language, is not deaf, and runs around all day hitting and biting and howling. What do we do with such a child?" I too am worried.

Important answers lie outside the domain of education. Our country and world need social planning and economic justice. Some answers would come with the obliteration of poverty from our country of conspicuous surplus and wealth. Other answers would grow from systemic educational reforms that reshape the physical size of schools and classrooms, and empower teachers to teach. In the meantime, class begins at 8.

The child who comes in sad may need a hug. The one who comes in discouraged may need a pat on the back. The hungry child may need a peanut butter sandwich. And the child who seems too quiet, or is never quiet, may need a conversation with her teacher. At times it takes only five minutes. We listen, we hear, we offer a gesture or word of comfort. At other times, it is a longer process, of noticing and seeking solutions. It is not the solution that is the answer. It is the responsiveness that answers. It is one of our jobs, in Sara Ruddick's apt phrase from *Maternal Thinking*, "to make truth serve lovingly the person known."

---

3 *Index of Social Health for Children and Youth,* Fordham University Institute, quoted in the *New York Times,* October 19, 1989.

9

Empowering Language: Say What You Mean & Mean What You Say

Early in my teaching career, trying to learn how to discipline, I observed a master teacher at work. Rose Thompson was known for her orderly classroom and her industrious children. Even more, she was known for a quiet dignity which radiated from her person and enveloped her classroom. I wanted so much to understand how she did it, this powerful woman, so small in stature. I observed in her room whenever possible. I noticed the quiet voice she used even when addressing the whole class; I noted the clarity of her instructions. I noted her attention to detail and the firmness of her expectations. And one day, I observed a crucial lesson, although at the time I was shocked.

The class was ready to make Halloween masks, abuzz with ideas and excitement. Mrs. Thompson had just handed out sharp scissors for groups to share. She carefully demonstrated how she wished to see them used, point down. "How will you hold them," she asked? Darrell showed the class again. Point down. The allocation of paste, the bins of paper, the place for finished work, were all reviewed before the start of the activity. "I expect to see you use things correctly," she cautioned, "or I will have to take them away for today." And then the children got to work.

Mrs. Thompson watched quietly, occasionally commenting or giving assistance. She was watching when Michael walked across the room, the scissors dangling precariously from one pinky. Michael was not holding them safely, the point was not down, the grip not firm. Mrs. Thompson beckoned to Michael. She quietly reached out her hand. Without a word, Michael placed the scissors in her outstretched palm. He had lost the right to use the scissors

for the rest of the period — no more cutting for that day. Michael went sadly back to his seat.

I watched, stricken. I wanted so much to restore the scissors, to give Michael another chance, to see the glow and smile return to his face. I am sure Mrs. Thompson did, too. After years of disciplining my own children and my students, I sometimes believe the cliche, "It hurts me more than it does you!" And if not more, at least it hurts.

But Mrs. Thompson didn't give in. She knew better. It was not only the safe handling of the tools that was at stake, it was the true handling of her words. Her class believed her. And because they believed her, they trusted and felt safe. It was an extraordinary gift she gave them. It required some extra thought and effort from a seven-year-old, but the gains were worth it. When she spoke, they listened, and never because she berated them or used harsh threats. Michael got the use of scissors back the next day, and I imagine that he and everyone else thought harder before they moved an inch. Michael and others learned to think carefully about most of what Mrs. Thompson said to them. They learned something about the value of words to say important things, and that some adults can be trusted to say what they truly mean. I was beginning to understand that compassion did not necessarily mean negotiating or relenting. It meant dignifying my arrangements with children by honoring my own words.

We tell children that when the bell rings (or the triangle sounds, or the lights flicker, or the teacher's hand goes up), the rule is to stop everything and listen. Stop. Listen.

The bell sounds. Immediately, the room is hushed, children look up from their writing or their books, cease conversations, stop moving around and turn to look at the teacher. Except for a few who continue their conversations, their drawing, or their trip to the water fountain. A few more face the teacher, but continue their chatter or their work on a project. The teacher begins her message, disregarding the activity in the room.

What will the two simple and concrete directions, "stop" and "listen," signify if we accept such "loose translations"? My own answer is that if we allow children to "sort of" stop, and "kind of" listen, we encourage the destruction of meaning. Our language becomes a shambles — and our classrooms may not be far behind. Rather than relying on a common and precise language, we develop a negotiable and idiosyncratic one — it doesn't matter how many times, or in what tone of voice we say "stop" if we don't attach it to a specific way of acting. We need to say what we mean and mean what we say. In general, the less we talk, the more children listen.

Children need to know that words have meaning. They need to understand that words correspond with actions. Here are some guidelines for using language to affirm meaning and action:

- Keep demands simple — keep them short.
- Say what you mean — make your demands appropriate.
- Mean what you say — dignify your words with actions.
- Remind only twice — the third time "you're out."
- Speak directly — tell children "non-negotiables," don't ask.
- Use words that invite cooperation.

Keep demands simple

Short, simple directions are essential if we expect specific actions. Here are some examples of times when simple demands are especially important.

To guide children through transitions:

- How much more time to finish — "You have five more minutes . . ."
- What happens next — "Who can tell me what you do next?"
- What will you need to do to complete and clean-up — "I want everyone to think to themselves, 'What do I need to do to finish up for now? What do I need to do to clean-up?'"
- Get ready for the next activity (lesson, class) — "What do you need to do to get ready to go outside? Who can tell us? Think to yourself what you will do."

To restore the proper noise level you need in the room:

- "It is too noisy. You need to use your 'indoor' voices, (conference voices, private voices)."
- "It is too noisy for our work time. Who can show me what a working voice is?" [Child demonstrates] "Now, everyone ask a question to a neighbor using your workroom voices. I expect those voices for the rest of this period."
- "It is too noisy. If the bell rings again, it will mean no more talking."

To introduce changes in room organization or schedule:
- Describe the change — "At one o'clock, Mrs. Marder is going to come in to do a special art project. She is going to show us ways to do watercolors. She will do it with everyone."
- Anticipate and reassure basic continuity — "I know that we usually do writing at that time. If you are in the middle of a story, don't worry, we'll figure out extra time for you if you need it. I think you'll all enjoy the art today, even if you have never done watercolors before."
- Ask children to repeat or paraphrase what they understand is going to happen — "Can someone tell us what is special about today? Are there any questions?"

To stop inappropriate behavior and redirect children to positive expectations:
- "You need to stop bickering, (fooling, chatting . . .) and get on with your work."
- "You need to follow meeting rules."
- "I expect to see you use a kindly attitude or this group stops."
- "I expect to see fair play or the game is over."
- "The yarn has become snarled and messy. Use it just the way you demonstrated before."[1]

Say what you mean

In the heat of the moment, it's not unusual to say things we don't really mean. Severe threats or ones we simply don't mean (or want) to carry out put teachers in a bind and discourage children.

Jeremy and Danny

Each day, a class of first graders went back and forth to the back hall where coats and lunches were stored. A heavy door separated the hall from the class. The hall was not heated so the door was kept closed in the winter. The children were unseen as they put away jackets and stashed lunches at the beginning of the day, or got ready for recess or to go home.

Jeremy and Danny were spunky six-year-olds. On their way from the meeting rug to the reading table, it was common for them to stop for a quick romp and wrestle. They were savvy enough to look to see if the teacher was watching, and mostly she was. However, by midyear, they realized the

---

[1] There are times when the brief, neutral voice must be abandoned. The magic and power of those times are in direct correlation to their infrequency. The fewer the sermons, the more powerful. Recently, a teacher of adolescents gathered them in a circle and spoke to them in a manner that cascaded from soothing to fiery for an entire hour. He spoke about their lack of kindness to each other, and their need to speak up and stop each other rather than wait for the teacher to step in. They sat transfixed, rolled their eyes, and wept. This type of guidance and moral authority must be there for children, as long as it is used with prudence on issues that they can't figure out for themselves.

potential of the back hall for excellent adventures. On some pretext or other — check a pocket, return a mitten, find a note — they ventured out again and again. Finally, one rowdy and mischievous activity left coats tumbled and lunch pails scattered. They got caught, of course. The utter shambles and mess upset the teacher. The poorly concealed grins of mischief incensed the teacher. "Do this one more time," she uttered, her voice low and threatening, "and you will miss recess for the rest of the week. Understand?"

The two heads nodded in unison. But what Danny and Jeremy really understood was a challenge, a test of their derring-do. The teacher had set herself up for disaster. What would she do with these two if she had to keep them in at recess? How would she deal with their energy and high spirits then?

The next day, Jeremy and Danny approached the back hall with renewed intensity and dedication. Coats were tossed to the floor, boots rocketed across the room. Lunches fell helter skelter. Of course, it was not long before their exploits were discovered. There could be no appeal. Recess had to go. The "imps" were chastened and deprived of their playtime. The teacher was chagrined, left to manage the spirits of her boys indoors. In addition, the children were resentful — and so was the teacher. The boys complained bitterly to their parents. Eventually, the parents were mollified and the boys repentant. They had learned their lesson and the back hall was left alone.

But suppose they had been more persistent? The pranks would have continued, followed by more lost recess time. And then what? Both the teacher and students would be victims of growing frustration or defiance — certainly not the ideal attitudes for the classroom.

This was not a case of endless warnings or futile speeches. But did the teacher "mean" what she said? Did she say what she meant? We don't always use our best logic or logical consequences in a moment of anger.

In this case, I would suggest two logical consequences. "You mess it up. You clean it up." Danny and Jeremy would take their free time, possibly their recess time, to return the coats to the hooks, line up the boots neatly, arrange the lunch boxes, and also to sweep and tidy the back hall until it was beautiful. That might discourage them from messing it up again.

Second, they would lose the "privilege" of going into the back hall. "If you can't take care of yourself in the back hall, you aren't able to use it." In spaces such as the back hall, bathroom or corridors, children must exert their own controls. They make decisions about whether to spray the water, toss the toilet paper, play tag in the halls, or take care of business. When behavior is not appropriate, they lose the privilege and trust for a period of time. Their coats and lunches would have to stay in the classroom for the rest of the week or the day. The privilege of using the back hall would be returned when the teacher agreed they were ready to be responsible for the care of the hallway and themselves.

◆

We need to anticipate problems in order to be able to say what we mean and mean what we say. We do "mean" to express anger and disapproval at key times, but we don't mean to carry through on the threats that anger alone may induce:

"No recess for a month."

"No more trips for the rest of the year."

"Stay after school and finish, and I don't care if you miss the bus and have to walk home."

And finally — "I'll kill the next person who opens their mouth." Tempting, but not so realistic!

When we anticipate problems, such as the invisible spaces that become irresistible to six-year-old testers, we are better prepared with logical consequences and a calmer, more rational mind.[2]

Mean what you say

Dignify your words with actions. If we ask children to freeze, continuing to draw or talk to a friend is unacceptable. It's not what we mean when we say, "Freeze." If we ask children to work quietly, calling across the table and laughing loudly is not acceptable. If we ask everyone to listen to a classmate read his story, staring out the window or playing with a neighbor's fingers does not meet our expectations for attentive listening.

If we expect our children to follow-through on their verbal commitments, we must follow-through as well. "The bell rang. What do you need to be doing?" the teacher asks. "Show me," she might say, early in the year. "Time-out," she says later in the year because children know the routines and are now expected to follow them. Consequences are more effective if they are anticipated and clear ahead of time. But most importantly we must be prepared to do what we say we will do.

There are times when actions communicate more clearly than any words. One class is highly familiar with the rules and conduct for a trip outdoors. As soon as we are outside, their voices get loud and partners begin to wander. I stop the class and return to the classroom without a word, signaling for the next period's activity. I see no need to lecture or review the events. The problems were clear, the alternatives are also clear. The next day, prior to the excursion, I might ask them to think what they will each do differently in order to enjoy the trip. My assumption is that they know the words; they now need to behave appropriately. It important to communicate to children that we know that they know! It is a way of giving them credit. It is also a way of giving ourselves credit and self-respect.

Sometimes, repetitions and incremental steps are the best way for learning to occur, but there are also times when learning must be put into practice and used. If behavior at meeting is silly and disruptive, discontinue the meeting. If the line-up

---

2 For examples of common problems reflecting developmental and age characteristics, see Appendix C.

is noisy and rowdy, sit down and wait. If writing conferences are giddy and unproductive, stop them for the day. It's often better to try again tomorrow.

Remind only twice

Ronald

Children were lining up to go outside. Ronald continued to work at his desk. The class would be kept waiting again, as Ronald slowly continued his work. Usually, I repeated my instructions personally to Ronald, hustling him along, nagging or yelling. Today I waited. The class, taking its cue from me, grew still. We all waited to see what Ronald would do. Ronald did nothing. He continued on as if either he, or we, were invisible. After an eternity, I picked up a ruler (the dreaded symbol of corporal punishment!) and advanced toward his back. I had no idea what I was going to do with the ruler once I reached his desk, but I gripped it tightly. After no more than a few silent steps, Ronald, who had not lifted his gaze from his papers, sat up and suddenly scurried off to get his jacket. Not a word had been exchanged. How did he know I was there? Or had a ruler? Or was moving towards him?

Ronald knew all along that we were waiting, and from prior experience he assumed he was waiting safely for the daily torrent of words that aroused him to action. The words, repeated especially for Ronald each day, had become a ritual. I realized that in many situations, repetitions had replaced the original message of the words. The words had lost their meaning because they were used too often. My classroom needed a change.

"Ronald," I recall saying, "Teachers and Momma's have patience, but only so much patience. They will ask you once NICELY. The second time they will ask in a stern voice. And the third time they will be angry." I realized again how irritating it was to repeat even the most routine expectations. Irritation eventually becomes sarcasm, shouting, or outright anger. Too often, we keep doing the very same thing.

As I spoke to Ronald, I realized that I had the rapt attention of the silent line of first graders, their eyes glued to the yardstick still in my hand! I had hit (literally) on something important. I turned to the class and repeated my now confident message, one which I use regularly, "Teachers and parents say things once, nicely. The second time they will be stern, and the third time, you are out. They will not say it again."

Speak directly — tell "non-negotiables"

Lorrie is joking and fooling around instead of doing her clean-up job. "Would you please do your job?" the teacher asks. Is this what the teacher means — "Would you?" Is it a choice for Lorrie to do her job or is it a "have-to?" Is it even a question? If it is a question, Lorrie might answer, "No, I would much rather talk." In an effort to be courteous and pleasant, the teacher's message is confused.

"You need to get the job done, Lorrie" is direct and honest. There is no mistake or confusion — it is a non-negotiable item. Non-negotiables are an integral part of every classroom and every community, although they vary from class to class, teacher to teacher, community to community. We need to make them clear and direct — they are declarations, not questions. We are not asking, we are telling. We may need to declare what we need the child to do, what the group needs the individual to do, or what the child needs to do for her own good:

"You need to sit down now."

"The group needs to come over quickly so we can start."

"You need to get ready now."

"You need to keep your hands to yourself."

"You need to get this work done."

"I need your help to get the room ready."

"I need your help to solve this problem."

"This class needs to listen to Becky now."

"The rest of the class needs you to be attentive now."

Use words that invite cooperation

The way we talk to children may invite participation or, unintentionally, resistance. I solicit cooperation with three techniques:

· Making it fun
· Asking for help
· Providing choices

Making it fun

Two teachers are trying to settle their class after recess as they line up before going inside. They know that the transition from outdoors to in is hard for some of their children. They prefer to have them regain their controls outside rather than charge back into the building.

One teacher, standing in front, begins to name all the inappropriate behaviors she sees. "Seth, turn around. Molly, stop talking. Dan, keep that ball still. Craig, hands to yourself." But it's like popcorn popping. As soon as Molly stops, Jennifer starts. As soon as Craig stops pinching Bobby, Bobby starts pinching Craig.

"Bobby," cries the teacher.

"But it wasn't me. He started it. What about him?" There is unbridled glee from the ones who didn't get caught, and they smirk at the ones who did. The ones who are ready to go are frustrated. Often the teacher gives up and takes the class in mild disarray upstairs. It takes another ten minutes before they settle down.

In general, the naming of misbehavior does little to inspire good behavior. Children, particularly in a transition, need to have a positive focus, one that sets the stage for immediate affirmative feedback.

A second teacher waits patiently for about three minutes, ignoring the bouncy bodies and gabbing, giggling voices. Then she says, "I'm going to close my eyes and count to ten and when I open them I expect to see a straight, quiet, beautiful line of fourth graders all ready to go back to their work."

Ninety-seven percent of the time this works! It works today, except for Randy who needs his own glance or hand from the teacher. Why does this familiar gimmick work so often? Perhaps it's the challenge of the "clock," the bounded amount of time to compose and ready oneself. It is finite, predictable and authoritative.

"Count to five and then I'll dive into the water," I always tell my daughter, who is begging me to swim with her and is impatient as I step gingerly into the cold water. "You didn't say 4 1/2 or 4 1/4," I needle my daughter. She complies, but I know that 5 will come and I will have to do it!

Teachers use this strategy for many activities. A count of three settles the class for meeting, as they move from chatting with friends to quietness. A count of twenty gathers a class from the four corners of the field into a circle. A count of five ("5–4–3 . . .") readies the group to leave meeting and go to their next activity, while they remember their "walking feet, thinking brains, and quiet voices."

Even much older children respond to the challenge of preparing surprises for the teacher, surprises like a quiet room, a perfect line, an orderly presentation. We encourage a pleasant complicity with phrases like "I'm going to close my eyes . . ." When the teacher closes her eyes, we transform duty into a contest. We avoid reprimands and inspire a challenge — one in which there are two winners.

"I'm going to walk out of the room for two minutes, and when I come back in it will be quiet and everyone will be at their desk ready to work."

"Let's see if we can walk upstairs so quietly and enter the room so silently that no one will know we are here."

I suspect that when we close our eyes, momentarily, we get children to open theirs and figuratively watch over their own selves. If we want children to rely on their own controls or skills, we must stop hovering. This challenge often works because we show implicit confidence in their abilities.

When I am ready to close my eyes and I know that my Randy or Sylvie or Grady will not be able to manage, I take them with me, literally or figuratively. We close our eyes, or step out of the room together. My hand may clasp Grady (and Randy too), or I encourage them with a whisper or by bringing them near me. For the majority, the count of ten is plenty of time to recover the necessary controls.

Asking for help

Sometimes it makes sense to invite cooperation directly. A teacher of a seventh and eighth grade group stands waiting for a few minutes as his class assembles and begins to slow down before returning inside.

"I need some help now" he says firmly. To Jess, who is still tossing the ball around, he says, "Jess . . . some help please." He doesn't say what help because he doesn't need to. Jess and all the children know. Most children willingly help adults who care for them, when they are asked directly. Asking for their help reinforces the reciprocal nature of the relationship and pays them respect. In fact, we do need their help. When they hold the ball still or hold on to themselves, they are helping the class and the teacher.

"Thanks for your help," the teacher responds.

Providing choices

Choices set boundaries. They mark out what *is* possible — the sky is not the limit! At the same time they give children some control and encourage responsibility. Choices are presented in direct, short, specific statements that avoid sermons or lectures:

"You can either work together and get done quickly or drag out this room clean-up and miss time later. Your choice."

"You can either quiet down and follow meeting rules or meeting will be stopped. What will it be?"

"You can either do independent reading or draw quietly at your desk. Talking is not a choice."

"You can either concentrate and get it done now or later, but it needs to be done before you leave today. Your choice."

"You can stay with your group and choose to follow the rules, or leave and work by yourself. What's your choice?"

If there is a clear consequence involved, it should be expressed as part of the choice. We ask children to decide, or after a few moments we say, "I see by your behavior that you have decided not to continue working with the group. You need to leave." And if the teacher has a clear preference, it too can be expressed — "I would like you to decide to join the group, but you need to figure out if you are ready."

Summary

Our words make a difference. We need to be clear in what we expect and communicate, and we need to honor our words by doing what we say we will do. If we use language precisely and honestly, we can expect the same from our students. Too often we're in the position illustrated by Holden Caulfield in *Catcher in the Rye* (Salinger). "I'm lucky, though. I mean I could shoot the old bull to Old Spencer and think about those ducks at the same time. It's funny. You don't have to think too hard when you talk to a teacher." However, we need to think hard when we talk to children.

10

Stress the Deed, Not the Doer

Eric and Vinnie

"Thanks for holding my lunch money for me when I don't have any pockets," says Eric to Vinnie.

Vinnie goes over to Eric, shakes his hand and says, "Thanks for helping me get stuff that I don't understand."

Eric beams. Vinnie giggles. Eric and Vinnie are nine-year-old boys in fourth grade together. A few months ago they didn't know each other's names — partly because they live on different blocks, partly because Eric is black and Vinnie is white. Now they are friends.

◆

"Stress the Deed, Not the Doer" is a technique that helps both teachers and children. It is a way to express praise and criticism, appreciation and disapproval, compliments and complaints while keeping the class safe. It is a specific approach to our use of language, but it is also an attitude that expresses respect for people even though their actions may disappoint us.

There are moments for heartfelt, global statements of praise or anger — "I just love seeing how you took care of yourself today" or "I get angry when I see that sneaky stuff!" But we must be careful about labels and grandiose implications. "You were thoughtful to include new people" is different from the label of "considerate student." "You did a sneaky thing" is not the same

161

as calling the child a "sneak." Labels tend to constrict and shrink potentials, even the favorable ones. We want to avoid imposing unnatural or unrealistic expectations for behavior. What happens if the next day, the child isn't considerate? We want to let children know that we like them — not because of their accomplishments, and in spite of their failings.

The focus of the praise or compliment, the criticism or disapproval is on the deed, not on the character or the personality of the doer. The emphasis is also on specific attributes or actions, rather than generalizations:

"Thank you for making our art shelf look so beautiful."

"It was a considerate idea to include new people in your game."

"I don't want to work with you when you are interrupting and disturbing the lesson."

"I don't like it when you make up excuses and don't tell me the truth."

"Your story really presents an interesting problem."

"Your patient explanation of the assignment really helped people get it."

"I like the way you added shading to give depth to your drawing."

"When you use that rude tone of voice, I don't feel like giving you the help you're asking for."

"I don't like it when you take things from my desk without asking for permission."

When we name the deed, we preserve the doer. "I like you. I don't like this behavior." And when we define the deed, we help to clarify expectations and set boundaries. As we narrow, define and specify, we show children what makes for a caring or considerate deed, a good piece of writing, an independent worker, a good friend. By pointing out the specific behaviors that work and those that don't work, children can begin to get beyond just the general categories of "good" or "bad person" or "good" or "bad student." When children come to see themselves as "bad," they often become defiant or defeated, or both. Many of our "incorrigibles" disrupt and distress our classrooms from beneath the weight of a broad, undifferentiated definition: "I am bad."

Using the "I voice"

Comments that reflect encouragement or disapproval should use the first person singular, "I." Using the "I voice" stresses the view point and opinion of the speaker, rather than a categorical judgment or command:

"I don't like it when you choose not to listen to my words" rather than the more automatic response, "You'd better learn to listen, young lady!"

"I feel angry when you make faces if I ask you to do something" rather than "You'd better wipe that look off your face."

"It bothers me that you didn't take care with this paper" rather than "You should have done a better job."

"I want to see you go down the stairs without hurting anyone else's body" rather than "Walk down the stairs and don't touch anyone."

"I want to know how you plan to get along with Sharon for the rest of the week and not hurt each other" rather than "You and Sharon better stop fighting."

"I would be sorry if you quit now" rather than "You shouldn't be a quitter."

When we use the "I voice," we take responsibility for our opinions and assert the importance of personal feelings. Conversations are personal because we establish a personal connection and personal perspective.

Helping children "stress the deed"

Children need a safe way to express their feelings, too. They can also learn to express feelings of appreciation and anger using the "I voice." They thrive on the praise and encouragement they receive from one another, and attend carefully to the criticism. Children need help expressing praise beyond their best friends or coveted possessions. They also need help expressing anger without inflammatory words and abusive names.

To teach children to name the deed, not the doer, we teach several techniques:
- To tell "what" they do or don't like, rather than the "who"
  * "I don't like it when you . . ." rather than "I don't like you."
  * "I hate it when you tell secrets" rather than "I hate you."
  * "I like it when you let me join your conversations" rather than "I like you."
- To narrow and specify
  * "I don't like it when you act like a jerk."

Teacher: "What do you mean about acting like a jerk?"
"Like when you have to make up all the rules. Like be my friend one day and not the next."
* "Thanks for being my friend."
Teacher: "Can you explain how he was a friend to you this week?"
"Well, thanks for being my friend and letting me play ball with you."
- To use their "I voice"
    * "I felt bad when you didn't let me play" rather than "You never let anyone play."
    * "I don't like it when you cheat" rather than "You always cheat."
- To acknowledge a compliment with a smile and "thank you"
- To accept criticism
One way to help children "listen" to criticism is to help them practice not arguing or rebutting. "Listen. Don't argue. It may not be what you see or remember, but it's what your friend (teacher or classmate) recalls. See if you can just think about it. You may say, 'I'm sorry' or 'I'll think about that.' But you don't argue."

The Compliment Club

A few years ago, I started a group for children ages nine to eleven with poor self-images (primarily children with learning problems) called a "Compliment Club." One task of the group was to give each other a weekly compliment. Names were picked from the hat. Each child wrote out a compliment, in a letter-like format:
"I think you have improved your cursive a lot."
"I think you did good in math this week."
"I liked the drawing you did. I think you are a good artist."
"You were a good friend this week. You helped me a lot with my reading assignment."
"I'm glad you picked me to be on your team. I like playing with you."
Several things struck me in the first months of this "club." First, the children noticed and recalled real things just as previously they had "ranked" on each other by noticing real faults. Now they picked up each other's true (not fabricated) accomplishments. Second, they quickly developed the knack of offering specifics:
"You are a good friend."
"Can you tell what made him a good friend this week?"
"Well, he picked me for his team."
One girl in the group, wrote "Thanks for being a good friend to me this week and listening to my troubles. You gave me some good advice, but mostly you listened."
Third, I was struck with how much they cherished the compliments they received. The letters were folded away and I would see them pulled out, read, and reread. It was a central part of building the esteem of individuals and also

creating a friendlier spirit in the group. The success of "compliments" depended on the capacity to notice and honestly describe by focusing on the concrete and specific.

♦

Children also need help expressing anger, without calling names. We've all heard exchanges like this verbatim record:

"You're a total smelly jerk."

"So? You're a nerdo wimp creep."

"So? You're so ugly even a rat looks good."

"Yeah. Well you're such a shrimp, you gotta' watch out or you'll get stepped on. Squish . . ."

Sometimes the one-upmanship gets so ridiculous it leads to laughing fits. Sometimes it hits too close to home, and sometimes it ends in a physical fight. What can you do if someone calls you a creep (or worse)? What can you expect from a creep, anyway? Both sides are stuck. The creep is not likely to say, "But I'm not a creep, I just acted like one." Children need to be able to name the ways they are creeps to each other, and they need safe ways to respond. Children can learn these skills through modeling by teachers, but primarily they will learn from doing. One way I involve children in "stressing the deed" is a special ritual in my classroom called "Center Circle."

Center Circle rules

I like Center Circle because it makes me feel happy when someone shakes my hand. When I get pounded, I feel a little worried because I know I did something bad to make someone feel terrible.

Kennedy, age 9

Center Circle was inspired by a dance improvised by a first grade class I taught. They moved in and out together, greeting each other with spontaneous and sweeping gestures of stamping feet, linked arms, together, apart, in and out, until they regrouped into a final circle. It seemed a very powerful and moving enactment of feeling for this feisty and creative group. A while later I read the book *Reality Therapy* by William Glasser, which further encouraged my belief in children's ability to help each other. My version of Center Circle is part dance and part meeting. This is the way I first introduce Center Circle to groups ranging from first through sixth grades.

"We all have times when we feel angry or especially grateful. Sometimes it's hard to share those feelings and tell people we appreciate their help or that something they did made us feel bad. Center Circle is a special time that we can share in our class where we try to work on these feelings."

"We also need to be able to share these feelings and still keep each other safe. To do that we need to follow the rules of Center Circle. You all need to listen carefully and know that you can make your best effort to use these rules. They will keep our Circles safe."

The class comes together in a circle, usually sitting on a rug on the floor. Bodies need to be relaxed and comfortable, but sitting up Indian-style, with room for each person around the circle.

"First, we need to know the Center Circle gestures. There are only three:

1. Everyone needs to know how to really shake hands — firm, not limp, strong, not hard. Who can show us a firm handshake? Everyone, now shake hands with the person on your left — firm, not limp, strong — not hard.
2. Now everyone needs to be able to make a fist and pound the floor in front of their body but not touching their body or anyone else. A good fist, a good pound but not one that hurts your own hand or touches anyone's body.
3. And we need to make eye-contact. Everyone needs to be able to look at someone directly, but not make a face. You will need to move your body in front of another person and look at them making good eye contact."

"Now that everyone has the three gestures, there is also some Center Circle language to learn. There are four rules about what we say:

1. 'I' comments: Everyone has to begin their comments with the word, 'I,' like 'I felt good when you . . .' or 'I felt mad when you . . .' or 'It makes me feel . . .'
2. 'I feel angry' comments: We will try to describe and tell what makes you feel angry at classmates this week.
3. 'I feel good' comments: We will try to describe and tell what makes you feel good and how friends have helped you.
4. Questions: You get to ask two questions — 'Why did you pound me?' or 'Why did you shake my hand?'"

"Remember you are going to describe actions and the things that people do, not describe people. I liked it when _____. Will you say, 'I like you' or 'I don't like you?'"

I generally model the procedures with several demonstrations. "Suppose Maggie helped me sort some papers and I feel appreciative. What will I say in Center Circle to Maggie?" The class will practice the language. "Suppose I was annoyed with Tommy because he kept us waiting this week. What will I say? Will I say, 'Tommy you were a pest this week'?" I keep practicing until I get very clear statements that follow our rules about language, such as "I didn't like it that you kept me waiting this week."

"There are a few more rules we need to understand before we can do our first Center Circle.

1. People may choose to go or not.
2. People may choose to raise their hands and ask, 'Why did you shake my

hand? Why did you pound me?' — or they may not.

3. People must use their Center Circle language.

4. There is no answering back. You may say 'Thank you' or 'I'm sorry' or 'I'll think about it.' People do not have to agree with the 'shake' or 'pound'; they only have to listen and remember that is how someone feels.

5. Center Circle is over the moment the teacher 'adjourns' the group. That means that there is no longer any discussion. Not later at recess or at lunch. CENTER CIRCLE STAYS IN CENTER CIRCLE.

6. Center Circle is 'confidential.' We do not share with friends in other classes. It is our private and confidential business." (But it may be shared with parents. I have often had parents come to watch out of curiosity and interest. They have always been very moved.)

Doing Center Circle

To me, Center Circle is a great way to express my feelings because if I pound someone I can tell the person how I feel without the person yelling at me. A person has to have a lot of courage to be able to pound or shake someone's hand . . .

Cherylee, age 10

In Center Circle, one child goes all around the circle, stopping before each classmate to pause, look, think and then use one of the three gestures. If she has something favorable to share, she will do her firm handshake. If she has something unfavorable, she will pound her fist on the floor in front of (but not on) the person. If she has nothing special to say, she makes eye-contact and moves on. This is not fast, but careful and slow. She moves all around the circle and then returns to her own place. Not a word has been said. When she gets back to her seat, hands may go up. She calls on the first hand. Below are a few excerpts from a fourth grade class that had used Center Circle only about four times.

First hand: "Why did you pound me?"

"I pounded you because you didn't share your jump rope with me."

Second hand: "Why did you shake my hand?"

"I shook your hand cause you helped me find my markers when I lost them."

Third Hand: "Why did you shake my hand?"

"'Cause, you've been a nice friend to me."

Teacher: "In what way is Cindy a nice friend?"

"You talk to me a lot."

Fourth hand: "Why did you pound me?"

"'Cause you make up things and tell lies and I don't like it when I ask you something and you're telling lies. But sometimes you don't and then I like talking to you."

I am always impressed with how serious children are in Center Circle. They learn the rules and procedures quickly. They are attentive and composed in their places. For their fourth Center Circle, these children were strikingly solemn and focused. As they become accustomed to the rules and procedures, they become more relaxed, as well as more open. It is only later that they begin to pound the teacher, for example.

They are generally thoughtful and precise, also. In this example, the teacher does intervene in order to clarify what was meant by "nice." Children are generally more specific about their anger and complaints, and general when expressing friendly feelings. In this case, the student doing Center Circle expresses a range of negative emotion. In the last comment, she is quite emphatic, but balances her reactions without the teacher's intervention. In this short transcript, I included only the positive and negative responses. In fact, this student revealed a strong agenda by only making eye contact with about a third of the group, rather than "shaking" or "pounding" them.

Gradually, the language and expressions of Center Circle begin to transfer to other spontaneous situations, although not immediately and not for everyone. But the ritual, guarded and preserved by the teacher, continues to be important month after month, even over several years.

Center Circle is not right for every child or every teacher. I find that the teacher sets the tone and creates the sense of purpose and conviction. If the teacher has faith in this process, the children will. If the teacher is doubtful or casual, the process gets sloppy or out of hand. If a few children aren't ready for Center Circle (they often self-select after listening to the rules and procedures), they may spend the time in another classroom. This is a non-punitive action. If a child disrupts the process after Center Circle begins, she must leave for a time-out, and perhaps miss the next session also.

Center Circle usually occurs only once a week. I find that thirty minutes is a good period of time. This means that only about three children get a turn each week. Teachers may set up a chart ahead of time, or see who is ready and willing.

Some children receive many pounds, from various children and over successive rounds of Center Circle. They will not always elect to raise their hands, and sometimes teachers need to remind them that it takes courage to ask. But my experience has been that most children do ask, "Why did you pound me?" And they do listen to the response. When the language is appropriate — "I didn't like it when you shoved me" — it provides important feedback. Sometimes after the session, I will have a conference with the student:

"I noticed that you got lots of pounds today. Does that feel kind of hard?"

"Sorta'," with a shrug.

"I hear that people are telling you that they don't like some things you do to them. Do you remember some of those things?"

"Yes."

"I'd like you to share what you remember."

"They don't like me to push . . . but they push me too."

"Yes. They don't like it when you push them or call names. Do you think they'd like it if you stopped doing some of those things?"

"Maybe, but they gotta' stop pushing me too."

"Do you want to work on that? Is there some way I can help you?" I try to avoid the "buts" and arguments and reinforce that the classmates are talking about deeds, not the doer.

Some children always get "passed." They are often the "invisible" or marginal members of the class, the children who don't interact or assert themselves in peer activities. They are excluded, not because they are mean or threatening, but because they are apt to be withdrawn. Sometimes children perceive them as "different."[1] I might intervene by shaking the child's hand when it is my turn, noticing something special about the student, or helping the student do Center Circle. Teacher and students are often surprised to find out the thoughts and feelings of the unknown peer.

A teacher gets pounded and pounds her class

Teachers do take their turn at Center Circle — often to model the language and behavior, but also to express and participate in the exchange of feelings. Here, Jan Doyle, a fourth grade teacher in West Haven, CT, describes the impact of her participation:

We had been doing Center Circle for three months, but no one had ever pounded me. I was waiting for that with some anxiety and worry. The past few weeks had been pretty hard with this class and I felt like this would be the time. But I was surprised when it was the quietest student, absolutely the quietest, who stopped in front of me and said in a barely audible voice, "I feel like I want to pound you and shake your hand." She stayed before me, poised, but still for some time.

Finally I said, "It takes a lot of courage to pound your teacher." She looked at me again as if to say, "Does she really mean it. Is she for real?!" So, I repeated, "It takes courage to pound your teacher." Then with slow, but sure, force, she raised her fist and pounded hard down on the floor. Suddenly in a great show of solidarity, or perhaps shared release, the entire class pounded the floor. It was a powerful moment.

"Why did you pound me and shake me?" I asked. She explained.

After this the tension in our room seemed to diminish. The next day it seemed that everyone was more relaxed, cheerful and friendly.

Some weeks later, I "pounded" the entire class. It was my turn to go in Center Circle. I was feeling angry with my class and thought it might be better if I didn't go since I wondered if the children were ready for me to demonstrate anger.

I explained this to the class. One of the children immediately said matter-of-factly, "Go ahead Mrs. D. You'll feel so much better." I did. I pounded the class as a whole, carefully explaining the things that were making me upset. And I did feel better, much better!

◆

---

1 By eight or nine, many children avoid peers they consider unpredictable or socially "different." A perception of similarity is a prerequisite for friendships.

When the teacher takes an active part (not just a leadership role), the children include the teacher in their shakes or pounds. I have found that rather than lessen authority, an intimate and still respectful bond develops. "It takes courage," as Mrs. Doyle reminded her student, to pound the teacher; it also takes courage for the teacher to expose herself in this way. After the pounding, we must raise our hands and ask solemnly, "Why did you pound me?" The child explains that the teacher didn't let her do such and such, but she let someone else do it. There are issues of fairness and sensitivities. "I didn't like it that you made me do a paper over just 'cause I made one mistake."

"I'm sorry," we might say or "Thank you for sharing." We do not get to argue or explain either. Some children do pound the teacher. More will shake.

With caution, I have included an "empty chair" in our Center Circle. Children use the chair to shake or pound siblings primarily. But the chair may stand for a student not in the class. "Who was in the chair and why did you pound it?" someone asks. "It was my brother and I pounded him because he started a fight with me but I got blamed by my mother." But it is important to focus Center Circle around school life, and not include open-ended family business which may be uncomfortable for the teacher and parents.

What happens if children take Center Circle out to the playground? Don't they threaten to beat each other up or get back at someone? In my experience and the experience of teachers now using Center Circle in other schools, the answer is that this doesn't happen. There is the strict rule about closure. Remember, "Center Circle ends when it is over," we say repeatedly. This is a most important precondition. If a child were to disobey this rule, there is a consequence — usually losing the privilege of attending the next session. The child is invited back after giving an assurance that he or she can follow the rules.

Generally children cherish this ritual and are careful to respect the rules, if the teacher is serious and observant of them as well. Center Circle should never be done casually or without the teacher's belief in the process.

Summary

Center Circle is one way to help children learn to express feelings and to learn to listen actively to the feelings of others. The central message is that it's important to share feelings, both positive and negative, but to share them in a way that is respectful and safe. We hope that the language and attitudes of Center Circle transfer to the playing field and the lunchroom as well.

But regardless of whether they become deeply ingrained or limited to a special time and place, I am still moved and glad when I see Eric, a shy nine-year-old boy, his face intense with concentration, look at Jeremy and say, "It makes me mad that you ignore me when I ask if I can play with you and Chris."

Jeremy, looking back, says, "Sorry, Eric."

I am moved by their courage. I am glad for Eric's assertion, and for Jeremy's moment of understanding.

11

The Changing Voices of Authority

All teachers use different "voices" of authority when they assume responsibility for the classroom. We must use these different voices selectively and in the right contexts for them to be most effective. I use three voices of authority in my teaching:

- The Golden Rule
- Rules for Safety and Order
- Personal Rules

Although the Golden Rule is the broadest and actually serves as a foundation for the others, all are important and legitimate voices. They are all necessary in a truly responsive classroom.

The Golden Rule

When we rely on the Golden Rule (or another code of beliefs) we call upon a higher and more inclusive authority to guide our behavior. We invoke the authority of ethical standards. These are not unique to one teacher, or one class, but principles which ideally guide and bind all of us in society. Ideally, a moral and ethical force guides us to become better individuals and better citizens of our school, community and world. We have "faith" — not that we always do what's right, but that we try to do what's right. The essential "authority" of the Golden Rule comes from its capacity to inspire faith. It helps us stretch our imaginations — we see ourselves, others, and our community struggling to

meet the highest ethical standards.

In an interview in *The Boston Globe Magazine,* Erik Erikson says, "As you go through the life cycles, every stage has to add something to the possibility of being able to obey the Golden Rule," which "expresses one's attitude toward the Other in a healthy way."

The Golden Rule doesn't tell us what to do. It lacks all specifics. It doesn't say that it's wrong to tease or call names. But the teaching and understanding of these specifics, growing from children's real-life experiences in school, is what forcefully involves children in ethical growth.

In the Greenfield Center School, a school devoted to a developmental perspective, the Golden Rule is the "one rule." It is discussed and practiced as the very first activity of the year. It establishes a focus and tone for the school. It governs us all. I remind older children that as we get older, the Golden Rule gets harder, not easier. As adults, we live in a society that too often holds the self-interest of a few far above the common interests of the others. And, as we increase our social involvement, social conflicts usually increase as well. It isn't a simple task to be able to take another's perspective while preserving our own autonomy.

Josie

A power struggle had evolved between a sixth grade teacher and Josie, age 11. She had become highly disruptive, trumpeting a negative and scornful

attitude towards everything her teacher said, did or tried to do. She rolled her eyes expressively when asked to come to a group. She whined that things were too hard or too boring, sometimes both at once. She whispered about unfairness and told her buddies that she was "picked on." The more her teacher reacted, usually with a consequence to leave the group or the room, the angrier and more provocative she became.

It was, of course, infectious. Some other children responded out of their own need for conflict. Some were naturally allied and sympathetic to Josie. Others were disturbed by the mounting tensions in the room. Although pre-adolescents identify strongly with their peers, and are overtly less attached to adults, they still need and depend on strong connections and supportive relationships with their teachers. At every level, the situation was divisive.

The teacher was quick to see that her strategies were not working. Although upset with the continued insolence and defiance, she was anxious and willing to figure out an alternative, one that would bring the student back into the class. She was concerned, however, about the contagion of Josie's hostility and its effect on others. Josie wanted to be back in her classroom and was willing to agree to conditions, but as yet acknowledged no responsibility. "I still think I didn't do anything. It's not my fault. She just doesn't like me. That's all."

It seemed clear that Josie needed time and professional guidance to work through some deeply-entrenched issues. In a social conference with Josie, we talked about self-control. We humorously dubbed her needs the "Keep-Your-Face-In-Place Motto," an instruction about what to do if she thought someone was wrong.

We also talked about the Golden Rule. "I hold a grudge," insisted Josie. "I stay mad." We talked about the capacity to stretch for forgiveness and let go of a grudge. It's not easy, we agreed. But it is the way to make peace.

"Do I have to do this?" she asked.

"To use the Golden Rule? To stretch yourself? Yes," we replied.

"I can't. I don't do things like that."

"You can make up with someone," we repeated. "You can make peace." For the moment, Josie was able to return to her classroom and extend her own "olive branch" — a peppermint candy in a napkin on which was written "Peace."

"It felt nice," her teacher said honestly. "It felt better." While Josie was having her "conference" with us, the teacher spoke to her class. She told them that she noticed that many were aware that Josie was having a very hard week and that she also noticed some of them were taking sides. She said that she understood that it was natural to want to take sides when there was conflict. She wondered, however, if taking sides was a way to use the Golden Rule. She reminded them that in our school, we were all bound to the Golden Rule and needed sometimes to make a hard effort if it was going to truly work.

"What would we do," she asked, "if we used The Golden Rule?" The children were able to see that there was a choice about prolonging a conflict or making an effort at peace. The teacher, rather than distancing herself, also admitted that some of the things she had done had created more conflict and thus were mistakes. "I want our classroom to be peaceful. I want our classroom to work better for Josie. I need your help too."

Many of the children were also able to see how they might help. Ideas included not talking about it anymore, or saying, "I'm sorry you feel bad. Do you want some help with your math?" They were basically offering comfort but not encouraging the conflict. Others were relieved that the focus was positive and supportive, which lifted the spirits of the entire group. By the end of the class discussion, the teacher felt that the children were ready to receive Josie with a more purposeful and hopeful attitude.

◆

This is only one, very fresh example, of a kind of conflict which surfaces in every type of school, every type of class, and with all kinds of children. One way to confront these issues is to invoke the Golden Rule. It doesn't tell us what to do, but it helps us create choices by seeing a higher purpose and social interest.

It is The Golden Rule, not the Teacher's Rule, that we call upon to decide whether it's OK to tease, or hoard the best blocks. It's the Golden Rule that directs us to consider the feelings of another person, to reach for a way to care:

"What can you do if you accidentally knock someone down?" (Shrug.)

"What would make you feel better? Say you're sorry? Help them up? See if they are hurt?" I don't necessarily expect five-year-olds to know what to say or what to do. Left alone, many would do just what we hope. Others might hasten away, either guilty or oblivious. But all of them can learn.

At eight, there are other important issues. The class is collecting toys and clothes to give away to those in need at Christmas. Some children bring in old, broken toys or torn and shabby articles of clothing. Again, I would invoke the authority of the Golden Rule. "If we use the Golden Rule, how will we decide what to give to another person, even someone we don't know? Do we give what we don't want — or something that we guess someone else might like because we know they'll enjoy it?" We present a germ of an idea — that the sacrifice of giving up something is rewarded with the satisfaction of caring for others and the self-respect that comes from a true act of generosity.

I see this approach as moral teaching, not moralizing, because the act requires a choice by the student. The Golden Rule provides a principle but also a choice. One must choose to use the Golden Rule. A child must actually choose to contribute a doll she still likes, or one she no longer plays with and sits in a closet. Even if, for now, the choice is the latter, we plant the seed for the next time.

At five, children may learn the basics of sharing (not grabbing), waiting for a turn, and then not hogging all the turns to come. At seven, some are able to pass a spinning top after one turn. Others pass it readily to a friend, but not to Josh, who can barely pass it at all. "But, his finger was in the way," cries Josh. "And it didn't get a good start. He made me miss . . ." At nine, they can pass the top easily and swiftly around the circle, but few remember to include new children in a special game or activity. The teacher can use the authority of the Golden Rule to help all of these children learn social skills and the gifts of caring.

I believe that we need to provide children with a higher moral and ethical authority, such as the Golden Rule. It is up to the teacher to help them recognize and name the possible choices. The Golden Rule is one voice of the teacher, but the teacher is not the Golden Rule — she didn't invent it or its practices. She accepts its authority and therefore gives it her voice. Her task is to transmit it through her own voice, so that children can then add their own voices to the larger community.

"When I see people in this class talk to the same friends every day and I see new people in our class not included, I think we are not using our Golden Rule. What does the Golden Rule tell us?"

Later, we hear a child's voice. "Would you like to join us and play a game?"

Rules for safety and order

"You need to be able to walk through the halls in a line as a class." That isn't the Golden Rule or my personal rule. It is a school rule. Children need to understand that there are rules which govern the well-being of the school and community. The teacher recognizes and upholds these rules, but they are not specifically hers. They are the rules which make for safety and order. We often refer to them when we say, "The rules say . . ."

It is important to be able to use a set of rules which are not arbitrary, but are not individualistic or readily negotiable either. If I want to play kickball, I need to follow the rules. These rules, like ethical rules, are for the common good, but they regulate practical matters such as physical safety, game procedures, and the allocation of rights and privileges. Permission or constraint come from the authority of the rules, not the authority of the teacher.

"You are out," says the teacher, "not because I say so but because the rule says so."

"The rules say you have to wait your turn in this game, even if you know the answer. That's not my rule. That's the rule of the game."

"The rules of our school say that if you want the right to chew gum, you have to wait until you're in the oldest class. That's the school rule."

"But that's not fair," protests a fourth grader.

"Well, who could you speak to if you want to question that rule?" I think that it's important for children to understand the source of laws or rules which govern their society. It's useful for them to learn that rules are man-made constructions and therefore changeable. It's an important exercise for children to pursue the reasons for such specific rules as no gum-chewing, bathroom passes, or lunchroom lines. In the process of exploring, children may begin to understand why rules are not always for individual convenience or satisfaction. If children's questions about rules are taken seriously and then followed up with a disciplined, orderly study, the quality of school life can be improved. Positive changes can be made in procedures in the lunchroom, halls or locker room. When children are involved, even on the classroom level, they generally gain respect for the process of shaping and making the rules.

When I use the authority of the rules, it is not my personal authority. When a child draws graffiti on the walls, I would avoid saying, "I don't like it that you wrote on the walls." Instead, I might say, "In our school, we need to keep the walls beautiful" or "The rules say we need a clean place to work and play." If children cheat playing a game of checkers, I might ask, "What do the rules say about jumping?" And then, "If you want to play this game, you have to do what the rules say." If a child argues with the referee, the rules says that the referee's call is final.

In a game of Capture the Flag with six-year-olds, one child says, "Teacher, I tagged him and he won't go to jail."

The teacher asks both children, "What's the rule?"

"Tagger's choice."

"But he didn't tag me."

"The rule says, 'If the tagger says he tagged you, you are tagged.' What do you do now?" If the "tagged" child chooses not to follow the rule, he loses the privilege of being in the game. These rules provide safety and order. The teacher facilitates and safeguards the rules, but it's the rules that "say," not the teacher.

Personal rules

There are two ways that I use the personal voice of authority. One has to do with personal "quirks" or values. People respond out of consideration, rather than moral choice or respect for the law. For example, at home I can't bear rock and roll music early in the morning. On the other hand, my children can bear it, and actually like it. I ask (actually insist) that there be no R&R music that I might hear in those brutal waking hours. My authority does not stand on morality. I can't argue that it is bad or harmful to human dignity — not logically anyway. I also can't invoke the rules of the state or legal proceedings. I can only say that it bothers me and disturbs my well-being. I need their consideration and respect as their parent.

I think it is important to request, even demand, consideration as long as the request is reasonable — something that is appropriate, that children can manage, and that truly reflects personal meaning. I wouldn't ask children to do their best work or to be nice just to please me. I would ask them for personal consideration by turning down the radio, letting me talk undisturbed with a friend, or helping me with a chore.

One of my personal rules for the classroom is "no war games." I do not make it a matter of ethics. It is not a school rule either, although it could be. I present it as my preference, something that I do not like or allow in my classroom.

The noise level is also a matter of personal consideration. I like it quiet in the morning. I need it quiet. Invariably, I begin the day with a quiet social time. Yet, one year I co-taught with a wonderful teacher who loved music and kept a piano in the room, which the children loved to play — endless four-handed beats of "Chopsticks" in the morning! My co-teacher didn't mind at all, and often joined in. It didn't work for me, so out of consideration, quiet music ruled the morning and "Chopsticks" the afternoon.

I also use personal authority for matters of strong personal conviction. These are most honestly expressed in the "I voice." I am not translating the Golden Rule, or the procedures of the school, but conveying my thoughts, my convictions and knowledge:

"It matters to me that everyone participate."

"I really care that everyone feels included in this class."

"I really want to see you finish a book this year. That feels very important for me."

These convictions may apply to goals for the classroom or for specific children. They are related to the Golden Rule, but we add the personal authority created by our relationships with children. Our personal authority is often our strongest voice with children, as long as we don't overdo it.

Summary

The various voices of authority serve as tools for the teacher in a variety of circumstances. The Golden Rule provides moral authority and helps stretch our power to care and attend to others. Rules for safety and order provide the permission and constraint of an external order. They give consistency and safety to the common ground. And finally, there is the personal authority of the teacher, which expresses both conviction and knowledge. Used carefully and sparingly, there is no stronger voice. It is the natural authority of a confident teacher — it springs from her inner strength and grace.

Section

III

Clear Positives

Introduction

What the effective people did seem to share was a quality I first thought of as moralism and later came to think of as moral passion. There were no laissez-faire teachers; the good ones preached, made demands and seemed to indicate that learning is a serious business.

Joseph Featherstone
Schools Where Children Learn

Parents [Teachers] must not only have ways of guiding by prohibition and permission; they must also be able to represent to the child a deep, an almost somatic conviction that there is meaning to what they are doing.

Erik Erikson
Childhood & Society

My best teaching comes from my deepest convictions. I believe that we are all strongest as teachers when our convictions infuse our teaching — our arrangements with children, the lessons we teach, the topics we study, the priorities of our schedules, the ways we organize our furniture and materials. When we strive to teach from a strong foundation of what we believe and value most, we insert what I call "Clear Positives" into the classroom.

Clear Positives are, first, a set of ideals or principles, phrased in positive language, that allow us to imagine and describe what it is we wish and hope to achieve. They are not necessarily complicated or many. Second, Clear Positives provide a structure for making decisions. We have reasons for what and how we teach, reasons that need to be based on belief rather than external pressures or curricular mandates.

The more we are able to translate our internal values into conscious and deliberate actions, the more we can make positive choices based on our beliefs rather than what is expedient or stylish — the short-term programs, flitting policies and facile solutions. Teaching towards our ideals takes endurance, and years of consistent teaching. We need conscious and clear-sighted criteria to make the best decisions. Clear Positives and the decisions they inspire are open to examination, but strongly rooted in a few, well-established ideals held with faith and belief.

Our Clear Positives are made real for the children by what we teach — explicitly in our words and even more strongly in the experiences we guide within the classroom.

Today it feels odd, naive or overly ambitious, to speak about our ideals in education. We live in a world scarred by attitudes of cynicism, resignation, and even blank despair. We have generations of young people defined by some as "spiritually empty." Critics point to the failure of the schools — faulty curricula, burnt-out teachers, ignorant students. Teachers find their authority chiseled away, reduced by systemic mandates, state regencies, and test-retest protocols. From time to time, most of us ask ourselves, "Why am I teaching?"

It is essential that we have positive answers to that question. These most fundamental answers are what we need to overcome the mood of negation, to show our conviction that things do matter, that there is meaning to what we do in school.

My father was a person who could not properly fix anything that was broken — he could not change a light bulb, hammer a straight nail, or make a meal that didn't come directly from a cereal box. Yet I turned to him (as did many others) when the world needed fixing. Not that he actually fixed that either, but he breathed new life into us, a renewed sense of courage and hope. He listened with interest, he expounded with calm reason and informed opinions, he touched lightly with humor. He had an abiding belief in the goodness of life and people, and an unquenchable human spirit. He made us feel good for asking. We turned to him when *we* needed fixing.

All children need some "fixing," and others need an inordinate amount to keep them exploring and "plugged-in" to their world. We must find, nurture, and project our faith. It is our task to fuel the spirits of children as well as direct their actions. By using Clear Positives, we hope to transmit our belief in life and living.

The process of using Clear Positives provides models and expectations that are:

- Clear — they provide direction for children and teachers, ranging from broad ideals to specific actions at specific times
- Positive — they frame the world positively and appeal to the deeper interests of children and teachers; they do not proscribe or prohibit

To use Clear Positives in the classroom, each teacher must begin at the beginning. Each individual must answer some basic questions: Why am I teaching? What is it that I truly want to teach?

Chapter 12 deals with finding those answers and forming them into a few basic ideals (which might also be called "values" or "principles"). These ideals then serve as a foundation for all of our subsequent teaching decisions and actions. They provide a framework for:

- Broad social arrangements and expectations — Ch. 13

- Class and group expectations for learning content and procedures — Ch. 14
- Individual expectations and contracts — Chs. 15 & 16

I would like to emphasize that this is not a process that is cut and dried, with clearly defined steps and neatly-tailored categories. Teaching is more intuitive and infinitely variable than mechanistic. But to teach with conviction, solve problems, and present a consistent approach to children's intentions and actions, we must know our roots. Ideally, each action and decision of every day in the classroom could be traced back to our ideals — our basic reasons for teaching.

12

Teaching by Clear Positives

Using Clear Positives assumes that we have positive reasons for teaching. Most people who become teachers initially have a vision of what they will add to the world through their teaching. This vision is often lost in the pressures, confusions, and constant demands that exist for every teacher in every type of school. But this initial vision, translated into a few ideals, is essential to teaching with joy and conviction.

In establishing and defining our ideals, we don't want to concoct laundry lists of aims for student behavior. At the drop of an eraser, any self-respecting teacher can produce at least twenty worthwhile goals: We want our children to be self-motivated, independent, reliable, careful with their work, invested, kind, polite, inventive . . . on and on. But these are too specific at first. I suggest looking at even a higher level. Too many ideals diminish the focus for teachers and children.

When I examine my own ideals, three have the most bearing on my teaching:

· Schools need to teach alternatives to violence and to stress nonviolence as an essential characteristic of the community.
· Children need to learn to think for themselves.
· We need to stretch, not track, potentials.

My list of ideals are not prescriptive — they need not be the same as the reader's. But I hope the discussion of my ideals will help readers reflect on their own and to use the process of Clear Positives in their teaching.

185

Teaching nonviolence

No school advocates the use of violence, but few would define nonviolence as a core curriculum. I envision schools actively engaged in a curriculum of nonviolence. I do not see this commitment as only a disapproval of violent behavior, or extra units of social studies. Instead, I see it is a distinctive way of acting and thinking that permeates the entire school.

Part of a nonviolent curriculum is teaching children to take an interest in others' lives and in views unlike their own. This helps children to develop a fondness for diversity, rather than fear or hatred. Our daily routines can encourage this type of caring — morning meetings that focus on actively listening and responding, writing conferences where one student attends to the meaning of another, and the process of training children as peer writers.

Sylvia Ashton-Warner wrote in *Teacher*, "To construct cooperatively is to lay the foundations of a peaceful community." We also teach nonviolence when we organize cooperative learning projects, class problem-solving discussions and team play. When children work cooperatively towards a common end, they come to rely on and to value differences.

Not long ago, I visited Central Park East in New York City, one of the elementary schools started by Deborah Meier. It is the start of the day and these sixth graders are working in small groups on numerous projects that include mapping countries in Africa, acid rain experiments, and pottery. There is a feeling of easy occupation. In each small group, I see children of color and white children, girls and boys together. In this city, a window on our country's racial and "have/have-not" tensions, there is a small society of young people creating maps, clay pots and chocolate chip cookies in utter collaboration and peace.

Children become conscious of differences spontaneously, naturally, and at an early age. Often it begins with recognition of physical differences within a group. The sixes notice that Jimmy stutters. They notice that Mark doesn't understand what their teacher says. They notice that Kimmy cries a lot. And they notice that Tara limps when she runs. Children are excellent observers and predictable commentators. But acceptance of diversity has to be constructed.

We may need to help them make space in their game for a classmate who limps and remember to talk to another who is partially deaf. "When I play with her she doesn't say anything and she just follows me around," complains one child about a peer with a disability. So we encourage inclusion, while also supplying tools to help the children work with each other. Sometimes an ordinary scuffle deteriorates further, revealing racial or religious prejudices fueled by the prejudices in our society. This can be a critical moment for a tactical display of indignation and righteous teacher wrath.

Research shows that barriers between groups of children are not always easy to dismantle and require deliberate and constructive teaching. There are

Figure 12.1

USING CLEAR POSITIVES

Clear Positives are:
- Clear — they provide direction for children and teachers
- Positive — they frame the world positively and appeal to the deeper interests of children and teachers

The process of using Clear Positives begins when we identify broad, basic ideals (values, convictions). These Clear Positives inform and guide all of our decisions and actions in the classroom. We can then create specific Clear Positives for specific situations.

Ideals

For example:
- Teaching Nonviolence,
- Children Learning to Think for Themselves,
- Stretching, Not Tracking, Potentials

Broad Social Arrangements and Expectations	*Goals and Expectations for Content and Social Groups*	*Goals and Expectations for Individuals*
For example:	For example:	For example:
• Sharing — crayons, etc.	• Science groups — "We are all scientists"	• Oral contracts
• Rewards — personal encouragement, not stickers	• Reading groups — "Book talk"	• Written "Jobs" contracts
• Universal participation — everyone plays	• Theme studies — Care for local environment before rain forests	• "Critical Contracts"
• Mediating conflicts rather than avoiding them	• Careful, efficient transitions	
	• Homework process	

now many programs for kindergarten through high school which teach appreciation for cultural diversity and attitudes that combat bias. I regularly do a simulation exercise which creates a group of outsiders and insiders. Seventh and eighth graders assume a given role and quickly respond in character when they are excluded. For many, the resulting insight and growth makes for a memorable moment, a highlight of their year.

Another approach teaches children to manage conflict. This is different than structuring situations to try to eliminate conflicts or leaving children to find their own solutions. I strongly believe that conflict resolution should be integrated into the curriculum — a lesson should be stopped or postponed so that a conflict can be confronted and discussed. Children learn, largely by necessity, as we lead them in considering issues of justice and equity.

Exciting programs that teach children to mediate their own conflicts (discussed in Ch. 5, page 88) have been started in many schools from third grade through high school. Both teachers and students receive special training and student-mediators are called to mediate problems with peers and between teachers and peers. There are also students involved in governing councils and "fairness groups."

A group of sixth graders that I observed identified name-calling as the central problem of their class and one that they most wanted to solve. Their first solutions ranged from corporal punishment to "If someone calls names they should have to stand up in front of the class and everybody call them bad names."

While many were nodding agreement, one lone girl asked, "Isn't that sorta' the same thing and maybe just as bad?" The dissonance effectively hushed the rash of ideas for penalties, but then there was silence. Most of the children still lacked the intellectual and moral development to move between two points of view, in this case the view of the name-caller and the view of the person called a name. They needed help from the teacher to stretch their potentials and explore workable plans.

Finally, I believe that we teach nonviolence by creating a model for children through the social arrangements of our school: the ways we treat each other; the priorities we give to social concerns and to a responsive, respectful environment; the opportunities for input into school government; the tone of the lunchroom, the playground and the hallways; our willingness to open the doors of the classroom to include the problems outside it.

Children need to see us, the grown-ups, behave decently and with integrity. I say to one of my students, "I don't treat you like that. I don't make faces or put down your requests. I treat you with respect, even if I disagree with something you do. I expect the same." And if I have, in fact, treated this child with respect in spite of his boasts and aggravating snits, I claim his attention. He may also move a step closer to internalizing a basic respect for others.

In a world too full of violence, we need to teach nonviolence. Schools do not create or advocate violence, and our best efforts will not eradicate the violence within or without. But teachers and schools can help instill peaceful alternatives.

Encouraging children to think for themselves

I want children to learn to think for themselves and for schools to become places where children learn to take charge of themselves and their learning. Children can learn to derive meaning from a text. But more importantly, they can learn to derive meaning from their schooling, which helps them to direct their lives and make good choices.

We do this by passing on skills and knowledge, but especially attitudes about looking, listening and speaking with one's own voice. We can arrange for children to *find out,* rather than to supply all the answers ourselves. We can balance analysis with experience, provide hands-on activities, field trips into the community, and opportunities to be playful and inventive. We can help children learn to define choices and become decision-makers in their own education.

I stress the ability to define choices and participate in decisions, but with caution. Recently, I worked at our school's construction site as part of an untrained crew of teachers. We waited nervously at the first meeting to allocate jobs, hoping to help in the remodeling of our new school building. I chose to work on clean-up. I realized how often I had assigned such a job to a student, and how often I had become irritated when the student wandered, dabbled, and chit-chatted his way about the room. Yet, here I found myself stumbling, aimless, and talkative. I began to realize that I had no idea what "clean" meant in a setting that was constantly producing debris and dust. What rubble didn't belong? What did? The whole was overwhelming, the parts almost imperceptible.

To be productive, to contribute, even to think about what needed to be done, I needed enough knowledge to focus. I finally got up the nerve to ask the person in charge what he meant by "clean." He started to give me a list. "No," I said, "show me." After he explained one part and was ready to move on to the next, I stopped him again, knowing that I would never retain more than one job at a time. Children also get lost in a landscape with too many possibilities, too little definition, and no place to start. Choices and decisions become random or disconnected. The confusion becomes painful, and there is often an anxious plea for order and direction. "Please, teacher, tell me what I do now." And too often, we respond by withdrawing the choices rather than teaching children how to make them.

Children are growing up in a world with frightful persuasions and terrifying problems. Rather than providing prescriptions for them, we need to make choices and decision-making part of the expected curriculum. There are many kinds of purposeful choices students may make in a regular school day. Some are important, but spaced irregularly: picking a topic for a social studies report, selecting a book to read, choosing a partner.

I think it's important to schedule regular choices as well, through a regular "choice" time. This is a period each day when students decide what they want (or need) to do, and then do it. They are expected to plan, and carry out their plan. It is not a fringe benefit, an incentive to finish assigned work, or a Friday treat. It is part of each day's steady schedule. Choices may vary from day to day or be ongoing. They may be solitary pursuits or include small groups, and may involve serious or playful activities. But they need to be a child's own. Children who are conditioned to expect easy or passive diversions may find it hard to make a plan of action or engage in it more than superficially. Some students are most idle and disruptive during choice periods. They cannot find diversion and engagement, so they bother others or wait for me direct them. Others may flit from one activity to another or perseverate, repeatedly drawing the same picture, tracing the same maze, or playing the same games.

In order to break the pattern, we may need to flex the four walls of the classroom, as well as find ways to develop children's capacities for choice. Sometimes I know that I don't see a child's true potentials. I may not encourage the choices that mobilize the most physically active students, who might spend hours shooting baskets. It's just as important to provide opportunities for children to tinker and fix things or stare through a microscope. By offering choices, we begin the process of identifying varied strengths and interests.

My ideal is for children to act as decision-makers in their own education. They can decide, in collaboration with teachers and parents, what they think is important to learn and share responsibility for that learning. One approach, explained in Chapter 16, is called a "Critical Contract." It begins with the question, "What do you most want to work on this year in school?" There are other goals, of course, but this one is self-directed. If I want children to share responsibility for their learning, I must be prepared to help them locate their own objectives and not merely to mouth my own.

We can also help children define choices and make decisions on ethical or moral issues. A few years ago, some schools used a program called "Values Clarification" to teach ethical thinking. Students were presented with contrived dilemmas and asked to imagine and discuss various solutions. The game Scruples has a similar popular appeal. Hypothetical, "what-if" games are absorbing, but most school days provide many *real* moral dilemmas for discussion:

Several pens were missing. The whispering voices have already indicted someone. "What should we do? Class?"

Tony is missing his trip money. There is talk of stealing and a scapegoat is emerging. "What do we do?"

No one wants to hold hands with Julie. Joshua is passing out secret stashes of candy in hopes of securing a friend. Andy cheats on a test. Only a few children dare to speak up during morning meeting. Some children can't get homework done at home, even if they want to, and need assistance from the class.

We need to seize these opportunities for discussion. Our classrooms can become places where children think about what they do, express popular or unpopular opinions, confront discrepancies and fallacies about things that matter. When we help children to think for themselves, we need to remember that they won't necessarily think the way we want them to think. Sometimes they suffer their own mistakes — and learn from them. Other times we must intervene. But at least they are thinking.

This type of thinking helps to build and sustain relationships — it helps create community as well as self-controls. It is intimately connected to my first ideal — teaching nonviolence.

A group of fifth graders were described by their teacher as having "chewed up and spit out" lunchroom aides during the year. The principal warned that they were now on their third and last one. In a class meeting, the students asserted that the lunchroom aide could not "cope" with them. They detailed several problems precisely. But, in the course of the discussion they began to realize that they could "cope" with themselves in the lunchroom. They could monitor themselves instead of challenging their aides. Soon after, their behavior changed. "They aren't wearing halos yet," reported their teacher, "but we all see improvement."

In this case, the children didn't develop an exceptional scheme, but they got beyond blaming and excuse-making. By naming the problem and giving it serious thought, they began the process of healing and change. Because they worked together, the bond between class and teacher grew stronger. The process helps children use their capacities for critical thinking as well. They can better manage the natural rifts between students and between themselves and teachers, aides, parents, or principals. The school climate ultimately depends on these relationships. When we develop our skills as a community to solve our own problems, we forge a unity of purpose that is too often fragile and elusive.

Stretching, not tracking, potentials

The development of a child's potential depends on the ability of the teacher to perceive the child's possibilities . . .

Rudolf Dreikurs
Maintaining Sanity in the Classroom

Our schools are full of writers, painters, scientists, athletes, breadmakers, fixers-of-things and dreamers. This is what we seek to inspire as teachers. To inspire, we need to help our children *do* even what they don't do well.

We often set up what we call "ability groupings." We have our high and low reading groups, our fast and slow classes, our "gifted and talented," our "special needs." We sort and sift children into teams, glee clubs and shops. It is not that our sorting is necessarily inaccurate, not that there aren't better and worse readers, singers or ball players. It's that this screening process depresses rather than elevates potential.

I recall a third grader once telling me with utter precision the skills (or lack of them) of every member of his class. He knew who could hit a fast ball, who was good at multiplications, who couldn't read, who could dance, who couldn't spell, who could fix zippers and who was good at cutting things out. He knew who could write neat cursive and who got in trouble most. So did everyone else in the class. Clearly, there are wide differences in aptitudes and skills within any group, as any third grader will tell you in the most matter-of-fact way.

The question is whether these aptitudes are the best criteria to determine what we do and do not do. "We are all operating at about 15% of our potential," wrote Dreikurs in *Maintaining Sanity in the Classroom.* Psychologist Howard Gardner, in *Frames of Mind*, documents multiple kinds of intelligences, many of which are untapped in school.

When I observe in a kindergarten, I note the ease in which one child will go to the easel, beat on the drum, race madly in a tag game, and solemnly recite a poem. As children get older, more advanced and mature, they often lose this global ambition for life. Their potential to enjoy a rich and varied life is limited. As children grow, there are external selection processes like ability groupings and an internal weeding — "I want to do what I do well. I like to do what I do well." We need to consider both.

There seem to be key moments in the natural stages of growing up when the sense of self is especially vulnerable and permeable. The seven/eight-year-old stage in school may be one of them. Sevens, for example, are especially self-critical and worry that their work isn't perfect. They write and draw in the tiniest circumference, their upper body hunched over in a protective shield. And then they whip out an eraser to blot out the "awfulest" mistakes it would take a microscope to locate, "'cause it doesn't look right." Everything that can be erased *will* be erased to do better. And by eight, the critical awareness extends to others. Children scrutinize and judge others' talents and skills, and rank themselves and others in pecking orders. Suddenly the child who loved to draw or spend hours on a craft project stops. The reason? "I can't make houses look real," explained Darrell. "Drawing is dumb anyway."

Maggie returned from a pond field trip complaining that it was "too boring." Maggie, often the quick one in the class, wasn't quick at spotting salamanders, nor was she an intrepid searcher in mud banks and pond bracken. Mostly she watched, inactive. She was perhaps "needy" for the first time in a school activity and didn't know how to ask for help. Rather than allow her to withdraw and decide that she hated science, on the next trip she was prodded in the art of turning over the rocks, poking her fingers into the ground, and cupping her hands to catch a frog. This time the trip was "OK."

Children — and adults — mistake ease of learning for the overall potential to learn. They confuse speed with facility. The product or end-result is overrated and the process is diminished. We are all so conditioned to end-products — the fluent reader, the super-athlete, the finished cloth — that the stages of production seem almost invisible and beyond our patience. We need to show respect for the doing, as well as the done, and for a slow and steady rate of acquisition. Children with learning problems, particularly, need to have the grit to struggle, to accept a slow and uneven gait of progress. The willingness to sustain effort and the courage to persist may be as important to achievement as any teaching methodology.

"I hate math!"

"I can't write!"

"I stink at soccer!"

These judgments, uttered emphatically by seven-year-olds, elevens, and thirteens, are all premature. Too often they represent only superficial exposure coupled with harsh competition and comparison. Too often they mask feelings of inadequacy and fear of failure. They become an excuse to avoid and withdraw from delightful and meaningful activities. As teachers, we need to struggle against these tendencies to narrow and constrict potential.

I rediscovered math as a teacher attending workshops and playing with manipulatives. I felt profound relief when I was able to manipulate fractions and understand ideas I had given up on long ago. I became a more lively math teacher because I was able to become an excited learner of math. I am not "good at math," not fast or particularly clever, but I am interested. I am not an accomplished runner or late-blooming tennis star, but I greatly enjoy jogging slowly in the early evening and intense tennis matches against "formidable" opponents! I believe it is more wonderful to play than to play well.

We can arrange our classrooms to stretch potentials and encourage participation. Here are some guidelines. We need to ensure:

- *Availability.* Every aspect of our programs must be available to every child.
- *Universal participation.* Every child participates. Block-building, sewing, and kickball are "have-to's." The expectation is that each student will do a careful observation of the cricket and that everyone will complete a story they want to publish.
- *Support.* We must provide support systems, and encouragement which sets realistic goals and emphasizes effort, progress and fun.
- *A responsive climate.* We must establish and protect a climate which cherishes diversity of input, mistakes, and peer teaching. Children teach each other, and cooperative learning is central to the classroom. The emphasis on cooperative (rather than competitive) learning does not blur differences in skill levels, but provides for self-acceptance and acceptance of others as both learner and teacher.

It's also important to confront gender expectations as we stretch potentials. I watched my daughter's class play a soccer game recently. Every member of the class is on the team. Some have exceptional skills. Some can barely run the length of the field or kick a ball. A few lose track of the direction of the play. And the goalie, a strong, but dyslexic boy, reversed his stance and sent the ball between his own posts. His team barely noticed. This motley crew was winning against a bigger and more selective team. They often did. There was a drive and spirit that sometimes seemed to compensate for a lack of skills, even in the competitive arena of sports.

As a mother of a soccer daughter, I watched with pride the beaming faces of the girls, their faces red with exertion, their chatter full of bodily complaints. But they held their positions and pushed their way down the field, standing their ground against boys often twice their size. Then they slumped down on the bench after the game, crying, "I was lousy but it was a great game."

A character in *Cat's Eye* by Margaret Atwood defines the world of girls:

> *I don't have to keep up with anyone, run as fast, aim as well, make loud explosive noises, decode messages, die on cue . . . All I have to do is sit on the floor and cut frying pans out of the Eaton's catalogue with embroidery scissors and say I've done it badly.*

This captures what we too often hear from our girls. But given a push, girls develop the sheer exuberance of playing, whether they ever say they're good or not. It may be a long haul: there are excuses, refusals to play in the games, a preference for standing and watching or gossiping during recesses. Given a choice at age eleven, most girls would stay indoors and draw. It may be with reluctance that they slouch out for their first days of soccer practice. They will fuss about positions, and detail a long list of bruises. But when their coach sends them out to play, they go.

I add one more example of ways teachers can stretch potentials. Jeff Phelps

was a young intern in a classroom of eights and nines. He was a skilled crafts person, and often wore sweaters he knitted or scarves he had woven. It was decided that he would teach the entire class to knit. The class, however, was at an age when girls and boys are reluctant to participate in tasks they consider not properly feminine or masculine. When Jeff announced his knitting project, there were many rounds of "snarly" looks and disgusted glances. Still, it was a "have-to" and Sean could tell his Mom as he sat knitting in the kitchen, "The teacher makes us do it."

In a few weeks, everyone had completed a knitting bag big enough for two needles and everyone knew a basic stitch. Soon they were busy with the "first draft" bookmark and were learning to "chain-on" by themselves. If they forgot, they could check the Knitting Tutor Chart to find a certified expert. The role of expert was new for Angie, who was used to getting, not giving, help. With remarkable patience and pride, she unknotted Donny's yarn, repaired his snarled stitches and showed him how to coil the threads around his finger. Soon, it was clear that it was not only the dexterous and nimble who took their knitting everywhere. I was surprised to see that Richie, who cried if he had to copy over lines of writing, would knit at every available moment. It became a room of knitters, complete with the clack of needles and soft murmur of voices. For a final project, Jeff bound together twenty-five colored squares (which were only "kinda' square") to form an afghan representing the work of twenty-five students. It was the centerpiece of the room, so that long after Jeff left the class, his knitters admired their handiwork and continued to turn out bookmarks, mini-scarves, or just more and more squares.

When we see children extend and deepen their interests, test their patience and endurance, tackle what's new or different, we are stretching potentials. We are getting beyond the 15%.

Years ago, the staff members of my school set a goal for themselves. The goal was to learn to do something new. My goal was to learn to speak in front of an audience. The first time my talk was terrible — long, rambling, and tiresome. The second time it was better, and now I speak before parent assemblies and workshops with more poise though still with apprehension and a dry mouth. It's not one of my favorite activities, but it does give me a sense of power. I believe this is true for children, too. We need to stretch, not track, their potentials.

Summary

As teachers, we need to know why we teach, and why we do what we do in the classroom. These ideals (or values) need to be conscious and clear. The process of Clear Positives begins by establishing these ideals, which become the foundations for our social arrangements and our expectations for content groups and individuals.

It's easy to lose sight of our ideals among the complex demands of every teaching day. If necessary, we need to go back and identify them again and again, recovering them from the piles of roll books, lesson plans and report cards — the "stuff" that may shroud our earliest spirit and most compelling desire to teach. When we truly know these ideals, we can use them to guide the specifics of our classrooms. I know that we are all strongest as teachers when our ideals inform our teaching.

13

Choosing Social Arrangements and Expectations

We can promote our ideals through our broad social arrangements and expectations for the classroom. By consciously choosing arrangements and expectations that are consistent with our ideals, we keep those ideals in the forefront. We continue the process of Clear Positives.

The crayons

In some schools in Maine, children bring their own boxes of crayons and markers to school. In other schools, the crayons are part of the communal property of the classroom. I discovered in a teacher's workshop that the question of sharing materials raises many central issues. Do you have to share with everyone or only with "special friends?" Here are some of the teachers' responses from the discussion that followed:

"If you make them share their markers with everyone, by the end of the day they are pretty much ruined. So, I don't insist."

"Some kids don't take care of other kids' things. I guess that would be like a logical consequence. If you're not careful, you can't use them."

"I say if it's too precious to share, don't bring it to school."

"Sometimes kids use their property as currency. I'll let you hold this, then you have to pick me for your team. OK?"

"This is a situation for me where there is a real fine line between children sharing and being polite and friendly to other people . . . but also being able to respect their own space and needing to have something that belongs to

197

them. Where do we stop telling a child, 'No, you have to share that or you have to let someone else use it,' because don't we *also* want to teach them there's a part of themselves they have a right to?"

"What about the child who never remembers her own crayons and always wants to borrow? Or the child with whom no one shares — because no one likes?"

This discussion brings up more than an "either/or" dilemma. Sharing is integral to the struggle to balance the needs of community and the "rights" of the individual. On the one hand, sharing possessions or communal property helps to create a friendly community, and promotes generosity and a concern for the welfare of others. On the other hand, we also want to demonstrate respect for personal boundaries.

Whether we offer communal boxes of crayons or have private supplies, conflicts over sharing will occur. How we help children negotiate these conflicting needs is crucial. I believe that our message about sharing should be embedded in a larger message. The larger message is that cooperative living is necessary and desirable, and that interdependence is the norm rather than the exception. We cannot ask children to be generous and depend on each other while at the same time we promote daily academic contests, regularly rank character, or challenge children to out-score, out-run, and out-pace the other guys.

Teachers can establish routines for sharing. Personal items brought to school can be passed around or set up for display for everyone. One teacher has her students sign-up on the blackboard for turns. The student remains in charge, a "teacher" of his property. Children bring in pets, remote-control cars, books and new games. With a few simple guidelines, they do a beautiful job giving turns to small groups of interested peers. The teacher may help set up the guidelines — how many in a group, how long each person gets to try the car — and then the group can be peer-directed.

Children don't internalize values by rigid enforcement. In a first grade class, during what was supposed to be a quiet drawing period, a group of girls waged a crayon battle. Usually the best of friends, they fussed no matter what agreement was reached in a moment of calm. Who had more crayons? Who hoarded the blue ones? Who had the box nearer to her side? Finally, the teacher divided the box into separate containers and insisted that they use only their own. It worked; the fighting stopped.

But after a short while, the teacher noticed that the single bins had mixed and all four were now in the center of the table as the children peaceably traded and shared. It seems that there are times when children need the reassurance of a safe boundary, even if that boundary is their own box of crayons. There are times when collective life is secured by attention to individual life.

◆

Children share space and activities as well as objects. Teachers must build habits and set up guidelines for friendliness, too. Friendliness transcends favorites or self-interest. We are expected to act decently even when we don't "love" someone, or perhaps even like them at all. One teacher reminds her five-year-old class, "We can't say no if we are chosen." I tell my twelve-year-olds we can't say no if someone wants to join a game, as long as they play fair. These habits of friendliness are often learned and used in the context of sharing crayons, a workspace, or a game.

Through these discussions about how to manage a box of crayons, we identified important teaching opportunities. There are no perfect arrangements for the markers or crayons as we try to balance community and individual needs. What is most important is that we inspire children to struggle with us, to search for the best possible balance. Their participation in the discussions can help ensure their acceptance of the process and its results.

Stickers

During a visit to a second grade class in an urban public school, I was struck by the large oaktag cards taped to each desk. "I am a Star" was written in the center of the placards. Some were speckled with glossy silver and purple stars, others were sparsely decorated. The teacher explained that when students followed the rules, they received a star and when they achieved a specific number of stars, they got to take home the card and show it off to their parents. There were other commendations and class prizes from their teacher as well.

Accumulated commendations earned special trips and festivities. For students who misbehaved, there would be fewer stars and stickers, accrued demerits, trips to the principal, suspensions and the loss of attendance on the special outings. The aim was to motivate appropriate conduct through the awards and privileges, as well as to apply negative consequences for misconduct.

"What do you do to earn a star?" I asked.

"You gotta' be good," responded a student.

"What do you do to be good?," prompted the teacher.

"Like if another teacher comes in the room and wants to talk to our teacher, you don't get out of your seat or talk."

"And you don't make noise," added another.

Another student pointed to a list of rules posted on the wall. "If you follow the rules," he began to read, "Raise your hand. Don't run in the halls. Don't leave your seat . . ."

Another student interrupts, "Hey, she can read. She's a teacher you know!" He smiles and bows to his friends.

The student reading the rules is now blushing and confused. He begins to stammer, "You do your work on time, you could get a star." He puts his head down on his desk.

I wondered, "Is kindness a rule?" I didn't note any exchange of stars or demerits at this point.

Teachers in this same school were concerned that their students showed a lack of incentive to do assignments (without tangible rewards) and little pride in their own output. School was a "low priority" for too many of their students. "We have 4th and 5th graders who are already planning what they will do *when,* not *if,* they drop out of school," one reported. As a group, these teachers felt that the school environment needed to become a more enjoyable social experience, and that children needed to develop intrinsic motivations to learn and behave. What was missing, the teachers reiterated "is a sense of responsibility and pride."

I observed a group of boys playing a lively and safe game of football during recess. Suddenly, an aide walked over and said to the boys, "Be good 'cause the lady is watching."

We must decide whether we are teaching children to be good because someone is watching or whether we are teaching "goodness" as a better way to get along with people. We must decide whether we intend to teach conduct that draws on inner as well as external sanctions. I do not think it works to equivocate; I do not think that stickers can be used to reinforce self-motivation.

Months later the same group of teachers met to consider specific classroom strategies to promote their goals of responsibility and sociability. The question of stickers came up. "Our kids need stickers," one teacher explained, because teachers and children often contend with overwhelming odds. Stickers offer tangible, positive feedback which provides immediate and visible short-term results. Children are excited and eager. They sit up, take notice and work. Teachers are reassured by their "interest" and better behavior.

What happens when the stickers become bribery to get the job done rather than a reward for a job well done? I've seen a student demand a prize for completing a single sheet of math problems! What happens when the children work for promised awards but show no investment in the work itself? Have we actually conditioned children to expect and value material gain rather than such intangibles as pride, competence, or self-respect? If we do that, then external gains and sanctions, like status with peers and money from selling drugs, have little competition from rewards like good grades or a low-paying job following a high school degree.

I fear that the prevalence of "stickers" means we have lost faith either in the inner resources of our children or our capacity to reach those resources as teachers. I sent one of my students off last summer with a "reading contract." I worried that the instant school was over she would stop reading — a realistic assumption. In order to be a bit more persuasive, I promised a payment. She would earn two dollars for each book she read. We went to the library and found three wonderful books. The contract was signed. On day one of the new school year, she greeted me saying, "I read my books!" She was beaming. "And I loved them." I didn't hear a word about money.

"I don't think a teacher should have to pay me," she confided to her mother. "It was fun!" I hadn't trusted that Lydia would be able to read for fun, only for money! I had underestimated her investment and capacity to assert herself. Lydia was a reluctant reader, but not a reluctant student. There are other children far more detached and disaffected than Lydia. Those are children we often feel need a motivational "carrot," an external incentive. Even when we offer "carrots," we must be careful not to lose sight of our basic goals, which are the value and meaning to the student of the work itself. The aim is not to accrue stickers, stars or money. The aim is to solve a problem, or enjoy a good book, or feel pride in competency or accomplishment.

"Tell me," I ask a student when I award a pizza-lunch prize, "how you managed to earn this treat."

"'Cause I finished all my books on time," he answers.

"What does that show us?" I continue. I want to emphasize the inner competencies and resources necessary for him to succeed with his challenge. "You were able to chose books you wanted to read and read them," I might begin. "You learned 50 new vocabulary words . . ."

We don't have to abandon all the short-term "carrots," as long as we keep in mind that the carrots do not take the place of the inner meanings. I use my pizza-lunch prizes or stickers to add a temporary element of gamesmanship and challenge and to take the edge off a fearful experience. For children who have encountered failure, stickers and prizes may help them overcome a strong avoidance.

Most of the time we say to children, "Give yourself a handshake. Give yourself a pat on the back. Be proud." And then we must help them to identify the reasons to be proud, the positives they have achieved:

"It's not easy to write a short story. And you did."

"It's not easy to listen when someone criticizes something you did that they didn't like. But I see you did listen."

"It's a strength to be able to stick to things and do things over until you feel satisfied and you did that. That's something to be proud of."

At a last resort, I will get out the stickers. But as a first resort, I will say, "Give yourself a big handshake. You should be proud of your hard work. Are you? Is it good?"

◆

Using Clear Positives means reexamining and restating our social arrangements and expectations so we can teach more directly. They should be consistent with our ideals and help keep attention focused on the things that are most important. I believe that children want to control themselves, to be responsible, to feel competent, to be an accepted member of the group. When they forget they want these things, we are there to remind them.

Figure 13.1 lists some other positive expectations for children. It is not by any means an exhaustive list. You will easily think of others. I believe that the more we appeal to the positive interests of children, the more peripheral stickers become.

Universal participation

A group of ten-year-old girls complain repeatedly about their recess time. They don't like the choice of games; they think they're stupid; they don't see why they *have* to play, anyway. Couldn't they just sit on the steps and talk, or draw? "OK, Mr. Sheyda? Can we please, pleeese? We won't bother anything, pleeese?"

The teacher in this situation has to make a speedy decision. He knows that the girls will behave. They will sit and draw and gab happily in or out of the classroom. They certainly don't need supervision, he thinks. Or do they? Would Mr. Sheyda readily agree to let a group withdraw from reading periods or math time because it was "stupid" or more fun to sit and chat? Would any of us be comfortable allowing students to avoid challenging academic tasks because they felt inept or unsure of themselves? Or would we try to help them participate?

I view this decision as one based on our ideals. It is not a matter of conduct or what is expedient for teacher or students. If Mr. Sheyda is to be a "nice" teacher, he will give in to the pleadings of the girls. If Mr. Sheyda is concerned with stretching the potentials of these students, he will help them to play one of the recess games. It is a chance to encourage them to investigate and extend their capacities.

Figure 13.1

SOME POSITIVE EXPECTATIONS

These are informed by my ideals — Nonviolence, Independent Thought, Stretching Potentials. I use them to guide specific classroom expectations and arrangements. I believe children want to:

- Be welcomed into the class each morning
- Be noticed in nice ways — "You really like baseball"
- Have choices in the course of a school day
- Have fun in school
- Be heard and responded to by teachers and peers
- Be able to talk with friends in school
- Gain competencies, skills and confidence
- Have others know they have certain skills
- Know they can think and solve problems
- Know facts about the world
- Have routines and a predictable order to the day and week
- Have appropriate tasks of independence
- Get compliments and give compliments
- Have a warm and supportive relationship with adults — at least some adults
- Have adventures — new challenges or risks
- Have rules for games as well as class
- Be able to get and give help
- Be able to resolve conflicts
- Be able to make and keep a friend
- Be a friend
- Be useful and contribute to their community
- Be able to make mistakes, break a rule or act wrongfully and then make amends, repair and recover their place in the group

---

In this example, the girls want to withdraw from the vigorous and active physical play and choose what feels safe and secure. They want to sit rather than run. They are secure in their conversation and relish their socializing, but they are also avoiding the risk of physical encounter. It may be that the choices for recess games, the swift dodge ball or intense basketball, are excluding and overwhelming. Perhaps the options need to be extended. But I want the girls exercising their bodies, playing on the field. They may need support to find appropriate choices and to contribute at their own

pace. They also may need to practice their skills. But they don't need permission to pull out.

Conflict

It is spring. The cliques and the games of "you're my best friend/now you're not" are at their fevered height in the fifth grade class. A rumor has started about K. — a rumor too awful to repeat, but everyone does. P. is blamed for starting the rumor. P. is indignant and tearful. She would never do such a thing. C. is also blamed, but asserts, "You're pickin' on me." Tempers are bursting and ill will is contagious, disrupting the work of the whole class. The group meets spontaneously to talk it out. There are more accusations, denials and hurt feelings. Telephone calls after school inflame the emotions even more. One mother tells the teacher that her daughter is crying and doesn't want to come to school. The group (about eight boys and girls) seeks permission to talk about the problem again, on its own.

The teacher says, emphatically, "No. I want to work this through *with* you." Social conflicts are not as secondary, trivial and repetitive as they sometimes appear. These dilemmas can involve children with real moral and ethical conflicts from which they can draw meaning and make choices. But even though the incident occurred over the weekend, not during school hours, I have no question that this is school business, part of the curriculum. My response would be to intervene, not to dismiss the problem or ignore it. While there are times when children must be left to figure out things on their own, there are other times when mediation is essential.

Although the children want to resolve their rumor problem, it is clear they are at a loss for solutions. This group is *stuck*. When children become stuck, they are apt to become more stubborn. It's harder to listen, harder to reconcile differences.

The children are stuck for several reasons. They're stuck because they are trying to attach blame, and at the same time to establish their own innocence. The view that solving a problem is like solving a crime is misguided. The search for culpability rarely provides the necessary release or leads to conciliation, especially when more than two are involved. Most likely the children, individually and collectively, need to gain insight into their roles in the situation, rather than to expose the culprits. If they didn't start the nasty rumor, they passed on harmful sentiments, relayed the gossip, added to the discontent and took sides. They sustained the conflict, which is interesting as well as hurtful. We may have to convince children that they want to (or must) resolve a conflict by ending it.

Another reason that the children are stuck is that one member of the group is acting out of a confused set of needs — a need to act out hurt and anger that supersedes her need for peaceful friendship. Even older children are overwhelmed and impotent in reacting to destructive impulses. Adult intervention is necessary.

Mediation is most effective when it defines responsibility rather than seizes it. Children still need to retain an active role in resolving the conflict. In this case, the teacher might ask each student two questions:

"What is one thing that you did that was hurtful?" (Some answers — gossip, told secrets, took sides)

"What is one thing that you could do now to help solve the problem?" (Some answers — ignore more stories, not talk about it anymore, be nice to everyone)

The teacher sets a tone that is contrary to blame. "We all do this. We all get caught sometimes. We all feel bad when our friends are not getting along. Sometimes when we mean to be helpful, we make things worse. How?" The group shares verbally or even writes the responses to the two questions. On a chart, the teacher may list some of the hurtful/helpful behaviors to give direction and guidance. Then the individuals can personalize them. An effective discussion of this type is:

- Short. The teacher goes around the circle quickly, hearing brief statements from each member.
- Focused. It is not an open-ended "What's the problem?" format. There are clear-cut questions and something for each person to do.
- Restricted to the "I" voice. "I did . . . ," not "you did . . ."
- Moved towards closure. Children leave the group with something they are going to try to work on that is positive.

Teachers may still need to set up limits and constraints. I might inform the children that for the next weeks, there would be no more talk about the rumors. I might even impose restrictions on bathroom and recess congregations. I might ask the children if they felt they would need help controlling their talk, because I know the temptations. We could role-play respectful ways to refuse to pass on or engage in rumors. I would also ask for help from parents, particularly to limit telephone access. And I would meet separately with the troubled student, and family, in order to explore other avenues of assistance.

Friendships are critical to children in school. At various times, they are as liable to produce grief as affection and happiness. Conflicts will not disappear, but children can grow, with assistance, to be better caretakers and friends.

Summary

Good teaching relies on reflection. Using Clear Positives means that I must look carefully at what happens in my classroom and assess the meanings, messages, expectations and rewards. I hope that I can trace each of my actions back to one of my basic ideals. My approach to the broad social arrangements and expectations of the classroom should point towards my ideals. How I approach sharing (crayons), rewards (stickers), universal participation, and conflicts should be part of a consistent environment that stresses self-control and community. If they don't, I need to rethink and reform my approach.

14

Introducing Clear Positives to Groups

Clear Positives are ways to explain to students why we do what we do in our classroom. They may be introduced to the whole class or to small groups, and they may frame specific content or direct children's behavior. They can give purpose to the study of geography or explain the nature of rules. They guide the outlook of individuals or groups, and can create a sense of purpose or help to recover one that has been lost. They may be established during the first weeks of school or evolve midyear.

Developing Clear Positives at this specific level can be a challenging and frustrating task. We must find the fewest words to convey the proper message, and eradicate "don't's," "not's" and negative syntax. Clear Positives provide a sense of conviction and challenge, but do not moralize or lecture. We define specific tasks we will help children accomplish and describe the attitudes we hope they will develop: for example, to show interest, to observe closely, to be careful or precise or more open-minded. By using Clear Positives, we continue to communicate faith in our children's will and aptitude, and our belief in the value of the undertaking.

A field trip

I was teaching a class of ten- and eleven-year-olds. We were studying the geography of our area in the Connecticut River Valley. I had planned an all-day trip with an outstanding local geologist as our guide. It was a beautiful day. Everything was set — except the children. As it turned out, they did not need

a geologist. What they really needed was a sheep dog to nip at their heels, herd them into a group and keep them reasonably on track. They wandered, complained about sore feet, and were perpetually hungry. When our guide, pointing to the river, asked, "Why do you think a river bends instead of going straight?" I noticed that half the group wasn't even looking in the direction of the river, let alone wondering about its contours! Not only was I exhausted by the end of the trip, I was furious.

I spent much of the ride home contemplating tortures: I could make them write, "I'll never wear new shoes on a trip again," one thousand times. Or, "I promise never to use my whiny voice in school again," ten thousand times. Or I could never let them leave their desks. The prospects were endless! Luckily, for them and for me, by the time we got back to school, it was time to go home.

After a very long night's sleep, I returned the next day refreshed. I realized that my class had no clear expectations for managing a trip. They had rules for safety, and they knew to put their names on their lunches and stick with their partner (sort of). But they had no true purpose and only a vague understanding of mine. Except for a very few "natural" geologists, the students had no clear focus. Their attention was easily scattered, and shifted from their stomachs to social conversations and back to their feet. And since they were not paying attention to anything consequential, they were, of course, bored!

I began again. I began by defining the purpose of these trips. I named it. It was a "field trip." A field trip I explained is a study that scientists and anthropologists — "Who knows what an anthropologist does?" — conduct in the field, rather than the laboratory. "Why is it important," I asked, "to study things 'in the field' rather than at your desk or from a book or a video?"

"To see things up close."

"To see for yourself."

"To know what is really there."

From continuing discussion and questions, we concluded that a field worker gets up close to find out answers to particular questions. We agreed that the questions might be very general, such as asking what is in the field, or specific, such as "Why do rivers change their course?" We defined the job of the field worker: to gather information. "What skills do you need when you go into a field that are different from desk work?" We decided the skills of the field worker are many. Children talked about observation, collecting, asking questions. These evolved into our Clear Positives:

1. We were doing field work, which is work that many kinds of scientists need to do.
2. The job of the field worker is to ask an interesting question, something they really want to find out.
3. To find out what they want to know, field workers need to observe, listen carefully, take notes and be interested in the field.

We never went on another field trip without these Clear Positives. The "ticket" for admission to a trip became "an interesting question," something each student wanted to find out. "No question, no ticket, no trip."

I considered a "good question" anything which showed a desire to know one thing. Not all children started off curiously or with a true question. Some questions were mechanical. But curiosity is contagious and they began to learn from each other's questions as well as from the exercise of thinking up their own. On a general level, it was the curiosity which I hoped they would develop. The question would give the curiosity focus. The two together would animate and enliven their work.

Most children *were* more focused and prepared for the second field trip. They at least pretended to attend and listen. But the "pretend-listening" led to sharing questions, spotting things in their environment, catching the contagion of discovery. Midway, I heard Justin exclaim, "Hey, this is interesting," as he ran off to locate an ancient mudball hidden in rock. As our guide complimented the group on their day's work, noting their attention and involvement, I was once again struck with how important it is to pay attention to, and teach, behavior. In this case, it was the behavior of interest. A strong Clear Positive is that I want the children to find their world interesting, even more interesting than the latest TV sequel. Many of the "interested field workers," became more interested students — prodding, probing, looking and listening.

When something isn't working in a classroom, it is often a signal to reconsider the Clear Positives. Here are a number of examples of Clear Positives and their use in various classrooms and content areas. They all deal with using Clear Positives to develop group expectations for content areas or routines.

A reading group

A group of nine-year-olds gathers, waiting to begin their first reading group of the year. The teacher asks, "Why do you think we need to have a reading group this year?"

"To learn new words?"

"To learn to read harder books?"

"To read things like mysteries."

"So you know if we read?"

The teacher acknowledges each of these responses and writes them on the board. She begins the discussion of the responses with "learning new words." "Words with many syllables," she adds, writing the word "literature" on a chart. The children take turns trying to decode the word, as the teacher exposes one syllable at a time. She tells them that they will learn ways to figure out some long words. She then informs them of a second task. They will also learn meanings for new words. That's called vocabulary, she tells them and adds that word (syllable by syllable) to the chart, giving time for the group to spell phonetically. "Does anyone know where to go to find out what a word means, if you don't know for sure?" The children identify and then try to locate a dictionary. Upon examination, they agree it's pretty heavy and might have at least 50,000 words. Soon, the group understands that they will be learning new words and trying to discover what they really mean by using a dictionary. Another new word is written on the chart.

Then the teacher goes back to the original survey of what they expect to learn in reading group. She agrees that they will be reading more books. "Someone mentioned mysteries. Is that a kind of book you like?" she asks, eliciting other kinds of books. The group responds with titles, rather than categories and there is a flurry of excitement as they recall and compare favorites.

"You know you will learn new vocabulary, use a dictionary and read more books, but there's still one more *special* thing I want this group to accomplish." The teacher carefully pauses, building a little suspense and anticipation.

"For our *literature* group," shifting the name from a reading group to literature, "I want Book Talk," she trumpets.

"Huh?"

"What's Book Talk?"

"Book-talk. Books don't talk," someone adds wittily!

"I want this group to have conversations about books." She goes on to discuss what conversations are and what it means to talk about books. She tells them about book clubs where people share "book talk." She weaves in a connection between the purpose of this group and a way that books carry over into the world. She wants to emphasize an interest in reading and a community of readers. She is concerned that although these children have reading skills, they do not read for pleasure.

"Every week we will have conversations about the books we are reading together. We will talk about what we think is happening in the story, or what you have found out about a new character. By the end of the year, I hope you will so like having book conversations that you will talk not only during our groups, but at lunch or even on the way to the bathroom. Once I remember telling some students to be quiet because they were disturbing the class and they said, 'But we were just talking about books!' Boy, was I in trouble!" The group laughs, their eyes atwinkle, imagining getting their teacher in such trouble!

Doing What Scientists Do — Ellen Doris

Ellen Doris, a teacher at the Greenfield Center School, initiates all science groups, whether with fives or thirteens, at the start of each year with the question, "What is it that scientists do?" Her masterful book, *Doing What Scientists Do*, gives detailed accounts of the different ways children reply to this question across the ages. The answers of the youngest children are literal and specific:

"Scientists look at things."

"Scientists make pictures of tigers."

"Scientists find bones."

As children get older, they say that scientists discover, experiment, conduct research in laboratories and search for medical cures or planetary life. Whatever the level of sophistication or prior knowledge, the next step is the same:

"Well, right now, you're going to do some science work, and here's where we're going to start. Scientists look at things."

She quickly establishes a connection between the work the children will do and the work that scientists do. The purpose of the group is to do the work of scientists. As young scientists, the children will learn to observe, question, experiment, record and see inconsistencies and errors (much in the same way as they construct meaning as they grow).

"What would scientists do," she asks, "if one scientist thought that crickets have four ears and another thought that crickets don't have any ears?" When some eight-year-old scientists complain that they are tired of observing the pond critters, they are reminded, "Do you know that there are some scientists who spend their whole life just studying one thing; they only study insects or even just one kind of bug? What could they be finding out, looking at one bug over and over?"

To name the students as scientists gives particular meaning and focus to their work. It helps to define the process of learning as the process of scientific method. For Ellen Doris, it is a way she can help children develop respect for a method of acquiring knowledge, which she believes "empowers scientists to solve new problems and find out new answers to new questions." This Clear Positive expresses a central faith — that there is indeed an interesting world out there and that children have access to that world.

A beginning theme study

Jay Lord's seventh/eighth grade class is preparing to study the rain forests as a year-long thematic project. They will be investigating many different areas, from weather and climate to cultures and world markets. They will do their own research, share readings, and build models. In the end they may organize a student conference or raise money to contribute to an international children's campaign to save the rain forests. Intellectually, these children are ready for thinking on a global scale; socially, they need frequent reminders to hang up their own book bags. Their teacher sees a connection. In fact, he believes strongly that we must all find connections between what we profess and how we choose to live our lives. He wants to communicate that connection to his students. He starts their rain forest study with the following assignment:

"You can not begin to take care of the rain forest until you begin to take care of your own classroom. I want each of you to think of a project that you would really care to do that would help improve or maintain our school."

It was a group of industrious and competent adolescents, who often left trails of discarded clothing, remnants of food supplies, and cluttered papers and books behind them. They were now thoughtful. A few had immediate ideas. Some wanted to improve the bathrooms; some, add plants, provide better containers, hang pictures, keep the school tidy and pretty. Someone suggested a recycling project. Someone else a mural. Another wondered if it would be possible to vacuum the rug.

The response was different than the usual blank nods given the usual clean-up lectures. There was a call to action, an enthusiastic commotion — the connection had been made. Many went to work right away, others began to assess their space. It was suddenly "their space." They had a task that demanded a responsible interpretation. What would it mean to improve and maintain? He also asked that students submit a proposal, explaining and defending their projects to the class, telling how or why it would work. In one case, a proposal for a loft interfered with student storage space. There were intriguing debates, and a compromise was reached.

The effectiveness of this Clear Positive — the connection between global philosophy and local or personal action — was its ability to merge action and reason.

A group of moody sevens

My class of sevens, in second grade, was becoming quarrelsome and cranky. Getting in line for a drink of water, sharing pattern blocks, playing a game, making room in the circle for everyone, involved minor but persistent irritations. I heard frequent complaints and tattling. The mood of the room was unfriendly and uneasy. I knew the tendency of sevens to be moody and negative and did not expect the exuberance of sixes or the effusiveness of eights, but I didn't like the tone of the class.

I was also troubled by my own tone, which was becoming increasingly cranky and impatient. After contemplating the schedule and the curriculum, I was reasonably sure that the pressures were not programmatic. The routine seemed secure, the transitions were working smoothly, the academic pace seemed challenging but not severe. It wasn't near Halloween and it hadn't been raining for a month. No. The social tone of the room needed to be improved. The group needed a "stretch."

I began by sharing with the class at our daily morning meeting what I was observing. I started with the positive things: the way I see children follow the routines, take care with their work, do a beautiful job with their science observations, come to meeting so efficiently.

"I see lots of good things happening in this class. There is *one* thing that is bothering me now. Something I notice that doesn't feel very good to me. I see people shove each other to get to the water fountain first; I see people save places in line for their buddies and not be fair; I see people make faces when they circle up and fuss about hand-holding; I hear tattling; I see unhelpful helpers, telling each other in rude ways when something is wrong."

"Raise your hand if you see some of these things, too. I'm not blaming anyone. I think we all do it. I know I'm feeling cranky, too, and then I snap at people. You might remember a time this week when you thought your teacher was grumpy. Perhaps we all have gotten a bit too grumpy. I wonder if someone has an idea about what gets them grumpy?"

Seeing the nodding heads, I knew that everyone had a grumpy story. I went around the circle collecting grumpy tales, but making sure that the focus and tone of this discussion was personal — in the "I voice" — not blameful. The grumpy narratives were spirited and amusing and relieved tension in the group. The children identified and reveled in their tales: rushing in the morning (anything short of an hour per sock is a rush!), waking up too early, having to eat the wrong cereal, not being able to find the paper you know you put just so. After everyone related at least one incident, hands were still waving madly. The subject was far from exhausted. We can appreciate Gesell's characterization of this age in *The Child from Five to Ten* as "inwardized," given to periods of worry, fear, and self-absorption. I would often greet one of my students, Lucy, with a "Good morning," and she would often respond, "What's good about it?"

To continue the discussion, it was not important to exhaust this theme of grumpiness but to focus on improving the tone of the classroom. I wanted to move on, saving further narratives for art or writing or other discussions.

"We all do get grumpy, I see. And when we're grumpy we aren't always so polite, or nice or friendly. I may be grouchy because my alarm didn't ring and then I yell at my son to hurry up. And it wasn't his fault at all, was it? It sounds like you do that, too." They respond with lots of nods!

I then state my Clear Positives. "I want this to be a friendly classroom. We spend so much time together in this classroom, I want it to be a place that feels friendly. I want to feel that I like to be here. I want to feel that this is a good place to do my work. It's not easy to work in a place that is cranky and grumpy. How can we make *our* classroom a place where we like to work and still know that sometimes we might feel grumpy. Who has an idea?"

At this point the children offered a number of ideas. Many had to do with *not* doing the things I had listed — not saving line spaces, not pushing to get water, not making faces.

I write the suggestions on a chart. "So we will agree to hold only our own places on line. We will wait patiently for the water, and Jimmy suggested that people shouldn't push to be first." I had automatically rephrased most of the "not-do's" into "to-do's" but I still wanted a more positive framework.

"We talked about a number of things not to do, a number of good plans to help with the grumpiness. What do we do if we want to act friendly?" It was easier to elicit antidotes to grumpy than examples of friendly. "When Kevin comes into the classroom and I ignore him, am I grumpy?" I role-play shuffling my papers.

"No."

"Am I friendly?"

"No."

"Why not?"

"Well you are just working. You didn't look at Kevin or say anything."

"What could I say?" To emphasize the point further, I ask Kevin to pretend that he is just coming into school with his lunch box, and I act out sitting at my table and ignoring his entrance. The drama captures the children and helps each to identify with Kevin, creating an emotional reality.

"Show me," I demand. "What would you do that is friendly?" Different children now act out a friendly greeting. From the passive response, phrased as a negative — a "not-to-do" — we are now thinking about active ways to generate friendly responses. The discussion has moved a long distance. I want to continue with other ways to respond actively later, but don't want to dilute the message or overwhelm the children now. I like their enthusiasm and want to make sure to preserve the mood. The meeting needs closure.

"I like the good ideas you already have about making our room feel more friendly. If we try hard to do that, I also think it will make our work site safer. We talk about a safe work site in blocks or outdoors. But we can make it safe for our feelings, too. And sometimes I know we will forget. But what happens when we forget? Will you yell at me or tell me in a mean voice that I am supposed to follow the rules? Suppose Julie says, 'Good morning' to me and I don't hear her or forget to stop my work, what will you say?"

"I'll say it again."

"I'd say 'Good grumpy morning.'" Everyone laughs and repeats a sing-song of "Good grumpy morning!"

"Let's see if tomorrow we can remember friendly greetings. Thank you for such a good meeting."

Transition times

Nancy Webster had twenty-eight third graders. "This is an extremely volatile class. Any part of the day that can go smoothly is valuable," she observed. The class had a particularly hard time making transitions from one activity to another. It was a clear issue as her class exhibited the outgoing behavior that often characterizes eight-year-olds.

"Voices become very loud, students are visiting and not getting ready for the next activity." She also noted, after observing closely, that children were using the five-minute transition times to finish work and then, at the last second, shoving papers back into their desks, wrinkling or tearing them or burying them in a heap. The system of filing which she had carefully instituted to help them order and preserve their work was useless. It took more time to search for the missing sheets or redo the ruined ones, which created further disorientation.

The transition time also revealed another product of their vigorous social agendas. The children who scurried most during transitions were making up for scattered work time. Instead of working, many had been gabbing. When the signal to end the period was sounded, there was a sudden frantic spurt as the short transition time turned into the work period!

Nancy focused on Clear Positives for better transitions in her class. "These children are just beginning to see the importance of organization and thinking and planning for themselves. This is one time of the day [transition] when they can exercise their new-found and developing skills."

In this goal, Nancy has identified an exciting and profoundly affirmative prospect — to help children learn to think and plan and organize for themselves. Suddenly, the task of transitions assumed a more-than-mechanical purpose. It is not simply a physical shift from one activity to another. Transitions also entail problem-solving and critical cognitive skills, such as anticipation, category-making, concentration and self-control. The recognition of learning processes embedded in the routines (or procedures) of our classrooms helps us teach children the skills and attitudes they need.

Nancy's procedure for working on transitions with her class began with a discussion. Transition time was defined. Expectations were clarified. A goal was declared — Efficient Transitions. The things the class would need to accomplish to meet the goal were established:

1. Transitions will take place in five minutes.
2. Papers will be put in proper folders and put away.
3. Appropriate folders for the next activity will be taken out.
4. Any other materials will be readied.
5. Pencils will be sharpened.
6. Quiet talking can take place within a group (if everything else is completed).
7. Safe stretching next to the desk is a good idea.

The class modeled and demonstrated "Efficient Transitions." Their teacher circulated and reinforced positives. Quiet talking, safe stretching, even "efficient" pencil sharpening were modeled repeatedly by teacher and students. Over the next weeks, everyone paid careful attention to transitions. They would stop and discuss transitions — what worked and what problems they or she noticed. The group took on the challenge. They enjoyed seeing their transitions become peaceful and effective. Their teacher observed that instead of prodding one another to mischief, they influenced each other in a positive way. She wrote in her journal:

I am sure that if children know what is expected from them, if they see it as reasonable and attainable, they will not only work hard for it themselves, but try to help other students to do the same. A student telling another student to hurry up or speak more quietly is usually more powerful than an adult.

Over the past few weeks the students have become increasingly more adept at calm transitions. My movements around the class have become punctuated by more "I like what I see" and "I like the way you . . ." than questions about "What should you be doing?" I feel good about this because we now have more time, and I have a few seconds to exchange a word or wink or hug with the kids. We still struggle with some students all the time, but now the students are helping me in the struggle. It is something we are all working on together in a positive way.

◆

Here are some guidelines for using Clear Positives for group expectations for content and routines:
• Make your goals clear for content groups and classroom routines.
• Recognize the learning process embedded in the routines.
• Discuss goals and strategies for implementation with children.
• Carefully model the behavior and attitudes you wish to teach.
• Continue to observe and reinforce effort and success.
• Use extra time to exchange words and give hugs.
• Remember to work together in a positive way.
• Realize that some children will continue to struggle, and recognize the steps — baby steps or giant ones — that mark growth.

Excuses

A number of children in the math group had not done their homework. Actually, one student had done it, but forgot he had done it until he started to do it all over again! It was only the second month of school and already the excuses came more quickly than the computations — and probably took more time.

"I forgot."

"You didn't tell me that."

"I didn't understand."

"I was late and my mom was rushing and . . ."

"I had practice and got home too late."

"My dog ate it."

This is a math group of ten sixth-grade students. They are usually motivated and excited about their math. They like a fast pace and enjoy challenging tasks. Everything goes fine until they are asked to appear a day later with work in hand. Somewhere between leaving their seats and the next morning is a "black hole."

"What do I do?" I wondered. If I send some of them out of the group to finish their work, then they miss instruction time and won't understand the next section. Should they have to miss something else to get the homework done? Is homework a reasonable expectation at this age? Should we make more time during the day instead of after school? What will we do? Everything in their day is important.

Clear Positives, which recall a sense of purpose and give direct strategies, needed to be reformulated. Did these students understand the reason for homework, other than as a system for capricious adults to torment children? Did they possess effective study skills for getting independent work done at all? Closer observation suggested that the students had little notion of purpose, but more importantly lacked independent work skills.

Generally, the purpose of homework is to reinforce skills and help children internalize ideas through guided assignments. It is contingent on independent work habits as well as academic competencies. The goal of independent work, similar to transitions, involves learning to plan, organize and think for yourself. In group lessons, the teacher provides that structure. When we ask children to work on their own, they must be able to supply the structure. I decided to try a paradoxical response with this group. I do not think it would work every time, but it helped illuminate the Clear Positives emphatically for the students.

I took away the homework. I told them that from all the lame excuses and poor work, I understood that they weren't ready for homework. Therefore, no homework. There would still be assignments, of course, but they would need to do them with supervision. Homework, I began to explain, was a "step up,"[1]

---

1 My colleague, Chip Wood, uses the metaphor of "climbing the mountain" as a way for fifth and sixth graders to understand the increased expectations.

a sign that they had mastered "not the content, but the challenging task of independent work." I also imported the image of a driving license as a proof of basic driving techniques. I wanted them to be "road tested" in homework before any more work would be permitted outside of school. (See Figure 14.1)

Independent work in school or as homework consists of three processes:

- Planning
- Organization
- Thinking for yourself

We worked together to define each of these terms.

Planning

We associated planning with anticipation and thinking ahead. The students differentiated "thinking work" versus "busy work," deciding that the first was

Figure 14.1

---

*Some pages of an Independent Work Manual — created **with** children.*

| jenny |

I-Work
Jenny
Manual

Advanced

Steps to Good I-Work

1. Plan
   Planning means
   I will organize my
   day.

2. Schedule
   Scheduling means
   I think when I need
   to do my math and my
   book reports.

3. Organize
   Organizing means
   I put things in the
   right place.

4. Problem Solver
   Being a
   problem solver means
   I figer out problems like
   whats the best name for
   my story.

harder for them. Planning also involves decisions about what is needed — materials, time and space.

Organization

Organization involved ordering the physical space, and then ordering the steps in the task. Children first need to organize a physical work space. Sometimes it is physical organization that is a problem — how materials are shelved or stored (scattered or carefully replaced and contained), how the important notebook or book gets home for homework and returned for school.

Second, there is the task of organizing one's own concentration and attention effectively, which may also be affected by the physical space — lighting or noise.

Third, the work process may need to be consciously ordered into steps. What do I do first? I have seen many a child flounder for want of a starting place, a way to hone in or narrow down. There are many different strategies to fit a range of styles — highlighting, key words, lists, verbalizing, webbing,

---

Wednesday

☐ I planned for my I-work

☐ I scheduled my I-work for _____.

☐ I organized my
   ☐ space
   ☐ materials

☐ I solved problems.
✱ Turn to problem solving appendix
   ☐ I figured out _____
   _____.

   ☐ I tried my strategy of _____
   _____.

   ☐ I got help by
     ☐ looking
     ☐ asking _____

☐ I made my brain pay active attention.

Problem Solving Appendix

Ask   What do I already know?
     I tell myself the facts.
     I write down the facts I know.

Let's Look for More
     What else do I need to know?
       ☐ who   ☐ what   ☐ when   ☐ where
       ☐ why   ☐ how
     Puzzling Words

Finding Out More   How will I find out more?
     I can look again in my book.
     I test out my ideas to see if they make sense.
     I can check with a friend to see if it makes sense.

I'm Still Stuck   I can try another way.
     I can see if it makes sense.
     Teachers (kiss) coffee.
     I can circle words I don't know.

     I can _____

outlining, and more. Some children verbalize, saying things aloud to themselves or to a partner, "This is what I will do." Others sit still and quiet, and then there is a flurry of work. Some work in spurts, others in a stream. Some work and walk, others talk and work, others prefer a solitary cave. We need to help children find their optimal arrangements and self-generating strategies.

Thinking for yourself

This includes interpreting directions, understanding questions, solving problems and applying information in different ways. Children need to be able to read and grasp directions. They need to be able to differentiate the aspects of a task they already know, from what they need to find out. Often they need to make a number of different kinds of judgments and decisions. For example, they need to know whether a question requires retrieving information or drawing an inference from what they already know.

Thinking for yourself does not mean that you work alone or without input from others. An important part is the ability to formulate questions. The questions may ask for certain kinds of help or direct your own inquiry. When we know where to go for information, when we know what information we need, we work with confidence. It's not answers that give confidence, it's the ability to ask useful questions, again and again. Children need to practice asking questions and locating multiple sources of information — teachers, parents, books, peers, themselves.

We then made a list of the features that depict "planning, organizing and thinking" using the students' own words. (See Figure 14.1) I suggested that each student assess their own performance for each type of task. It was interesting to find, when the personal evaluations were done, that many more had difficulty with physical space — losing things, forgetting their assignments or books — but felt confident about their thinking skills. (See Figure 14.2)

No homework would be assigned until each student demonstrated proficiency with assignments in school. The issue was important enough to rearrange the schedule, to make time for what I called with great originality "study hall." Study hall was a forty-five minute period when everyone brought one assignment to work on. They would be supervised, but given assistance only if they asked. It started with students arranging two storage units, one for in class and the other for transporting work — a book bag or knapsack. Second, each student had to identify the assignment they were going to work on and produce a plan that included:

1) the assignment
2) the materials to do the work

Figure 14.2

HOMEWORK SKILLS SELF-EVALUATION

This sheet is often used to help children prepare for and evaluate the skills needed for homework.

Planning, Organizing & Thinking for Yourself

Self-Evaluation Sheet

> Key: Rate 1–5
> > 1 = Most Difficult
> > 5 = Mastery

1) Planning

_____I anticipate what I have to do for homework.
_____I know my assignments.
_____I remember to bring my books and papers from school.
_____I remember to return books and assignment papers.

2) Organization

_____I organize my work space.
_____I organize my materials. (I know where they are; I take care of them).
_____I am able to organize the steps and parts of a problem. (I know what I need to do first, second and third. I complete my work.)
_____I show good attention for a *sustained* work time.

3) Thinking for Myself

_____I read and understand directions.
_____I am able to locate information.
_____I think about what I need to find out.
_____I know how to get help from other people.
_____I know how to use other references.
_____I can *generate* new ideas using what I know.

Signed:_____

Figure 14.3

This sheet could be used to help children plan and assess independent work on a single assignment.

Name: _____   Date: _____

CLASSROOM ASSIGNMENT PLAN

PLAN

My Assignment is: _____

_____

I will need the following materials:

_____   _____

_____   _____

It will take about _____ minutes.

My workspace will be: ☐ solo desk ☐ group table ☐ rug

☐ other: _____

Questions: ☐ For Myself ☐ For Teacher ☐ For Classmates

RESULTS   [kEY 1 - 5 Poor - Excellent]

Rating:

☐ Attention (Stayed on task)

☐ Organization
      Chose good work space
      Had correct materials
      Followed directions

☐ Thinking
      Solved problems
      Did careful work
      Used good ideas.

Comments:

I feel good about_____

I had problems with_____

3) space and amount of time needed
4) attention requirements — would they need to talk over their work or work on their own.

Head-phones, breaks, etc., might also be part of the plan.
    During the following weeks I regularly asked, "Did your plan work? Was

it helpful?" During this period children became more aware of their own needs and abilities to organize themselves. My next step was to provide less supervision. I did not circulate about their "hall;" I did not redirect students who wandered; I did not monitor the noise level or offer words of encouragement. I read my own book, stepped out of the room, took care of other business. For some, it was an invitation to shift their attention, to talk to friends or stare out of the window. Others kept on with their work. Most saw a direct correlation to the work completed and their efforts to stay on task. Most exerted the inner controls needed to stay focused. These children were ready to become "certified home—workers." They were graduated from study hall.

Some would still need the encouragement and support of an external structure. (See Figure 14.3) While I wanted children to feel the achievement of taking on new responsibility, I also wanted everyone to accept the process for developing skills. Study hall was not a punishment or a sign of teacher disfavor. I had to be sure that this "experiment" was seen as a learning exercise, not as a detention. Two keys were my tone and the use of student self-evaluation. My tone stressed my own mistake as a teacher, and my desire to help them learn critical skills before they got to college or high school. It was presented as a common endeavor.

The self-evaluation enabled children to pinpoint some of their own weaknesses — such as not putting away materials properly or becoming distracted — and to identify areas that needed improvement. It also reinforced the positive spirit which transferred to their work and to one another. There were nice reminders and many cheerleaders. When Debby left her folder on the table as she scurried to another activity, a classmate reminded her. When one day, weeks and weeks after we had begun this campaign, everyone in the entire class remembered their homework, a roaring cheer erupted. It was a genuine burst of joy for a job well done.

I do approach homework with one caution. I am not convinced that homework always serves elementary children well as a way to acquire independent study skills. There are children who tell us frankly that their home life is too tumultuous for school work. Other children, weary of school, need the time for vigorous play or relaxation. I don't think a responsible educational approach is implemented through an arbitrary homework policy. We need to assess the readiness of students and their families for support and also consider their needs for recreation, play and family time. At the same time, helping children to plan, organize and think through independent assignments is a vital feature of curriculum.

Summary

Clear Positives provide a sense of conviction and challenge, but do not moralize or lecture. They are clear — on a general or specific level — and always stated positively. We want them to clarify a sense of purpose and give children an understanding of the reasons for their work. We can define specific tasks we will help them accomplish and describe attitudes we hope they will develop. Using Clear Positives helps us communicate our faith in children's will and aptitude, and our faith in the value of the undertaking.

15

Clear Positives for Individuals

Clear Positives work with individuals as well as groups. Identifying them for an individual often helps us identify them for the group as well. Clear Positives can be made specific through a written or oral contract.

A written contract

My illustration of this process involves a single student named Jenny. Most teachers encounter a child similar to Jenny at some time in their professional lives. My Jenny was a scarred and battered nine-year-old who appeared to have almost no capacity to interact constructively. She had few positive social skills. Her primary skill — and it was a skill — was knowing how to alienate others. She had a keen knack for getting everyone to dislike her. She had already transferred from two schools and was starting over in her third. It was only October, but she was well on her way to antagonizing her new group of peers and adults.

Jenny was sneaky, negative, sour and selfish. She hardly ever listened, asked question moments after information was given, refused to do her fair share of jobs, made nasty comments to other children, and at least four times a day complained that someone was "picking" on her. She had, of course, left her other schools because everyone "picked" on her. I recall our first meeting, asking her if she would help me open a small box, thinking she would like to be helpful. She shrugged and looked at me as if to say, "Open it yourself!" She did say, "I don't know how to open boxes" with a whine I would hear

repeatedly. When I foolishly persisted, she opened the box so that its contents spilled and tumbled every which way. Her stubborn scowl indicated that I deserved to pick the things up. It was clear that if Jenny was to succeed in her new school, she had to become more likable. That was going to be a challenge.

We decided to try to teach Jenny directly the acceptable behaviors for our classroom, assuming that she had internalized only negative ways to interact. We would organize our expectations in the form of a "contract." We called the contract "Jenny's Jobs," signifying that it was *her* work in school and her ownership of that work.

The "jobs," which outlined explicit expectations, covered only three areas of the classroom. For both student and teachers, we wanted a focus which was easily monitored and perceived. When we brainstormed Jenny's jobs, it helped us rethink our approaches to Jenny and make concrete Clear

Positives for all our nine-year-olds. We had to define what it is that enables a child to behave constructively so we could help Jenny develop new patterns of relating in her classroom. The process of setting up this contract may be a useful model for your Jenny's; it is also a way to think about forming Clear Positives.

The three areas selected for the contract included a whole-class activity, a small-group work time, and the area of friendship. (See Figure 15.1) For each area we wanted to define a major purpose and appropriate expectations. We also needed to clarify how each expectation was accomplished. If we were to say, for example, that we wanted Jenny to contribute to her group, then we felt that we had to be able to define what we meant by participation. Did we mean to sit quietly? Did we mean to express thoughts and feelings? If we wanted "nice" comments, what did we mean by "nice?" How do we know (and how do children know) what constitutes "nice?" As we built the contract, we began with general expectations and followed with the individual focus for Jenny. The general expectations are similar to those used for groups — they reflect broad purposes and aims within the framework of developmental needs and abilities. The individual focus reflects specific needs. I urge readers to imagine their own expectations and objectives for each of these areas and how they would apply to various age levels. A discussion of each area follows.

Morning meeting

The first area in Jenny's Contract is a whole class activity, morning meeting. Children come together at the start of every day. Meeting activities include greetings, individual sharings of personal "news," a group activity (singing, a game, etc.) and daily announcements.

General Purpose and Objectives:
- Build a sense of group and group belonging
- Set a tone of friendliness and social interest in the group
- Provide transition and orientation from home to school
- Establish expectations of attention, listening (to peers as well as teachers), participation and inclusion
- Reinforce predictable routines and meeting rules

General Expectations of Morning Meetings:
- We expect children to follow meeting rules — to come on time, find a place in the circle ("the place" for nines is not always the same place, next to the same people; boys and girls may sit next to each other), raise their hands, attend for a thirty-minute period.
- We expect children to share "news."

Figure 15.1

JENNY'S JOB CONTRACT

Morning Meeting:

1) *Jenny will follow meeting rules.*
   I show I am following meeting rules by coming on time and taking the first place I find in the circle.

2) *Jenny will listen at meeting.*
   I will show that I am listening by:
   > Looking at the person speaking.
   > Asking a good question.
   > Making a nice comment.
   > Following directions.

   Example of a "good" question: How long did you stay there?
   Example of a "nice" comment: I like your story.

3) *Jenny will share news with the group once each week.*
   I will tell about my own experiences. I will share something I want the group to know.
   Example of sharing: I tell about dancing class.

Math Group:

1) *Jenny will come to group prepared with all her materials:*
   List of materials: pencil, folder, assignment.

2) *Jenny will ask one good question.*
   Example of a good question: I tried to do it myself and now I'm puzzled about _____.

Friendship:

1) *Jenny will share a friendly comment with her lunch partners.*
   Example of a friendly comment: I had fun at recess. Did you?

2) *Jenny will invite someone to play a game with her each week.*
   I will choose a game that I like and think is fun to play.
   Example of a game: Connect-4
   Example of an invitation: Do you want to play Connect-4 with me?

- We expect children to listen. We know they are listening because they ask questions, make "relevant comments," participate, and follow directions.

Jenny's specific jobs at meetings

1) Jenny will follow meeting rules.

The specifics are following the rules by coming on time and taking the first place she finds in the circle. Jenny tended to disrupt the meeting by being the last to arrive and then attempting to switch seats several times.

2) Jenny will listen at meetings.

She will show that she is listening by looking at the person speaking. She will also show good listening by asking a *good* question and making a *nice* comment.

It seemed vital to help Jenny understand how to ask questions and make more acceptable comments. If she could learn to do this in a structured setting, it might carry over into her conversations and spontaneous interactions with peers. "Good questions" usually, at this age, expand on a detail — "How old is your dog? What kind of car did you get? Do you like your cousin? What was your favorite present?"

There are also pattern questions — "How long did it take you to . . . ? Where did you get it? Did you like the . . . ?" Jenny's example was drawn from a teacher's model. She was able to ask about a general detail. The teacher told about a visit to New York. Jenny asked, "How long did you stay there?"

The nice comments were also modeled. "I like the . . ." was the most comfortable pattern — I like your story. I like the part about the . . . . I like your picture. It was important to keep in mind that all the nine-year-olds were learning to be responsive. We worked with them to avoid redirecting the sharing of their peers to tell their own tales. Being responsive also meant responding to classmates even if they weren't your very best buddies, and attending to the content of narratives. It meant communicating interest by asking relevant questions and giving compliments or making comments that express appreciation. The examples were discussed with Jenny. Her own example, using her own words and writing, was entered into the contract.

3) Jenny will share news with the group once each week.

Jenny will tell about her own experiences. She will share something *she* wants the group to know.

The teacher discussed with Jenny appropriate sharings, recalling information about her swimming or dancing or visits to grandparents. She was redirected from sharing her usual "misery" stories. The teacher at first made an arrangement to go over a sharing for each week together.

Math group

General Purpose and Objectives:
This group was learning to solve problems using basic number concepts and operations. An objective was to evoke interest in the process of figuring out problems, not just getting "right" answers. "I want you to learn to be problem-solvers, not just answer-grabbers!" I told them.

General Expectations:
- Come to group on time and bring all your materials.
- Concentrate on your work for a thirty to forty minute work session.
- Listen to directions, observe demonstrations, use manipulatives.
- Try more than once before asking for assistance.
- Learn from peers.
- Be able to work independently and in cooperation with peers.

Jenny's specific jobs in math group

1) Jenny will come to group with all her materials.
Jenny compiled and wrote in the list.

2) Jenny will ask one good question.
Jenny often asks questions instead of thinking or listening. She uses questions to draw the attention of the teacher or the group instead of applying herself to the work. The tone of her asking is also significant — she seems to want to manipulate people instead of information. She uses a whiny voice and a helpless posture or affect. Rather than seeking to find out, she seemed to be seeking a way *not* to find out.

It is hard to provide a comprehensive model of questions involving critical thinking, so we tried to establish some simple steps in the process of forming a question. The steps we reviewed with Jenny were:
- Read the directions.
- Observe the demonstration lesson.
- Try the problems yourself.
- Listen and watch others in the group.
- Ask for help if you are puzzled.
- If you have an interesting solution, ask to show your group and your teachers.

Jenny phrased the "puzzled" question as, "I tried to do it myself and now I'm puzzled." The word "puzzled" was lighter and less serious. It was also different, which might relieve the whiny, helpless attitude. By having her review the steps, the "I don't know" reflex was somewhat diminished. She had a number of set things to do. We established expectations for what she knows and how she can find out. We wanted to communicate firmly that she was capable of performing the work if she wanted.

Friendship

General Purpose and Objectives:

This was the most difficult of all the areas for us to define for Jenny. And it was clearly the area which would be most challenging for her. We needed to be very specific about the skills children typically exhibit by this age, as well as about our image of positive social behavior. How do children express their needs to have, and be, friends?

When I ask teachers what they expect in the area of friendship, they easily come up with the ideas of sharing, helping each other, taking turns and making friendly comments. Cooperation and consideration are also common terms. Often overlooked, however, is the importance of play. Even at nine, children want and need playful encounters. It is a currency of social life. Some of the play is conversational — sharing stories, news, jokes and feelings. Other times children enjoy rule-governed games — board games, outdoor activities, word games. Some play may involve well-rehearsed, companionable tasks or spontaneous and open-ended activity, such as fantasy dramas that occur with Lego blocks or dress-ups. With all of these, there is intrinsic gratification — a pleasure in the doing more than the outcome.

We expect children to have a repertoire, more than one playmate and more than one game choice. We expect reciprocity —the ability to take turns picking the game, being the dealer, going first, deciding on the adventure, or being the captain of the team. We expect children to have fun most of the time. We expect quarrels some of the time.

We expect, by age nine, that children care about the rules and fairness, and that they have some regard for another point of view. We expect children to try to resolve conflicts on their own, and to be successful some of the time. Still, some will not want to be part of a game unless they are in charge. Some quit, if they don't get their way. Some cry, if they lose. Others will only join if asked and never take the role of asker. And sharing friends may still be an ordeal.

Jenny is not unique in her struggles in the area of friendship, though her needs were more acute and disruptive. Jenny was unable to play, unless with much younger children, who she tended to boss. Her conversations with peers were notably unsuccessful, antagonizing rather than befriending. "Didn't Heather get an ugly haircut?" she might observe. "Maggie kisses boys," she gossiped. "I hate Neil, don't you?" Her tactics were to outrage or insult. Yet without friendship, Jenny would never achieve a sense of belonging.

General Expectations:

Our goals for Jenny were twofold:

· We wanted her to be able to play and follow the rules.
· We wanted her to be able to have an appropriate lunch-time conversation.

Jenny's specific jobs for friendship

1) Jenny will share a friendly comment with her lunch partners.
Jenny supplied her own friendly comment, with some prompting.

2) Jenny will invite someone to play a game with her each week.
She would choose a game that she liked and thinks is fun to play.

We were prepared to help Jenny find a game she liked — or to like a game that she had chosen! We were prepared to help her decide on playmates and how to ask someone to play a game with her. Our emphasis to start was on short board games, games of chance more than skill. We modeled expressions such as "Oh! It's your lucky day," stressing luck, not cunning; and stressed complimentary remarks, like "You played well," "I liked playing with you," or "That was fun!" We needed to help Jenny understand that the purpose of these games was enjoyment.

Procedure for the contract

Jenny's Contract was stapled into a notebook, which she kept in her work cubby. Each time she "forgot" a job, she would need to get out her notebook. The signal that she "forgot" continued to be a time-out. But for Jenny, time-out included getting her notebook with the contract. She would then locate the correct job, and then on a separate sheet in her book, copy over the terms and example of that job. She was welcome to return to her activity when she showed that she remembered her "jobs." She was thus expected to know and identify the jobs without assistance. She was expected to use them at all times.

Although I anticipated some confusion or an attempt to feign confusion, she was never confused. Sometimes she stalled or pouted. Eventually she returned to the group, resumed the activity and followed through with her jobs. It would be wishful thinking to say that this process transformed Jenny's behavior. Her behavior improved gradually. She was more apt to share a pleasant comment, offer a compliment, or enter a conversation properly. She was more involved in the content of the classroom. She continued to avoid her part of the clean-up, to demand more help and attention than was strictly necessary, and was a poor team member. Complaints about Jenny were not exactly rare! But on the last day of the term, as she started out the door, Jenny turned and reentered the room, calling out to no one and everyone, "Bye. Have a nice summer. See ya'!" She was smiling. Others were smiling back.

A verbal contract

The Clear Positives had to be framed into a written contract for Jenny. For most

children, they can be used in a verbal contract, which helps provide the following:
- Reasons and meaning for the work of the classroom
- Expectations
- Methods to accomplish the expectations
- Faith in the ability of all children to work towards a Clear Positive

Joseph

Joseph entered Mrs. Mariani's kindergarten class midyear. His mother, passing over a bundle of records, reported that Joseph had been a "troublemaker" and a fighter in his other school. He often had to sit on the "naughty rug" or got sent to the principal's office. Joseph confided, as well, that he had been the "baddest" kid in his class.

Mrs. Mariani bent over and whispered softly, "I hope you like your new school. I think you will."

◆

Perhaps that is our primary Clear Positive — that children will want to come to school, and will like their teachers, their classmates and even their work.

"But Mrs. Charney," one of my students said seriously, "no kids *like* school."

"I hope you will!" I said without flinching. "I know you won't like it every day. Even teachers don't like it every day. But I hope there are days and hours when you just say to yourself, 'I feel good' or 'I am so excited about my drawing' (or something else) or you just can't wait to get back to work on a project or just can't wait to tell your buddy what you figured out about the science stuff! That's what I mean by 'like.' I hope you do like school this year. But don't worry, you won't have to tell anyone that, 'cause maybe they'll know anyhow!"

Making a student job contract

Brandon is ten and in the fifth grade. He has trouble paying attention, particularly when the teacher is working with a group and he has to work independently at his seat. He tends to get up and down, and is easily diverted and diverts others at his table with silly chatter or idle behavior. Brandon does OK in highly-supervised groups and gets along well with other children in his class. His teacher is tired of scolding and reminding. She wants to try a contract. What are the Clear Positives for Brandon? The following is a sample of the process for making a contract. These might be self-questions or a dialogue with a colleague.

Q: What is the main goal or focus for this contract?
A: We want Brandon to develop work skills, even without the immediate supervision of the teacher. We want him to be able to be productive and able to take care of his work when not in a teacher-directed setting. We might consider naming our goal "A good independent worker." We might call his contract "Brandon's Independent Work Jobs."
Q: What are the skills and expectations for independent work for children at this level?
A: At ten in the fifth grade, we expect children to:
  * Be able to get the materials they need for their work
  * Be able to stay in their seats
  * Be able to pay attention to their work
  * Follow written directions
  * Be able to concentrate (in spurts) for thirty minutes at a time
  * Be able to refocus
  * Be able to work quietly
  * Enjoy the company of others, but be able to focus more on the work than on the company
Q: What does it mean to pay attention to your work? What is this quality of attention?
A: It includes:
  * Thinking about what you are doing at the time
  * Keeping your mind on the task
  * Thinking about the problems in your work, not others that might be on your mind
  * Looking at what you are doing

* Going back to your work again if you stop to answer a question or talk to someone
* Caring about what you are doing
* Talking about the work, not social chit-chat

Q: How do children show they are paying attention?

A: Their work shows effort. They get most of it done.

Q: How might you model for children what you mean by "good attention?"

A: By demonstrating working on a task. I'd get the materials, sit down, work, maybe look around for awhile and then go back to the job. Or I might do that and also talk to myself, "Let's see what do I have to do first . . ." Or I might do the opposite and get Brandon to model "good attention." I would get up and walk around, chat, draw pictures of creatures and then say, "I'm paying good attention, right?" Brandon would show me what I'm doing wrong. The paradoxical approach is funny and effective.

Q: What do you think the most important jobs for Brandon would be to help him start to become a "good independent worker"? Will you worry about neatness, accuracy, long stretches of concentrated activity, . . . ?

A: Attention and concentration.

Q: How do you want to phrase that for Brandon in Clear Positives?

A: I would identify the three job areas like this:

   1) Brandon will stay in his seat during a full independent work period.

   2) Brandon will pay attention to his work. He will show that he is paying good attention, by getting most of the work done.

   3) Brandon will work quietly. He will talk to his friends one time about his work if he has a question or an idea about the work.

This would be the suggested procedure:

* Review the contract daily with Brandon. The goal is "Good Independent Work." I would give checks or a rating (1–3) for each of the three areas in his contract.
* Accumulate points (from the ratings or checks) each week. Have Brandon figure out possible outcomes.
* Share weekly outcomes with parents. For example:
   "Brandon earned thirteen points this week. He has been getting most of his work done and is quiet. He forgets to stay in his seat sometimes. Next week, he will work harder on that."
* Set a goal that spans two to four weeks.
* Establish a way to celebrate the goal with a privilege, something related to school, or shared with parents. The contract could end with the statement, "You are now a good independent worker."
* Expect improvement, not 100% perfection. When Brandon "forgets," say "Show me your good independent-worker skills. I *know* you know how to be a good independent worker."

Figure 15.2 provides some general guidelines for the process of creating job contracts for individuals, partners and groups.

Figure 15.2

CREATING JOB CONTRACTS

For an Individual Contract

Narrow the jobs
List two or three "jobs" that describe the positive behaviors you want in language that is clear to the student. For example:
- Raise your hand to speak in the group.
- Use your "good" words when someone bothers you — not your hands.
- "STOP AND THINK," then follow directions.

Create a chart
Write the "jobs" in a bold, clear chart for the student to follow. The chart should be easy to find and read, but private.

Check the jobs
Set up a system for checking each day. For example:

	Monday	Tuesday	Wednesday	Thursday	Friday
Job 1 Hands					
Job 2 Words					
Job 3 Directions					

Report to parents
Set up a system for daily reporting. For example:

_____ did his jobs today.

I'm sorry but _____ did not do his jobs today. Tomorrow we hope he will do better.

Specify consequences
Specify where the student will go when jobs are "forgotten," and for how long (rest of work period, morning, day). In general, it's "3 Strikes & You're Out." (You may want to arrange for reminder signals, below.)

"I hope that you will choose to follow the rules of our classroom. You show us that you want to participate in the classroom by doing your jobs. If you forget to do your jobs, you are choosing not to be in our class. I will give you two reminders. The third time you are out."

Welcome student back
Teacher may briefly express regret that the student chose not to follow the rules, and faith that he or she will be able to try again. Use a firm and kind manner — not apologetic or lecturing. Note progress, such as a steady decline in the number of times consequences are enforced.

"I'm sorry you had to leave. I hope you'll choose now to follow our rules and do your jobs so that you can stay with us today."

Use reminder signals
Teacher and student decide on signals to use for reminders when a job is forgotten. They should be clear and simple, and should not disrupt a lesson or call attention to the student. For example:
- When the teacher tugs on her ear, it means that the student is forgetting one of the jobs.
- Cubes may be placed in a container when a job is not followed: a red cube means raising your hand to speak, a green for using words instead of hands, a blue for following directions.

Celebrate success
A certain number of check marks or smiling faces earns a celebration. This may involve some privilege the student enjoys, such as the chance to play a special game, work on the computer, or share a treat with a friend or the class.

Prepare a beautiful "Certificate of Accomplishment" to reinforce reaching important goals.

For "Partner Jobs" to Solve Continuing Conflicts:
- Students must leave activity and figure out how they will solve a conflict before they can return to it.
- Options may be suggested by the teacher and are modeled with teacher's help.
- Students share their solution with teacher.
- Students resume their activity when they show they have a workable solution.

For Class "Jobs"
The process can be used to build better listening, decrease bickering, improve transitions, etc.
- Teacher notes and describes a class "job" in positive language.
- Teacher sets up a code for keeping track of "forgetting" or succeeding — for example, a slash mark on the board each time a lesson is interrupted to tell students to listen.
- Marks are tallied at the end of each day.
- Teacher sets up a class "challenge;" for example, "Five consecutive '0' mark days means we can celebrate becoming good listeners."
- Teacher may graph the tallies for the class, hoping to show a steady decrease/improvement.

Summary

We have many Jenny's in our classrooms — children who do not know how to play, make friends, get along with adults or peers. They may have deeply entrenched patterns of evasion and relentless misbehavior. There are more Brandon's who need work on a narrower area of academic or social behavior. A written or verbal contract names the areas for work, provides specific expectations, and establishes a way to gauge progress. We define our Clear Positives for our Jenny's and Brandon's — and in the process define them for all of our students as well.

16

The Critical Contract

My most important work this year is to make friends.
My parents think that the most important work for me this year is to enjoy going to school.
My teachers think that the most important work for me this year is that I enjoy my first year in school.

Darrell, Age 5.

My most important work this year is to work on reading, because when I read words, it makes me feel all grown up.
My parents think that the most important work for me this year is to enjoy my new class.
My teacher thinks that the most important work for me this year is to share my good ideas with my classmates.

Nina, Age 6.

My goal for myself this year is taking care of myself and not being sent to time out.
My parents' goal for me is to follow directions better.
My teacher's goal for me is to be an interested worker.

Kevin, Age 8.

My goal for myself is to make friends.
My parents' goal for me is to read more and enjoy it.
My teachers goal for me is to learn math and enjoy it.

Rachel, Age 9.

The most important thing for me this year is to gather 2-3 more friends.
My parents' goal is for me to be a helpful and thoughtful friend to classmates.
My teacher's goal is for me to be an honest worker, to do what I say I'm
going to do.

Jamaal, Age 11.

My goal for myself is just to be a good person and keep to my own
standards and not lose control like getting behind and forgetting things.
My parents' goal for me is to work on my spelling.
My teacher's goal for me is to be able to spend time with a lot of people
in the class and not just my best friends and not to be cliquey.

Andrea, Age 13

At the Greenfield Center School, we call it a "Critical Contract" because it answers the "critical" question: "What do you most want to work on this year in school? What is most important to you?" It contains three goals for the year. The first is decided by the student, the second by parents, the third by teachers.

The question is not "What do you need to do better?" or "How should you improve?" Instead, the question asks for a focus on what is of greatest interest, what matters or is most important. It is intended to instigate a search by students in these areas. It generates a more personal connection to school and a responsibility for work. It also initiates an educational partnership among teachers, parents and student. The Critical Contract is another way to know children — to know their wants, their hopes, even their fantasies for themselves in school. The more children feel known in school, the more we can be their teachers. We use the Critical Contract to help shape our expectations and objectives for each student for the year.

Goals in the contract

The Critical Contract begins with a leading question: "What do you most want to work on this year in school? What is most important to you?" The respect that is implied in this question makes it critical, too — we believe that when we ask children to think seriously about their education, about what is most important for them in school, they will. In the beginning, it is the question, not the answer, that I most prize. It is the question, not the answer, that I want each of my students to study and ponder.

There are several aspects to that question. The first requires parents, teacher and students to focus. To focus, we need to be able to set priorities and organize our time and energy to reflect our priorities. What do we want for ourselves or our children? Where do we want to go this new school term? Often we fall short of our resolves, not because we try to do too little but because we try to do too much.

Criticle Contract – Chris

At first when you told us about the Criticle Contract (or however you spell it) I imedietly thaught of writers circle, to get it vnder controll so I could be a well rounded student. But after awhile I got to thinking that the reasons why I havn't had much luck with it, (at least for this year) is that I either put it off, or lose it and have to do it in a rush. And the same with alot of other subjects. Also I kept loseing my notebooks. So I realized I need to ~~arig~~ orginize my work and get things in order.

A second aspect of this question involves making a judgment. When we ask children to think about what they most want to work on in school, we ask that they take a serious look at themselves. Even our fives and sixes, given time to think, respond with discrimination and self-possession. Their responses to the question remind us that even young children find serious questions a validation of their involvement in school. As children get older, their ability to reflect their own needs and aims is often impressive. This statement was written by a twelve-year-old boy:

"At first when you told us about the Critical Contract, I immediately thought of writing, to get it under control so I could be a well-rounded student. But after a while, I got to thinking that the reasons why I haven't had much luck with it is that I either put it off, or lose it and have to do it in a rush. And the same with lots of other subjects. Also I kept losing my notebooks. So I realized that I need to organize my work and get things in order."

Not all statements will be as practical or insightful as this one, but rarely will children be glib or silly. To be able to single out one thing that is most important to work on involves judging what is doable as well as desirable.

Teachers and parents must make judgments, too. We often present children with generic "laundry lists." When we define a specific goal appropriate for an individual student, we reveal our own understanding and awareness. The teacher's goal is based on understanding the student in various contexts.

Teachers' goals attempt to name a single, specific, verifiable area of growth for an individual student. It is important to be clear and straightforward about the reasons for the goal. Do we want to see a child stretch — take a risk and move beyond a familiar pattern, make new friends, or try out a new skill? Do we feel a student is ready to improve specific competencies, responsibilities or habits of work? Do we want to see a change in how the student behaves with others or his or her role in the group?

"I'd like to see you complete more of your projects this year," I might say to one student. Yes, I think, I want this student to continue to read, write and get along, but an important issue will be to finish more of what gets started without all the delays and digressions. "I'd like to see you write a story this year," I tell another student, recalling her strong interest from last year and knowing her need for a satisfying project for this year. "I'd like to see you work hard on some of your projects and feel good about working hard," I might state as a goal for a student who is easily frustrated and discouraged.

I want to affirm the growth and strength of the student. It is much easier to form these goals when we have two-year classroom cycles and children return to us for a second time. But, it is also possible to draw on observations from the first six weeks or by a selective review of records, as long as we are careful to balance what *was* true with what we currently see.

Parents also need to make judgments to identify their special issue or aim for their child. Parents are generally very aware of their children's strengths and weaknesses and have many hopes for the coming year. But we ask them to single out one special focus and help them give it a positive wording. Their focus may reinforce the school's goal or it may be unique. For example, a student may be developing independent work habits both in school and at home. Or, the parent may single out math competencies while the teacher's focus is on study skills.

Sometimes, the school and parent goals appear incompatible. For example, a teacher may want to focus on getting a reluctant writer to write more willingly while a parent may want to emphasize spelling. Forming the contract offers a chance to discuss educational decisions. We may need to find ways to phrase the goals so that they are not contradictory or divisive. "Your parents want you to bring home a paper every week that shows beautiful spelling," and "Your teachers want you to find five topics you are excited to write about," may be a way to reconcile expectations. The process of discussing the goals allows teachers and parents to think aloud together, to discuss points of view and reasons. The aim is not to contest or argue, but to understand and communicate. Children witness this serious consideration in educational planning, but are participants as well as listeners. The partnership of school and family can be one of our most powerful unions, and one of the most difficult to establish. A Critical Contract is one approach to building cooperation and trust.

The three goals (Student/Parent/Teacher) form the Critical Contract. After discussions, each goal is written by the student into a contract for the year.

Goals can only be actualized if there are realistic opportunities to act on them. Therefore, along with the goals, there need to be ways to accomplish them. But I don't believe children's performance in relationship to these goals should be strictly evaluated. Instead, I suggest that we review the goals, and revise and reinforce them. We can help children get to their goals but are careful to show patience with less realistic claims and difficult challenges. Our assistance may only consist of noticing — "I see you are trying to finish your work before you start on something else," or "Remember, you wanted to work on reading this year and yet you don't have a book. How can we help with that?"

The first Critical Contracts in the Greenfield Center School were informal. We held parent and student conferences to share expectations before school began. Students filled out a worksheet at the start of each year. Parents also were asked for written comments. We learned what our new students liked to do best in school and what they didn't like or found hard the year before. The last blank, "This year I want to _____," was duly filled in and then filed away in a folder. We often lost sight of this important information during the course of the year. A formal contract and more conscious procedure was implemented more recently. It is still "in the works," as teachers explore ways to develop and use the contracts. We need to remember that we are not only learning to construct contracts, but developing a method to deepen the involvement of our children in their own educational lives.

I trust that readers who find this a tantalizing and practical idea will also feel free to experiment and adapt the Critical Contract to best meet the conditions of their community and group. In the following pages, I will show how teachers in the Greenfield Center School use the Critical Contract — how they write the contract, how they share it, how they insert it into the work of the year. There are further details and explanations about this process for primary levels (ages 5–6) and upper levels (ages 11–13) in Appendix D.

Throughout the process, we follow these guidelines:
- Goals are positive expressions.
- Goals are specific rather than general.
- We offer help with realistic strategies.
- We evaluate and share progress.
- We share goals with parents.

Goals are positive expressions

We must help parents and students to make their goals positive. We want expectations that will inspire. They are Clear Positives — they establish guidelines for desirable behavior and purpose. When we tell children to stop acting like clowns or stop being sloppy with their work, we are scolding.

Goals are specific rather than general

What does it mean to become "organized" or "independent" or "good readers" in first or fourth grade? Does "independent" mean to know how to

With these sixth, seventh and eighth graders,
the Critical Contract involved an exchange of letters.

Chris,

My goal for you is that you take as much pride and interest in your writing as you do in your math. You are a good writer and I want you to acknowledge it and work at it, just like you do in math.

Critcal Contract
for
Chris
1989-90

My Goal for this year is: to get more orginized, not to lose homework or forgot to do it, and try to do work beforehand, not at the last minute. I need to get my school work in order.

My teachers goal for this year is: to be proud intorested and enjoy my writing as much as my math.

My Parents goal for this year is:

come by a sharp pencil on your own, to go to the bathroom on your own, to find answers to questions, or to use free time? At home, does it mean entertaining yourself on a Saturday morning without TV, or making a lunch each morning, or managing a paper route? If we are concerned about a social issue such as bossiness, for example, how will we specify what it means *not* to be bossy? To find the right wording, I often visualize classroom interactions. I can see the child's tendency to give orders during a cooperative activity. I can then visualize what I would like to see — "Be a good partner who gets the scissors instead of telling others to get them, and who can accept other people's ideas as well as contribute her own." I think that the more we clarify what we mean by consideration, organization, friendliness or even active reading, the easier it is for children to grow.

Offer help with realistic strategies

Offer to help children with realistic strategies whenever necessary. "How to do it" may be a separate issue from setting the goals. Sometimes students have their own ideas, but sometimes they need help. Joel wants to become more organized, to not lose things so much, but may need to acquire a system to

---

Mandy,

My goal for you would be that you would have a real friend who is a boy who doesn't have to be a "boyfriend." I want you to know boys without it having to include coyness, flirting, and silliness.

Jay Lord,

I think that sometimes I need help getting my work organized. Like when we have a full schedule of work, for someone to sit down with me, maybe Mary-Beth for a short time at the begining of the week. Desingling my week by having me do work for particular classes durning free periods.

My teacher would like me to work on having more boy friend boys who are just friends.

make order. I observe how Joel organizes himself now. When he wants to straighten his desk he dumps all the contents out and is confronted with a huge mess, a chaos which dismays him. I ask his parents how he cleans up his room at home. Does he go about it randomly or does he start with all the toys and then the clothes, categorizing as he works? Strategies may accompany the Critical Contract or evolve during the year.

Evaluate and share progress

By evaluating, I mean reviewing with children — noticing, commenting on successes, helping them work toward their goals. Teachers most often notice the gains. "I see you are remembering to let others be in charge of a game. I hope you feel proud of your work." They may also nudge a bit, "Remind me how are you coming with your important work to take turns in group." They will also notice and reinforce the growth children make with the goals posed by teacher and parents. I worry that if we interject traditional ways of evaluating these goals, we will end up scaling down the objectives to what is most easily graded.

One way to evaluate progress is to ask children to reflect at the end of the year with the question, "What is the most important thing you learned this year?" This technique developed spontaneously in Debby Porter's primary classroom at the Greenfield Center School. The year-end reflection and the goals of the fall may be quite different. But there is no attempt to make them the same or to limit children to initial goals. The ease with which children identified important learning led the teacher to observe, "Fives and sixes knew a lot about what was important. More than I realized."

"The most important thing I learned this year in school was about myself, because I learned what I could do and what I couldn't do," declared one six year old.

"I usually enjoy being with my friends now and I don't get angry as much as I used to. I know that I could still improve in a lot of my social places but I think I have fulfilled my goals for this year and I have fulfilled them pretty good," reflected Alfred, age 10.

As part of a regular midyear progress report in one class, nine- and ten-year-old students reviewed their contract and commented on it with these guidelines:

___I am working on my goals and think they are appropriate.

___I need to change or revise my goals.

___I want to choose as a new goal:_____

Not all goals need to be continued throughout the year. Sometimes by mid-year, children shift because they change their mind or have finished with something. If a goal is difficult and the student shows a keen avoidance, I want to redirect the student rather than erase the goal because the student is resistant or scared. We may need to break it down into smaller steps or provide additional support. "You told me that you wanted to learn to read better, but I don't see you reading. What do you think you need to help you with *your* goals?" "How can I help?" is not replaced with "You have to . . ." If children work toward improvement, rather than perfection, they will often be able to accomplish what is most important for them that year in school.

Finally, we must notice and celebrate the achievements and accomplishments. In some cases, as soon as the times tables have been learned it's best to continue the momentum right into long division. At other times, it's better to practice and enjoy the fruits of victory before beginning the next campaign.

Share goals with parents

Our school schedules a pre-school and late-fall conference. At the first conference, parents are asked to think about their priorities for their child. "What do you feel is most important for your child to work on this year in school?" Often the parents share compelling insights, pertinent history, lingering anxieties and deep aspirations. We find out about children's interests, habits, attitudes and struggles.

We are all sometimes afraid for our children, fearful that lacking certain accomplishments, they will not hold their own in the world. These worries and hopes can produce a flood of demands on top of existing teaching prescriptions which assess and measure numerous discrete skills. If we are not careful, we start the year preparing for a marathon. When we ask ourselves and parents, "What is most important?" we intend to shorten the list and highlight a plan. The more we identify a focus, the better able we are to devote attention and effort to a course of improvement. And the more tangible successes children experience, and parents and teachers witness, the more pride and hope we create.

Children are responsive to the concerns and expectations issued by their parents and teachers. "I don't like the math we are doing right now," explained Tyrone, "but I know it's important for me." He "knows" because his parents have emphasized his need to improve his accuracy and proficiency with operations. He cares, not because the material provides intrinsic satisfaction or interest, but because of his authentic desire to please. It is the collaboration of interests and perspectives that makes the Critical Contract strong.

Helping students form goals

What does it mean to "form" or "construct" a goal? One meaning is to find a way to "stretch your potential." A colleague, fond of baseball metaphors, explains to his sevens that Wade Boggs is a great hitter, but perhaps one year he wants to get better as a fielder. That becomes his goal. "You already know that you love math, but this year you want to try more art," he explains.

Another meaning is to pursue a strong interest. What are you interested in finding out this year? What do you love to do and want to continue to do this year? How will you further your interest in insects? Some children choose to deepen and extend a special area of interest.

Another interpretation envisions a personal change. "Last year I was ... This year I want to be more ..." Many older children articulate "change" goals, often involving social issues — having more friends, becoming more outspoken in a group, being less "cliquish." One eleven-year-old stated that he didn't want to be the class clown. A girl wanted to be friends with boys. A teacher of fives and sixes noted that many of her children chose specific goals related to the way they used the Golden Rule. For example, "To tell when you are mad, so they can say sorry, and say you're sorry when you are mean to somebody."

The fourth kind of goal is a wish to improve a skill or attitude — to write better, to learn to spell, to get work in on time, to be organized.

Procedures for a critical contract

Students begin work on the contract after the first six weeks of school. They need a chance to adjust and teachers need time to get to know their class. I

A Critical Contract for ages 5, 6.

The place in the Prime Blue room that I like the best is Drama because I like to imagine.

The place in the Prime Blue room that I don't like is Math meeting because it is long.

have started earlier when I have a group for a second year.

These procedures can be adapted to work with different age levels. Here, I describe the procedures we use for nines and tens. In Appendix D, I describe the methods at a primary level (fives and sixes), and an upper level group (elevens and twelves). There is no "correct" format; rather, we explore ways to make the contract meaningful and exciting, to involve children and focus on the critical goals as part of the ongoing work of the year. You may decide that what we do for nines and tens can be used for sevens and eights as well. With nines and tens, we use three steps:

1. Mapping
2. Representing
3. Reviewing and producing final drafts

1. Mapping

The process of forming goals starts with a mapping exercise of the classroom. The idea is to enable children to *visualize* their classroom, and see themselves in relation to it. Children are asked to draw a rough map of their room. They are given large sheets of manila paper with crayons (many quickly grab a

My parents think that the most important work for me this year is to enjoy playing by myself and with others.

My teacher thinks that the most important work for me this year is to make lots of new friends.

NAOMI

I think that the most important work for me this year sis reading because when I read words it makes me feel grown up.

pencil instead). Large paper and crayons suggest broad strokes and strong lines. It is a sketch rather than a lesson in precision mapping; however, a wide range of mapping skills is evident. Some children reveal a keen sense of scale and proportion. They capture a bird's-eye view and a three-dimensional field. Others draw a side view, with everything anchored on the bottom of the page. I set time limits to release children from over-investment in the mapping task. Most will do a "final draft map," giving more care to the drawing. It takes one or two forty-minute periods to work on the maps.

When the maps are complete, I will ask the group to locate three things on their map for which we will need a "key." We will have a short discussion about the definition of a "key," and the use of symbols on maps. I will ask them to invent a symbol for each of their three targets. The three things I want the symbols to signify are:

1. What they like to do and find most interesting in school
2. Something they don't like or avoid
3. What they think is most important to work on this year

They will make the key and design their symbols. They then try to associate the symbol with a specific area of the room map.

Each of these questions is discussed in the class as a whole. Students brainstorm and share interests, likes and dislikes. This is usually a lively and animated discussion, with increasing specificity as ideas are generated. If some children only like recess, I may prod them, but generally the input from other classmates sets a tone of positive responsiveness. A few hold out. There is nothing to like in school. "I hope this year is better," I will suggest and then go on.

For a first-time contract, it works better to discuss each question and then identify the corresponding area on the map before going on to the next question. It is also likely that there will be some confusion between the verbal image of "what you like" and the physical entity of the map. Some children are so literal that they will take the question to mean a kind of furniture or part of the room arrangement. When Laura placed her "not-like" symbol in the loft area, she was thinking more abstractly about the way girl/boy secret-telling in the loft had upset her the year before. A clump of tables symbolized "group work" for many children. The meeting area represented feelings about meeting activities. For most of the children, the maps were a springboard, a chance to remember.

The third question, the goal-setting, involves discussion and examples. I will model various kinds of goals. I want to make sure that the children understand that a goal is not always getting better at something. I may model this on a map that I draw. I point out that last year I didn't teach much science, and I explain my reasons. But my new goal is not to focus on science. "I really want to work on play-writing. I am excited about teaching people to write their own plays." Still many children will choose improvement goals. Many parents' and teachers' goals will stress improvement or change. I want to encourage children particularly to think about stretching themselves and developing strong areas of interest. I point them in that direction, but they don't always take the hint!

They have now drawn their map. They have included a key and created symbols. They have placed their symbols in the proper areas of the floor plan. (See Figure 16.1)

2. Representing

Representing is a way that children may extend and revise their thinking by sharing their work. As they explain the points on their map, they are making

Figure 16.1

In this map for a Critical Contract, this child liked working on art projects, didn't like (long) meetings, and wanted to work this year on math.

the inside become the outside, giving an appearance and stability to an inner logic. And as they communicate, they organize and edit, finding words and order and reason. As they listen to the sharing of others, they find commonality and difference. In short, they construct and transmit knowledge.

We start the representing in pairs. I assign partners to describe their maps to one another. Then — and this is the "hard part" — partners will explain their partner's map to the whole group. I have two children model an interview.

"I like the science observation table."

"Why?"

"I think the crickets are fun to watch . . ."

The most important thing I learned this year was that I could do projects all by myself.

The partners take turns and switch roles. The challenging part is to listen carefully and recall the information. Time limits are effective ways to help children stay on task and remain focused. I allow about ten minutes for this part of the representing, before asking them to return to the circle. As the partners are conferencing, it is a good time for me to reinforce cooperative learning — quiet conversational voices, attentive listening to your partner, focus, and mutual regulation.

Now, in a meeting of the whole class, the group is interested in each child's choices and decisions. They see the maps. They listen to the content of the answers to the three questions. It is important that this sharing is respectful and that ground rules for representing work have been previously established. Maps that are more crudely drawn, speakers who forget some words receive help only if they wish. The job of the audience is to listen, and ask a question if necessary. But it is probably enough to hear and learn what others are thinking.

3. Revising and producing final drafts

After the group sharing, there are final drafts of the maps and a time to consolidate or revise the goal for the year. Children may wish to revise their goals after the representing meeting because of a new idea or recent insight. Changes are a part of the process, as long as they have not been manipulated. There is also time for personal conferences between the child and the teacher as children work on drawing their maps and copying over their goals for the contract. This is a chance to check in and help if some students need help clarifying or defining.

Children complete the statement, "My goal for myself is _____," in their own words and handwriting. The final draft means that both content and form are satisfactory. Maps will be mounted for display; the contract is ready to share with parents. The contract will not be complete until teacher and parent goals are added. These are discussed together and then written down by the student to form the year's Critical Contract.

"It used to be like it was just the teacher's room. That everything was how the teacher wanted it. I guess I like making a goal, too," observed Maddie, age 10.

Summary of steps for all ages

1. Pre-school query asking parents for their goals
2. Students work on first and final drafts of their goals (October)
3. Conference to discuss parent goals and current teacher and student goals
4. Parents discuss their goal with student
5. Teacher discusses goal with student
6. Student prepares contract
7. Contract is sent home for signature and copied for home and school
8. Contract is reviewed — continuously or at specified times

Summary

If we are no longer trying to teach children what we value through the force of our command and the sheer strength of our authority, what is our force and strength? I believe our greatest strength is in our convictions and our ability to make the lives of children in school meaningful. I suggest that our task is to inspire and enliven through Clear Positives — they guide us through broad ideals and specific expectations for groups and individuals. We continually need to communicate our faith in ourselves, our children and the process of learning. Clear Positives renew promise and hope, which we find over and over again in the work of the classroom.

"This year in school I want to . . ."

Conclusion
Authentic Teaching

We were never the carriers of our own stories. We never trusted our own voices. Reforms came, but we didn't make them. They were invented by people far removed from schools — by "experts." Such reforms by-passed the kind of school-by-school changes, both small and structurally radical, that teachers and parents might have been able to suggest — changes that, however slow, could have made a powerful difference.

Deborah Meier
"Good Schools Are Still Possible"
Conflicts and Constituencies

I conclude with the idea of authentic teaching, which is central to every approach, technique and guideline in this book. Change and reform, as Deborah Meier stated, need to reflect "real issues" recognized by the "people who made up the roster of school life — parents, kids, teachers, principals . . ." And real change, she went on, needs the "kind of detailed specificity that teachers could offer . . . ," concrete and practical changes rather than the broad, general, often vague changes that policy-makers favor.

This book tells one teacher's story, which is really a collage of many teachers' stories. It is dedicated to the concrete change, the "detailed specificity" which comes from the perspective and voice of real teachers teaching in real classrooms. It assumes that teachers are skilled and knowledgeable, and that they need to regain more of the control over their curriculum and their workplace. Teachers need to be able to decide what they want to teach, when, and for how long — freed from a manic pace and cluttered day mandated by those far from the classroom. They need to be able to make critical decisions and give voice to the central concerns of their children.

Teachers currently have few choices. Budgets, schedules, and curriculum are imposed, often by state regents or invisible bureaucrats who never see or

meet the teachers or children they are supposed to serve. Few teachers even have a tiny "slush fund" to go out and buy a four-dollar paperback on King Arthur or Wilma Rudolph for that child who needs a special recognition.

But teachers have also let choices slip away by being afraid to advocate for their children or themselves, uncertain of their own knowledge and rights. To use every bit of their power, teachers must acknowledge their authenticity — they must be empowered by confidence in their own perceptions and values. When we are able to infuse our teaching with the dynamic force of our perceptions and values, we teach with strength and resounding voices — we teach authentically.

Teaching is an extension and projection of a person, not just transplanted skills or acquired methods. Every day we reveal ourselves — our manners of organizing, habits of dealing with frustration, entrenched patterns of thought and interest. Just as we aim to teach the whole child by responding to affective as well as intellectual development, so we also aim to teach *from* the whole teacher — the cognitive, social-emotional teacher. The inner resources of the teacher register deeply in the climate of the classroom and the weathering of the students. Schools as they currently exist often stultify and stunt the passions and dedications of their teachers, battering them into indifference and silence.

If teaching is to be infused with conviction and joy, the best hopes and creative powers of teachers need to be nourished. In the last five years, I have met with many teachers in workshops across the country. There are some who come only because it is required by their system or for the credits that affect income differentials and promotions. But so many others attend out of sincere interest in their work. This group is a mix of all types of teachers, young and old, new and experienced, from public and private schools. I particularly recall a group of teachers in Maine, sitting in a warm, dusty classroom, two days after the end of their school term. They were full of humor and laughter, eager to learn a new way to do science or blocks only days after school let out in June. Whether their hands were covered with "oobleck" or they crouched on the floor erecting sturdy buildings, their stamina and exuberance for teaching was apparent. And it became contagious.

How do we hold on to that exuberance? How do we keep it at the center of our teaching? It is certainly an essential resource for our children, and it can't be falsified. I believe it will survive and prosper where there is permission and potential for authentic teaching, and for authentic teachers to teach.

To teach authentically, we must accept the realities of teaching and of who we are — including our limitations, our frailties, our mistakes. One of the hardest things to get used to as a teacher is being observed by parents, visitors, and supervisors. It is hard because we reveal so much. I recall the first time I had a lesson videotaped so that I could study it to discover things about my children. Instead I watched myself. I noticed the hard set to my jaw, the excessive use of my hands and the way my hemline rode up over my knee. When we teach, we reveal far more than a lesson plan. We reveal aspects of our deepest selves. We reveal our vulnerabilities, whether we want to or not. One masterful teacher wrote in his journal, soon after an observation, "I have met the enemy and it is me!" He wanted to give his fifth grade students more responsibility. He needed to combat his natural inclination to direct and explain — he would have to learn to "bite his tongue."

As a child I would sometimes dream that I was naked in a crowded room. As a teacher, I dream that I am shorn of all power in a room crowded with children who run around despite my cries to be seated. As authentic teachers, we must accept that the practice of teaching is one which often leaves us semi-dressed. Just when everyone is watching (and often when no one is), everything goes wrong. Our best plans fail. Our best controls crumble like cookie dust. We cry; we yell; we suffer shame and we grieve. We want to cover up.

We take our responsibilities seriously. When the principal yells at my class, which is behaving in some outrageous fashion, my feelings are mixed. I feel pangs of shame for not handling them well enough; I feel anger that my children made me look bad in front of the world; and I feel resentful that the principal intruded upon — "violated" — my brood. I might stand up for my children and protect them from the misperceptions or intrusions of other adults, or I might scold them soundly, or both. Through it all, I must realize that sometimes children act badly no matter what I do or say. That is not "our shame"; it is our job. Facing these realities, without guise or cover, is essential for authenticity to survive.

Authentic teaching requires individual courage, as well as courage and trust from administrators. Teachers must have license and sanction to make mistakes and risky decisions. Parents may disagree with things we do. The children themselves repeatedly challenge us. And we always face scrutiny from supervisors. But the most intense scrutiny comes from within, because we are usually our harshest critics. Authenticity rests finally on our capacity to make mistakes and to admit error rather than needing to cover it up.

Accountability never seemed to me to be primarily an issue of public record, but rather a private matter. We can continue to be accountable to ourselves only when we feel safe to make mistakes and safe to make the mistakes known. I believe the single most important factor in the preservation of a good teacher is the courage to admit failure, rather than to deny it in order to feel like a "good teacher."

Vulnerability seems to me a constant, only partially relieved by experience. Children will always be there to unravel us or our plans. Sylvia Ashton-Warner captures the fragile confidence of even experienced teachers in *Teacher.* "If only I had the confidence of being a good teacher. But I'm not even an appalling teacher. I don't even claim to be a teacher at all. I'm just a nitwit somehow let loose among children."

Because authentic teaching is founded on our acceptance of limitations and vulnerabilities, it allows for our unique strengths and passions as well. Authentic teaching permits an individuality and personal style to emerge. We share our love of birds, or history or photography with children. We reveal and share our personality — humor, playfulness, concentration, quietness, investigation. We share much more than skills. We share our passion for learning in our own unique ways.

Some teachers have a quiet and soft-spoken manner, while others are more emotive and dramatic. One teacher in our school is known for the force of her "glare," another for his booming voice. Some teachers thrive on organization and detailed planning, others are more spontaneous and flexible. Some of us tend to be more directive, others more non-directive. We may be more playful, or more businesslike. We may love to sing with children or invent puzzles.

I don't want to imply that our style must be one thing or the other, e.g., organized or disorganized. A style is composed of many shades and attributes. I happily copy and repeat what I learn from colleagues, but it is filtered through my voice and perceptions. The virtues of sound teaching — patience, attention, the capacity to structure, the flexibility to individualize — are conveyed through a multitude of styles. But affection and respect — for children and for ourselves — are only conveyed when we are willing to trust ourselves with others.

It is important to distinguish authentic teaching from self-promotion. When teachers become self-promoting, children become instruments to aggrandize the teacher. The teacher, consciously or not, seeks to gain from the children a sense of importance and love. Authenticity is not about getting children to love or obey us, or even to admire our talents. Authenticity is about knowing oneself well enough to allow others to know themselves.

We cannot teach authentically without the capacity to like children as they really are. My friend, a kindergarten teacher of fifteen years, collapses into the nearest kitchen chair, saying, "I don't understand how some days I just can't stand it. And other days, I feel so good." To like being with children does not mean ignoring or dismissing the frustrations and failures. It does not mean denying those rainy days, pre- or post-Halloween days, or just hellish days for whatever reason, when classroom survival is a dubious proposal; it doesn't mean denying those times when our own worries and preoccupations — with family, the world or self — have depleted our mental and physical resources. It doesn't mean denying times when we feel like a pincushion, poked by children, punctured by parental criticism, prodded by administrative fiats.

To like being and working with children, we must acknowledge the difficulties. It takes humor, patience, stamina, conviction. We can preserve our authenticity by confessing the irritations while maintaining our care. This care for children is both a burden and a gift of our spirit.

Authentic teaching requires and encourages personal authority. This authority is not so much an office as it is a way of acting. We stake a claim — in the classroom and in the larger context of schools and systems — to what is personally, intimately known and felt. Personal authority means that perceptions and values are not easily repudiated or pushed aside because others — even those with official authority — disagree. Disagreements may spark investigation and spirited discussions, but they can't force denial of our thoughts and principles. Authenticity involves accepting our personal authority — and the risks that go with it — so that we can be agents of the changes needed in our schools.

The majority of elementary teachers that I see in schools, conferences, and workshops, are women. The majority of administrators are men. This fact, which mirrors a general social norm, contributes to a disenfranchised community, with teachers (mainly women) having little say over the most elementary resources of the work site. In order to achieve a stronger role, it is necessary to change the structures of school society for both men and women. I do not mean that women must become administrators in order for these changes to occur. I do mean, however, that administrators and policy-makers must become more integrated, more dependent on the classroom "experts" than they currently are. For that to happen, teachers must be willing to raise their voices, to say aloud to administrators as well as students, "Listen to me, I have something to say."

We raise our voices when we find courage, not in certainty, but in the authenticity that springs from belief in ourselves and our task. When we teach children through our own disciplined and caring actions in the world, we take an authentic stance. We use the most basic and fundamental principle of teaching: Our actions speak louder than our words. It is then that *children* say, "I see you, I see everything."

Appendix A
Horse

This story I'm about to tell you is mostly true, though since it happened more than a week ago it may have come into some changes. I shall tell you what I heard.

◆

Well, it happened that Horse was leading Fox, Dog, Rat, Sheep, Goat and other gentle beasts from the old forest to the new. It had been a long winter, but the day was grand and Horse pranced along, his mane flying in the wind, as if a flag-bearer. At times, the shorter-legged creatures would climb aboard her back and rest when weary as the procession continued. Suddenly they came to a rushing river. Across the river there fell a log. The log was just long enough, narrow enough and high enough to need careful feet to cross safely. Horse was first and he stepped up. No sooner did he have all fours on the log than he was filled with dread. Suppose he slipped? Suppose he lost his balance and fell over? Suppose the log began to shake with his weight? Horse backed off the log. He turned to Goat and ordered, "You are lighter. You go first."

Goat was nimble, a climber of steep cliffs. He was over the log in no time. Even Donkey did not pause or ponder. He swayed a bit, his hind quarters seeming to go on their crooked way apart from his fore quarters, but soon he too was across. And then there was only Horse. He considered swimming the river. The current looked swift; the waters were icy. There was no telling where he would end up or if he would end up. Now the others were waiting. Horse could not go forward or backward. Could he stop here and make this his new settlement? He knew there were better places ahead. Could he go back to the old place? There wasn't much food left. He would not — could not go on. While he stood still in uncertainty and fear, the other animals were meeting.

"Horse has left us," cried Rabbit.

"Horse doesn't like us," said Sheep.

"Horse has found the best spot and wants to keep it for himself," said Turtle.

"Horse is scared stiff," said Beaver.

Horse scared??? The other animals couldn't imagine that! What is he scared of? It couldn't be that something they accomplished would trouble the fast and strong Horse.

"Perhaps," murmured Mouse, "a monster lurks in the depths of the river and only Horse knows. He let us almost die," thought Mouse bitterly.

So for the next long time all the animals stood still and watched Horse being scared. Finally after a forever long time, Fox cried out, "Horse? Are you thinking?" And Horse said, "Yes."

"What — if I may ask — are you thinking about?" said Fox.

Horse answered, "The log."

Fox said, "The log? What about the log, Horse?"

Horse sighed, "Why must a log be round on all sides, Fox?"

Fox replied, "Round it is, Horse."

Horse: "I was thinking it would be better to make logs flat."

Then Rat piped up, "Horse are you coming or staying?"

Horse said in a soft voice, not at all usual for him, "I would come — if I could come — but I can't come."

And Beaver repeated, "He's scared stiff."

So the animals stood silent for awhile more and watched Horse being scared on the far shore. Then a creature who had not yet spoken said, "Let's help Horse cross the log."

The other beasts opened their eyes as wide as possible and grinned a most incredulous grin. "We cannot pull Horse. We cannot push Horse." And the small but knowing creature said wisely, "We can keep him company."

So all the animals, big and small, sure and awkward of foot, returned across the log. They explained the plan to Horse. Then they all lined up. Donkey, seeing Horse tremble a bit, went over and said in a quiet tone so only Horse could hear, "Just pay attention, Horse, to what's most important."

"What's that, Donkey?" said Horse.

"To keep going," said Donkey.

And so it happened that there was a trail across the log and Horse was in the middle, Fox holding his tail from behind and Horse holding Goat's stub of a tail in front. Slow and slower and pause and slow they marched until each and every animal crossed the log. Safely.

And that is — from what I heard — how it came to be that the animals came to the new forests where they have been for some time now. Which goes to show that there is always some point, often along the most important journeys, where fear is great and the best care from others helps us make it. And, perhaps *we* must also remember to pay attention to what's most important.

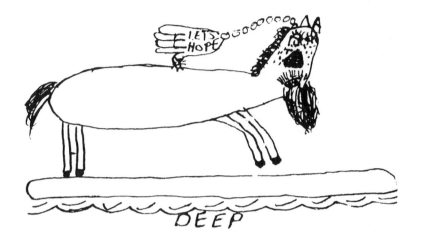

Illustrations by Apple Lord, then age 9
Story by Ruth Charney

Appendix B
Holding a Social Conference: Some Typical Problems

Although every situation is unique and must be geared closely to the individual child, classroom and teacher, here are a number of common problems and a possible social conference format. I suggest these as an exercise or practice with formulating "could it be's" and possible solutions. Remember that every conference is more of an improvisation than a set script. The examples are organized into:
- Noticeable behaviors
- "Could it be" formulations
- Generating alternatives

1. Attention-seeking behavior

Behavior

The teacher notices:
- Child shows off, may brag a lot (even lie) about accomplishments or possessions.
- May be clingy, show EVERYTHING to teacher, make a general pest of him/herself.
- Asks unnecessary questions.
- Repeats silly, mischievous bids for approval and teacher's time.
- Inappropriate noise-effects and antics.

The student notices:
- Kids don't pick me.
- Teachers ignore me or don't explain things to me.
- I like to tell jokes, it's funny when I . . .

Could it be?

- You wish people would pay more attention to you?
- You think the only way that people will notice you is if you bother them or act silly?
- You think the only way the teacher will notice you is if you act very good and show all your good work.
- You feel you need to impress other people to get attention.
- You wish people knew certain things about you and noticed you more.

Generating alternatives

"How do you think I might help you to stop asking so many questions (acting like a clown, being a nuisance, etc.)?" Teacher proposes some alternatives:
- Child needs concrete activities (board games, project, job) to do with a small group to help gain acceptance and inclusion.
- Child needs help making a friend. You may want to set up a specific friendship goal that includes being a friend, as well as making a friend. I outline three tasks for this goal:
  * Notice and list a number of friendly qualities in yourself — things I like to do, things that are nice about me, things that make me a fun person.
  * Name one person as a possible friend — I would like to be friends with _____ because she also likes to _____.
  * Invite "the friend" to do one thing — play a game, do an activity, sit together or share a class activity.
  These steps usually involve rehearsal and feedback from the teacher.
- When acceptance by the group is an issue, perhaps because the student has been a disturbance, working with the class as a whole may be necessary. One aim is for the group to become more accepting, without putting up with the nuisance behaviors. For example, the teacher might lead a discussion about acceptance. I ask children how they show, and don't show, that they accept others. I ask if most kids want to feel accepted, and if everyone in our class does now (the responses to this are often very honest).

  I recall one reply, "Well if you act like a jerk, then people might not like you." That led to a wonderful discussion in which I asked that everyone name one way they act like a jerk and one way they act that is nice. "If everyone acts like a jerk sometimes, is that a fair reason to not accept people?" The class was willing to try to use their accepting behavior to help include others. We also talked about things to say if someone is "a jerk."
- If the student thinks he or she needs to be known better, I might ask, "What do you wish people knew about you that you like or can do well, and they don't know?" I will help the student publicize a strength or hobby, or enact some special responsibility, demonstrating skills or interests, helping to create a more positive image or role in the room.

- If the child thinks she needs more time with the teacher, we might call this a need for "quality time," meaning a short, positive way for a child to check in and be noticed. For example, a journal that the child keeps and the teacher responds to once or twice a week; or a short ten-minute "visiting" period, each day or a few times a week. (Sometimes the child is given tickets which she passes in when she needs her visit, rather than have a set schedule, which also gives the child a sense of control.) The child needs to understand that this takes the place of the other frequent nudges and bids for attention.

2. The defiant one

Behavior

The teacher notices:
- Negative, critical, frequent objections about peers, work, teacher — "Oh God, didn't we just do this last year?"
- Contradicts, argues about facts, methods or what was said last month!
- Makes faces, passes knowing glances, or rudely mumbles when asked to do something. May accompany poor and incomplete work.
- May ignore minor rules, test each and every limit (bell rings and keeps on talking, walks out of the room at will, take things from teacher's closets, tells lies about handing in work, denies doing what was just observed, ridicules efforts of others).

Student notices:
- Teacher picks on me.
- Teacher isn't fair — doesn't like me as much as others.
- Teacher doesn't give me a chance.
- Stuff is too easy for me.
- Stuff is too hard for me.

Student generally wants to prove that teacher mistreats or is wrong.

Could it be?

- You need to show your teachers that you can be a boss, too?
- You want to impress your teacher or other kids by showing us that you can do what you want and don't have to follow our rules?
- You feel angry because you think grown-ups don't understand something important about you?
- You feel not so good about some of your work in school, so you worry that people won't think you are a strong or smart person.

These work on an assumption that defiance may sometimes mask feelings of inadequacy.

Generating alternatives

"What do you think you would need in order to use your strong self (or ideas) to be more constructive?"

In general I think we want to validate and find some positive outlets for the child's need for power and control, as well as to place limits and not give in to the badgering or disruptions. Solutions seek to validate strengths and establish boundaries.

- The child needs the teacher to know that he/she can be a boss. "I notice that you like to make up your own mind about things" or "You like to have your own way" (give your opinion) or "You aren't afraid to stand up to me. When you argue with me, it makes it hard for me to teach a lesson. Let's see if we can think of a way you can give your opinions."

- The child needs to show independence and control. "You are lucky to have these strong things inside of you. That shows you probably have the skills to be a good leader (or a fine debater, executive, problem-solver, etc.). How can I help you use your power to accomplish and build, not to knock down?" The metaphor of the builder or architect works particularly well for some children. I will even go so far as to use blocks and design a structure, inviting the student to help me make it sturdy and beautiful, talking about our potential to create.

- The need to impress and the need to feel good about some work often come together and continue from the second solution. Plan something together to build: capitalize on strengths. The child needs to think of one or two things he or she wants to "build" or accomplish. As "architects," they need to use their good thinking and power skills to design the task. The teacher may need to provide some options, using what she has noticed about strengths or interests. It might be to use the artistic talents of the student to create a beautiful bulletin board for the class; find a way to learn and then teach chess to other members of the class, because the child loves strategy games; organize a way to help with math or reading. Older students with learning problems often make wonderful tutors of younger children, sometimes in the very areas where they have struggled.

- The child uses power to do some hard work. When we validate a child's strength, we also reinforce their resources to tackle hard work or "tricky" controls. Sometimes this means helping a child confront and work on a perceived difficulty. If the disruptive behavior covers perceived or real inadequacies, avoiding them confirms the sense of helplessness. We may offer choices about how to do the work, but not about whether the work needs doing. "You need to work on your writing. Do you want to work on it at home, with special homework, or in school? Do you want me to help you with it or would you like to see if Mrs. _____ might be able to tutor you?"

- The child needs the teacher to know . . . . Often the child needs the teacher to know they are smart or good (despite appearances). Teacher may be able to set up a "contract" that allows the child to achieve success in some area.

The teacher provides a challenge or a progression of tasks that allows the child to advance or demonstrate aptitudes in conduct or skill. "I'll know you can be responsible if you show me for the next two weeks that you will line up quickly and collect all the balls" or "I'll know you are able to do harder reading if you read the next two chapters and can answer three questions." It's usually important to make the challenge realistic but something that gives success.

- The child uses power to build "hard" self-controls. "I see that you have many strengths inside of you, so I believe that you can control your own giggling (silliness, mean comments). What are some ways that you can think of to help that?" (such as seating plans, practicing helpful comments, taking a self-imposed time out). Teachers may prompt or redirect with shared secret signals that mean time to change seats, while urging student self-awareness.

- The child gets help from parents. The best results involve parents. When parents also support the particular attributes of the child and agree with the goals of the teacher, the objectives are greatly reinforced and the changes more immediate. I will often write up a statement listing the Clear Positives for the student — goals, expected behaviors — and consequences. A copy goes to parents and a copy to the student, to be discussed, and decided in concert. The collaboration itself supports growth.

- The child needs immediate feedback. We notice the progress. We also notice the unwanted behaviors. We need to act immediately on both. Children need to see that we mean what we say — we mean for them to stop bothering, talking after the bell, making nasty comments. The consequences go into effect.

3. Poor sports

Behavior

The teacher notices:
- Outbursts of temper, bullying, cheating, quitting, tears, especially during games or recess times.

The student notices:
- Teams aren't fair.
- The referee is lousy.
- Kids don't play right and don't follow rules.

Could it be?

- Hard for you to lose?
- It feels bad if you don't do as well as you always want to do?

- Hard for you to follow the rules and accept the decisions of referees, partners or the boss of a game, if the boss isn't you?
- You have trouble taking care of yourself when the teacher isn't there to help you?
- You care about the game so much that you get frustrated when others on your team don't play with as much interest as you?

Generating alternatives

"What do you think you would need in order to enjoy playing more?"
- Children need to play and lose. I discuss "fun and fair." Do children know what it means to play for fun? How do you know that you are having fun? How do you know that others are having fun? How do we make games fun? This alternative explores and seeks to teach children the challenge of making a game fun. Children may need to make a chart listing their ideas about "fun" and "fair" and then rating themselves after a game. This has also been effective on an individual basis, with personal rating sheets.
- Children need to play by the rules and accept the decisions of adult or peer referees. Disputing the rules or the source of the rules is a common source of misery. Twelve-year-olds playing Four Square, a game with a rotating referee, flexible rules, and judgment calls can reach unprecedented levels of squabbling and disputation, particularly with intense players. The need to accept, without controversy, decisions of other children, as well as teachers or "professional athletic arbitrators," is a security system to be learned, with consequences to follow if it isn't learned. Formal agreement on a written set of rules for the game may become a special committee assignment, ratified by the class along with guidelines for referees and players. "Anyone who argues with more than one decision leaves the game," was a policy decided by the class. It worked.
- Children need help to play by a standard rule. Set up standard rules and group participation. Play involves children in ongoing issues about standard rules, practices and consequences for conflict. School-wide rules such as "taggers choice," make a big difference — Taggers Choice: "If the tagger says he tagged you, he did. You are caught." Fives are still "inventive" rule-followers, apt to make up or invent as they go along. Sixes often test the rules that they know by heart. Sevens may become overly competitive and need to play games which emphasize cooperation rather than winning and losing. Eights may take an entire game time to refine and dispute the rules and the fairness of sides. Older children may have trouble balancing skill levels and participation — on the one hand hogging the ball, on the other, quitting games that are difficult.
- Outdoor and indoor games may demand self-regulation. In most schools, recess is managed by adults other than the teacher. When children are playing checkers or Go Fish, it is in a peer-directed setting. These are wonderful opportunities for children to acquire and practice individual

controls and interpersonal rule setting. We need to help children follow guidelines, without intruding or taking over. We encourage self-controls such as keeping your body and others' safe, controlling voices and words, using the game rules (not cheating), taking turns, making fair teams, etc. When the controls break down, it is important to know which controls: Are children swearing, kicking too hard, taking too many turns? The "privilege of being in the game" means using these controls. At times, teachers play games with the children, modeling the behaviors they wish to see. For example, I will emphasize "luck" in games, saying "Oh gosh, it's not my lucky day!" Another teacher is wonderful in the way he models "playfulness," a combination of keen involvement and fellowship as he roots for others in the game.

- Some children (even with the supervision of their teacher) break down if they lose or don't do well enough in a game, or if others don't play with equal vigor and intensity. They become abusive, throw a tantrum, or withdraw from play. We need to make it absolutely clear that this is unacceptable. Immediate feedback or immediate time-outs are implemented. It may also be important to prepare children for various levels of play. Some games are to be played with loose rules; some may be more serious. We need to help some children know the difference and act flexibly, and to learn acceptable outlets for frustration, such as stamping a foot.

4. Tattling

Behavior

The teacher notices:
- Daily tattling and concern about what others are up to — He called me names. She pushed me. He took and didn't ask. He's making stupid sounds and we can't concentrate . . .
- Whining complaints.
- Frequent interruptions to report trouble.

This may also apply to the class in general. The teacher notices a lot of tattling going on in the classroom.

The student notices:
- She's not following the rules.
- I tell them to stop but they don't listen.
- You said . . . and they shouldn't . . .

Could it be?

- You want me to know that you know the rules and know how to follow them? (This is not uncommon for fives who crave approval and acknowledgement from teachers.)

- You want to see those children get in trouble? (Our children love to sing the Rosalie Sorrels song, "I'm Gonna' Tell on You:" "I'm gonna' tell. I'm gonna' tell. I'm gonna' holler and I'm gonna' yell. I'll get you in trouble whatever you do. Cause I'm gonna' tell on you!" This may be the six-year-olds' theme song!)
- You have asked people to stop and they aren't listening to your words? You feel that you need my help (in situations where a child is involved in a conflict directly).
- You are feeling a little jealous and maybe angry when you feel that you are not included in what others are doing? (This may apply to the child who wants to be accepted by the group, but isn't.)
- You are worried that children aren't taking good care of our class rules?

Generating alternatives

"What do you think you will need in order to help each other and not tattle?"
- Children need help with expectations to understand that tattling is not a way to gain attention and approval. When teachers are attentive and affirm positive efforts in an ongoing way, children tend to have less need to seek out that approval. Thus, we might want to think about whether the claims for attention are excessive or whether we have overlooked this quiet, compliant lad or lass. It is important to sanction small actions, and not wait for final products. If tattling continues, the teacher may need to provide other options.
- When children tattle, the teacher may need to determine the causes of tattling. They tend to change with age. Fives are apt to tattle in order to affirm their own law-abiding status. Sixes may be more interested in making trouble and testing the punitive possibilities. Sevens may worry if the slightest rules are disobeyed. In general, I try to distinguish with children a difference between "tattling," and telling. I use the word "tattling" to mean when you repeat stories in order to get others in trouble; "telling" is when you need help from the teacher. I would try to set up specific criteria for "telling:" an emergency, a conflict you really can't solve on your own or together, a problem that you think needs adult attention (like if someone is hurt or fighting).

The teacher may further state that "tattling" is not an acceptable way in her classroom to take care of yourself or others. "Telling" is important. She knows that sometimes children will have to think to themselves first, "Hmm, I wonder whether this is a tattling or a telling." She can also model or try out examples. A "Tattling/Telling Quiz" can be done in good spirit and humor.

When the child comes to the teacher and just begins her tale, the teacher will ask, "Well, Jennifer, is this a telling or a tattling? What do you think?"

Sometimes Jennifer will accurately self-monitor and self-correct. Or another time, she may not. When her interpretation is mistaken, the teacher can go back over the questions. Does this business concern you? Is there an emergency? Are you just trying to get someone in trouble? In some cases, the issues are discussed with the whole class. When it mostly affects one child, it is discussed and worked out individually.

- When children tattle because they are left out, they may need help asking to join or being included.
- When children are worried that rules aren't followed or when tattling is intrusive and pervasive, the teacher may need to examine the tone of the classroom. Sometimes a wave of tattling is indicative of tensions in the room, perhaps from too much competition or pressure. I have found that tattling (when it involves numbers of children) can be symptomatic of unclear expectations or expectations that children feel unable to meet. They may become "frantic" and upset about the rules. An unclear expectation may also occur when we say "No teasing" but ignore or fail to act on incidents of teasing. It is also true that tattling accompanies the evolving concerns of children for the rules, and their responsibility for abiding by them. It is part of growing up. We need to deal with it firmly and kindly.

5. Losing and forgetting

Behavior

The teacher notices:
- Student doesn't remember lunch money, bus pass, books, homework, directions, instructions, where he/she just put work, etc.
- Student can't find lunch money, paper, book, where he/she just put report.
- Student floating and wandering about classroom.
- Messy desks, messy cubbies, trails of belongings.
- Parents running in with forgotten trip money, lunches, homework assignments.

Could it be?

- You have trouble organizing your things?
- You don't remember well when you just try to keep everything in your head and your head needs some help?
- You have so many things to think about right now?

Generating alternatives

"What do you think will help you to remember and take better charge of your own things?"

- Some children need to organize their physical space. Some children work well in the clutter they love to create. But when we notice disorganization, it's time to step in and get the physical space organized. This may include systems for holding things (files, notebooks, pockets, notebooks with pockets, etc.). It may also include a system for order, such as a checklist taped to the desk. The checklist reminds children about the "when's and where's," putting things away before starting on the next activity, and in the proper container — knapsack, desk, trash.
- Some children need help organizing objects. Younger children may benefit from practice with categorizing and organizing a shelf in the room, a set of books, a bin of art materials. Some children more naturally tend to organize by clustering and grouping, while others may do better with sequences and a first, second, third ordering of information. It's effective to notice how they best organize and then help them apply these strategies to specific areas of school work.
- Some children need to remember. They may need help learning to plan and to keep track with written memos. Many adults who have several things to keep track of depend on their lists, daily planners, week-at-a-glance calendars and computers to remind them of what's ahead. We can also help children learn different planning and mnemonic strategies. One thirteen-year-old is learning to use a memo book, which he slips into his back pocket. He writes in it first thing in the morning — the "have-to's," the schedule, and materials he will need. He blocks out his long-term assignments to show expected school and homework schedules. Since beginning, he has gotten his assignments in on time. He has remembered what he needs to do, most of the time, although I'm pretty sure I saw his Mom rushing in with a forgotten lunch just the other day!
- Some children have a lot on their mind. "Forgetting" may be a sign of preoccupation with other concerns, fears, problems, burdens brought in from home. (It also may be a more serious appeal for help that requires further investigation.) When anxious or worried, children may daydream in school. Their fantasies give momentary comfort and relief, even when it may put them at odds with their classwork. Where we notice ongoing preoccupation, we try to redirect the child, at the same time setting up times for drawing or writing or daydreaming which will not jeopardize participation. Children who continue to withdraw may need family or guidance services. I find that we can show compassion, yet act in the best interests of the child by redirecting their energy into school projects, rather than away from them.

6. "Escape to the bathroom"

The teacher notices (like Derek in Ch. 8):
- Avoids work, specifically during independent work times.

- Loafs, likes to hang out without doing much, has trouble making choices.
- May go to the bathroom a lot, or wander around the room, be slow to get going, be lethargic or easily distracted.
- Talks or fools around instead of doing the assignments.
- Offers excuses for not doing assignments, needs a lot of reminders and direction.
- Asks questions but doesn't seem to listen or apply answers.

The student notices:
- Teacher didn't explain what to do.
- I can't concentrate in here when there are other people.
- I don't understand what to do.

Could it be?

- You find this work so hard you feel you don't like to do it?
- You like the subject, but you feel bad because you're stuck on something and it's easier to avoid it than to figure out how to get unstuck?
- You have trouble concentrating when you have to work on your own?
- You feel not so interested and you don't like to do things that don't seem interesting?

Generating alternatives

"What do you think you need to feel more independent or confident about your work?"
- When students find the work is hard, we need to help them recover self-esteem. Try to analyze, with the student, the specific hard part — "What part is hard?" — rather than the general, "Math is hard." Sometimes, a simple diagnostic battery is useful to pinpoint areas of strength and weakness. Otherwise, I brainstorm with the children. What part of reading is hard? Is it remembering the story? Is it recognizing new words? Children are comforted and assured by concrete information about their skills. "You are good at phonic decoding, but have trouble recalling words by sight." Inventories of math also help discriminate strengths. When we can show children what they know, they begin to show themselves what they know, which is the basis for self-esteem.
- When children feel stuck or confused, we may need to arrange the environment in such a way that they feel more secure and autonomous. Self-doubt is not conducive to independence. But it is not just what teachers say to children that creates confidence, it is what "children say about themselves to themselves" (Sheila Kelly).

    What a child needs in order to feel more independent in the classroom will vary. Some children may need the option of checking in with the teacher about instructions. Some children may need to have a buddy to show them what to do when they are stuck. Some children may need more modeling or a moment to just watch. Others may need something written down that they can read. Again, we need to look at the skills and aptitudes of the child and then look at the arrangements of the classroom.

- When children avoid their work because "It's boring" or doesn't interest them, they may need a way to be interested. "Bored" is often a catchall, a code word for many different things. One thing it covers is fear of failure. Another is a lack of imagination, by which I mean the child doesn't yet imagine the possibilities. In this case, we want to reveal the possibilities, stretch children's thinking and find connections between the child and the subject.

  When the child avoids rote material — times facts, spelling lists — we may need to provide some individualized requirements. Some children may work better with shorter, smaller chunks given intermittently than with a steady diet of twenty problems to a page.

7. "Restless & on the move"

The teacher notices:
- Hates to sit still, is inattentive, grabs, knocks into things, bumps into people.
- Interrupts, starts talking to the teacher regardless of what she is doing.
- Wanders from a task, from a desk, from thought to thought.

The student notices:
- Meetings take too long.
- The worst thing about school is when you have to sit and sit.
- My hand just flies up.
- My words pop out of my mouth.
- There's so much waiting, and I hate to wait.

Could it be?

- You have trouble being the "boss" of your own body? You want to sit still, but your body wants to get up?
- You have so much energy and your muscles just need to work hard?
- You have trouble telling your mind to pay attention. You start thinking about your own work, but then you notice other things, other children, the teacher and the moving clouds you see through the window?

Generating Alternatives

"What do you think you need to do to pay attention?"
- Set up short and intermittent periods of sitting and listening — five minutes if that is what will work. Reinforce this at home, as well as at school. If a

child is expected to sit still for ten-minute spurts at school, have similar expectations at home — child will stay at the supper table for ten minutes, for example. Rather than work backwards, build up gradually, reinforcing effort along the way. "It's nice to see you sit still with us for a few minutes today," is more effective than a punitive sanction for less than the ten-minute goal. "I see you worked to use your brakes when you got up after meeting." "I see you use your good listening." "It's good to see you keep your hands to yourself for the first part of the games."

- Some children attend better when multi-sensory channels are engaged. Some listen better when able to chew gum, knit, doodle. Sometimes older children attend better when encouraged to take notes or keep a record of key words. Hand gestures (raising their hands, learning to sign) may be used in many different ways to add emphasis, transition, and attention. Self-talk helps some children — saying a direction or phrase to themselves; vocalizing through a chorus, chant or paraphrase. "You need to bring scissors and ruler to the group. Tell yourself what to bring," I say.
- "I tell myself to stop and think." Take three deep breaths, count to ten, repeat to yourself, "Stop. Stop and think." Impulsive children benefit from lots of practice with self-monitoring and self-correcting techniques. Again, every small gain needs to be encouraged and sanctioned along the way.

This is a small sample of classroom events that might generate a social conference. It is in no way exhaustive of events or constructive responses.

Appendix C
Issues Reflecting Age Characteristics

This is only a partial listing of common issues.

Some issues at five — self control

Children may:
- Have difficulty with body and mouth controls
- Not be able to sit still for more than fifteen minutes
- Have trouble keeping hands on their own body
- Raise their hands to speak but call out anyway
- Get physical when they don't get their own way
- Shout and/or use baby-talk
- Have difficulty sharing
- Take more than their share — of snack, blocks, etc.
- Take things that don't belong to them because "I want it"
- Want to always be first
- Want teacher's undivided attention
- Have trouble taking turns
- Need to be seen and released to a task
- Need constant approval
- Be afraid to try new things or make a mistake
- Tattle in order to get approval or show that they know the rules

Some issues at five and a half — self control

Children may:
- Experience language control
- See teacher as "a jerk"
- Shout "I hate you" at a buddy
- Have poor impulse and motor controls

- Move from tears to tantrums more easily
- Have a shorter attention span — more wiggly, fidgety and floppy
- Be more clumsy — fall down, out of and into things
- Grab, push to get out the door first
- Have conflicts with friends and peer
- Shout "You're not my friend anymore" — a friend one moment, an enemy the next
- Always give in or never want to give in
- Use few common rules in game situations
- "Invent" rules as they go along
- Lose interest and quit if rules don't work in their favor

Some issues at six — self control

Children may:
- Test out limits, particularly when they think teacher doesn't see them
- Value quantity over quality — very speedy
- Avoid fix-ups or changes to finished work
- Be sloppy in their haste to finish and do more
- Be very talkative, sassy, noisy — they often need self-talk to direct their thinking
- Use self-talk and chatter to begin drawing or writing, but talk soon takes over
- Converse rather than take care of transitions
- Worry and fuss about every little ailment
- Need lots of band-aids and comfort
- Get frequent stomachaches
- Be highly sociable — want to work together more, and experience more trouble working together
- Be bossy rather than cooperative in play
- Cheat in games
- Love "power games" — good guys vs. bad guys — but may become mean
- Make up frequent stories and lies — enjoy fantasy and storytelling, including their own stories
- Lie when confronted with misdeed

Some issues at seven

Children may:
- Be perfectionists and need to be released from a task
- Erase until paper is "holey," start over endlessly
- Need to dot every "i," but never complete a task
- Cover their work because nothing is good enough

- Not be able to take any criticism
- Cling to routines, avoid changes, fear the unknown
- Worry about a bus accident when a trip is announced
- Get frequent tension headaches or stomachaches
- Be very competitive
- Hate to lose
- Want to do everything right and well
- Be self-absorbed, poorly attentive when others have their turn
- Continue the fascination with themes of power and identification with superheroes — may try to boss and bully

Some issues at eight and nine

Children may:
- Feel a strong sense of gender identification
- Avoid holding hands with opposite sex
- Be teased or excluded from friendships and activities if they continue androgenous activities
- Have awareness without empathy — they may take care of each other's bodies or possessions, but be unclear about feelings and uncomfortable with differences (yet show a cognitive interest in cultural diversity, and belief in Golden Rule)
- Comfort Joe when he hurts his arm and Diana when she loses her book, but be unaware that Jeff is left out or that they treat Shannon differently
- Call names and be cruel concerning appearances or mannerisms — "Foureyes," "Fatty"
- Compare self and others — strong judgments about what one, and others are good at and not good at, want to avoid the things that are hard or that they are not so good at
- Say, "I hate art (math, tag, etc.)" — Translation: "I'm not so good at art"
- Repeat choices and self-planned activities more often
- Feel the importance of peers and friendships
- Begin cliques and clubs — often based on who is *not* "in" rather than a positive function or identity
- Be very concerned about issues of "fairness," particularly in terms of their teacher and in games
- Frequently complain, "That's not fair"
- Use "He (she, they) isn't fair," as a frequent alibi
- Show greater interest in telling secrets and gossip
- Form class hierarchies in which some children dominate or have too much influence

Some issues at ten and eleven

Children may:
- Have friendship conflicts that are intense and bitter — mostly "My friend isn't fair to me" while just beginning to ask "Am I fair to my friend?"
- Show interest in working things out with friends, but still limited in their ability to see another point of view without help
- Identify class scapegoats and exclude children socially —will stick with the same friends unless partnered by the teacher with new or other classmates
- Begin to feel peer pressure, often to side with a friend against another friend
- Use common interests as a positive factor in selecting friends or grouping-up, but may harshly reject others with different interests — often defend prejudices, such as picking on people who are short, fat, quiet, etc.
- Strongly relate self-esteem to achievement and performance in school or athletic field, and ability to attract attention
- Fear inferiority which may lead to reluctance to expose weaknesses and take risks
- Want to fulfill gender stereotypes — girls want to avoid physical activities, boys avoid crafts and handwork
- Be afraid to explore and solve problems
- Be afraid to offer ideas and give opinions
- Need to feel more in charge of themselves, but still rely strongly on teacher authority to set realistic goals and set workable limits
- Test limits and routines
- Worry that things are "babyish" and demand privileges or responsibilities they are not ready to handle
- Challenge and criticize teacher or school codes
- Handle small responsibilities poorly, yet lobby for big ones — not consistent or logical

Appendix D
Critical Contracts

The process of using a Critical Contract is covered in this appendix with this outline:

> I. The Process — All Ages
> II. Examples of the Process
>> A. Fives and Sixes
>> B. Elevens and Twelves
> III. Parent Conferences
> IV. A Summary of the Steps
> V. Some Sample Forms

I. The process — all ages

The process of using a Critical Contract includes:

A. Generating and writing individual goals
B. Sharing goals with teachers and parents to form the contract
C. Evaluating progress

A. Generating and writing individual goals

These may be generated with questions or a standard form. Parents will generate goals also (see Section V). Some examples:

My goal for myself is _____.

I think the most important thing for me to work on this year is

_____.

Students, teachers, and parent usually work through a first and final draft. Some examples of first drafts:

Student's First Draft
"Not being sent to time out. Taking care of myself."

Parents' First Draft
"I feel Kevin needs to organize himself and become able to follow instructions better. Kevin has worked more on reading skills this summer and has done a good job. I feel he needs more help expressing himself."

Teacher's First Draft
"I would like Kevin to come to his work on his own and to show real interest in at least three projects this year."

B. Sharing goals with teachers and parents to form the contract

Parents choose one goal and share it with their child. The child writes the goal in his or her own words. "My parents' goal for me is to make my work neat and bring it in on time and to listen to directions better."

Teachers form their goals based on knowledge of their students gained over a period of time. Usually, they present their goals at a formal conference during the latter part of the fall. It is important to be clear and straightforward about the reasons for the goal. Do we want to see a child stretch — take a risk and move beyond a familiar pattern, make new friends, or try out a new skill? Do we feel a student is ready to improve specific competencies, responsibilities or habits of work? Do we want to see a change in how the student behaves with others or his or her role in the group?

I share specific strategies and expectations — what I will be asking and requiring. I also tell parents what they can expect to see and how I'd like them to help me. Generally parents are highly supportive of teachers' goals and may only have doubts about a detail — "How/when will he learn to spell?"

If students are going to be able to put our goals into their own language and writing, they must understand what we mean. (Fives and sixes are not asked to rewrite goals, but the goals will be read to them and they are asked to repeat them. The student shows that he understands the other two goals clearly enough to recite and write them.) Both parent and teacher goals stimulate a conversation and explanation. Do you understand? Is it clear. Are there any questions? Can you tell me what you understand that I want or your parents think is important for this year in school?

Finally there is the formal contract, hand-written by students and signed by student, parent and teacher. Some examples:

Name: Kevin
> My goal for myself this year is not being sent to time out. Taking care of myself.

My parent's goal for me is to follow directions better.
My teacher's goal for me is to be an interested worker.

Name: Meg

My goal for myself this year is I want to read at least 5 books this year.

My parents' goal for me is to feel good about myself and improve in math.

My teacher's goal for me is to be more confident and share feelings.

Name: James

My goal for myself this year is to get better at the computer, to write a play, to make a few more friends in my class.

My parents' goal for me is to take more risks.

My teacher's goal for me is to balance my work and play time and relax for a period of each day.

C. Evaluating progress

I do not conceive of Critical Contracts as another instrument of measure. It is most important that the goals children generate for themselves are not graded. Instead, I suggest that we review the goals, revise and reinforce them. We can help children get to their goals but are careful to show patience with less realistic claims and difficult challenges. Our assistance may only consist of noticing — "I see you are trying to finish your work before you start on something else," or "Remember, you wanted to work on reading this year and yet you don't have a book. How can we help with that?"

We will help children reach their goals, but most important is the role the goals play for the children, the meaning they assume in their school life when they are free of external judgment. I worry that if we interject traditional ways of evaluating, we will end up scaling down the objectives to what is most measurable or reachable.

Nine and tens, or other ages may evaluate progress with the question "What is the most important thing you learned this year?" (See Ch. 16, page 246)

We need to help children develop standards and measures of progress. I want to reinforce the idea that paying attention to the goal is what I credit and value most, not finishing, completing, or achieving. Marnie felt she was done with handwriting because she had learned all the letters. I suggested that now she was ready to use her skills to write her compositions.

Not all goals do need to be continued throughout the year. Sometimes by mid year, children shift because they change their mind or they have finished with something. But I don't want to erase a goal because it is difficult or scary, I want to redirect the child's effort.

II. Examples of the process

A. Fives and Sixes

The procedure for the younger group begins towards the end of October. It is important that the children have time to get to know school and become familiar with routines. It begins as a whole-class exercise and it begins with drawing. Children start by answering three questions.

The first question concerns *what they like to do in school and why*. They will brainstorm as a group to generate ideas. The teachers find that it helps the children evoke their own ideas when they truly picture the areas and activities of the room. So they draw a picture.

The second question asks them to think about *something they don't like and why*. They brainstorm in the group. They review the different things they do during the day and may even sit in the area they are thinking about. Then they draw their picture. "The place in the Prime Blue room that I don't like is math meeting because it's too long." Fives will dictate their answer to the teacher. Sixes write, using invented spelling for the first draft. At each step, they will also represent, first with a partner and then to the whole class.

The third question asks, *"What do you think is the most important work you have to do this year and why?"* Teachers try to give children a way to think about this question, rather than provide lists of examples.

"What do I mean by most important?" the teacher asks.

"You like it a real lot."

"Like if you want it and your mom says you can't have it then you really get mad."

"Yes. 'Important' is something that you care a lot about. What do you care a lot about working on in school? Before you think, let me ask one more thing. You know that word I used just now, the word 'working'? Well, that's also a special word. What do you think it means to do important work in school?"

"You learn stuff."

"You get better at knowing things."

"You can do things you couldn't do before."

"You know things and your Mom is proud of you."

"Like you do hard things, like count to a trillion and stuff."

"These are all very good ideas about important work in school. You told me that you learn new things and get better at things and people are proud of you and perhaps most of all you will feel proud of your own self for doing this important work. So now I want you to start to think about something you want to work on this year in school that is important and that will make you feel proud of yourself."

The children may still need some modeling and examples. Teachers often share something important they want to work on. One teacher describes how she really loves art and thinks it's a very important way to show things you feel and think. Last year she didn't do very much art and this year she wants to teach more art. They may also role-play thinking aloud about the question. "I wonder if it is important that I work on my writing. Well, that's OK, but I don't know. I really wish that I had more friends . . ."

Once ready to work on their individual goals, the children begin with the drawing. Again the fives tend to dictate the sentence that goes with the picture. The sixes use invented spelling for the first draft. The final drafts are typed, hand written or beautifully copied by the children. The illustrations will also be done in final draft using markers or crayons. All three pages are bound together in a folder and presented to parents for a November Conference Period.

One teacher of fives and sixes noted the fact that the children took the question seriously. "No one talked about lunch or endless recess," she said and many chose goals connected to the Golden Rule. One six-year-old boy wrote, "The most important work for me is the Golden Rule because that's everything." Other children talked about doing projects, building strong buildings, making friends and learning to read. Everyone gave voice to important work, something they cared to do in school and something to share with classmates, teacher and parents.

B. Elevens and Twelves

The teacher of the seventh and eighth grade class designed a different format to build Critical Contracts. He chose letters. Parents would write a letter to their child and teacher. The teacher would write a letter to the student and students would write a letter to the teacher. The three goals presented in each letter would be transcribed by the student into a formal contract that included, "My goal for myself, my parents' goal for me, my teacher's goal for me."

At the beginning of the semester, the students were told that they would be expected to set up a goal for themselves for the year. They would have time to reflect and consider during the first six weeks. Then they would compose a letter that includes the nature of their goal, the reasons for selecting it and how they plan to accomplish it. Some students preferred conferencing privately with the teacher to set up their objectives. Others relished peer feedback and recognition. The teacher gives students a choice. You may read your letters to someone else in the class or share them individually with the teacher. The written communication takes the place of a more public dialogue, which enabled the younger students to represent and revise thinking. At this level, the goals were highly validated by incorporating them into a contract. Some examples:

"What I most want for myself this year is just to be a good person and keep up my own standards and not lose control, like getting behind or forgetting things," wrote one twelve-year-old.

"I want to be more respected by other kids this year and I guess that means I have to say what I think more, not be so quiet all the time," stated another student in what his teacher felt was a particularly difficult and apt judgment.

"I want to know I can do hard work and not have to be pushed," proclaimed Erik, who often delighted in last-minute dashes or flippant attitudes about such things as tests or papers. Erik's goal was well-grounded in the reality of his transition year before high school.

Most students at all levels were able to formulate a powerful goal for themselves. They were able to project a hope and want for their year at school. They were serious hopes and serious wants. In the process, they gathered information about themselves as learners and shared information with their teacher, a part of the exchange that allows children to be known and teachers to become better teachers. The next step involves the communication of parent and teacher goals, which may be the second most vital incentive for the learning to come. The first is the student's own sense of contribution to the plan.

III. Parent conferences

Our school schedules a before-school and mid-fall conference. Parents are generally very aware of their children's strengths and weaknesses and have many hopes for the coming year. But we want to ask them to single out one special focus and to help to give it a positive wording. Their focus may reinforce the school's goal or it may be unique. For example, a student may be developing independent work habits both in school and at home. Or, the parent may single out math competencies while the teacher's focus is on study skills.

Sometimes, the school and parent goals appear incompatible. For example, a teacher may want to focus on getting a reluctant writer to write more willingly while a parent may want to emphasize spelling. Forming the contract offers a chance to discuss educational decisions. We may need to find ways to phrase the goals so that they are not contradictory or divisive. "Your parents want you to bring home a paper every week that shows beautiful spelling," and "Your teachers want you to find five topics you are excited to write about," may be a way to reconcile expectations. The process of discussing the goals allows teachers and parents to think aloud together, to discuss points of view and reasons. The aim is not to contest or argue, but to understand and communicate. Children witness this serious consideration in educational planning, but are participants as well as listeners. The partnership of school and family can be one of our most powerful, if fragile, unions. A Critical Contract is one approach to building cooperation and trust. In general, we want to foster discussion. There is discussion with parents about their goals and teacher goals. There is also a discussion between parents and students in order for them to share their goals. I have found parents reliable and responsive to this format, willing to come to school and willing to work at home. There may be more openness to process than the usual arrangements where teachers talk and parents listen.

During the second parent conference, the three goals are reviewed. All of the goals are expressed in positive language. "Not wasting time" may need to show what is intended by constructive use of time, in school or at home, if it is to be a positive goal. "Not arguing so much" is converted into a positive use of will power or learning respectful debate. "Not getting assignments in on time" becomes a challenge for self-monitoring. We mean to encourage and inspire — not criticize or undermine.

Not all parents come to school. The percentage tends to drop as students get older, with less than 50% after first grade in some school systems. Parents who come to school tend to have children who come to school. There is no substitute for the active, visible involvement of families in the school lives of their children.

Poverty and despair are formidable obstacles. Helping to close the gap between the home and the classroom is a central concern if we are to reform our schools. I know that there are no easy or quick solutions where alienation in the community is entrenched. I know that when children are excited about school, they are apt to bring parents in, too. Occasions, displays of fine work, plays and festive productions are apt to get a far bigger turn out than conference nights. Parent-to-parent programs have had some striking successes and schools which are open as community centers have also increased parent turnout and involvement in regular activities. I have never implemented a Critical Contract in a school where parent involvement is an issue. I can only envision its positive impact.

IV. A summary of the steps

1. Pre-school query asking parents for their goals
2. Students work on first and final drafts of their goals (October)
3. Conference to discuss parent goals and current teacher and student goals
4. Parents discuss their goal with student
5. Teacher discusses goal with student
6. Student prepares contract
7. Contract is sent home for signature and copied for home and school
8. Contract is reviewed — continuously or at specified times

V. Some sample forms

Fives and Sixes:

(1) The place in the room I like the best is _____

(2) The place in the room I don't like is _____

(3) I think the most important work for me this year is _____

My parents think that the most important work for me is_____

My teachers think that the most important work for me is_____

Nines & Tens:

The Critical Contract

Name:_____
Date:_____

(1) My goal for myself is _____

(2) My parents goal for me is _____

(3) My teacher's goal for me is _____

Signature Student:_____
Signature Parents:_____
Signature Teacher:_____

Sample Parent Query:

Please answer the following questions to help us plan your child's program for this year. Teachers and students will also be responding to similar questions. At our fall conference, we hope to share all of our answers.

1) What do you feel was the most important thing your child accomplished last year in school?
2) What do you feel will be most important for your child in school this year?

Ages 5, 6

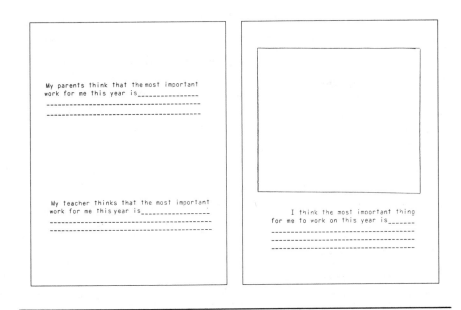

My parents think that the most important
work for me this year is_____

My teacher thinks that the most important
work for me this year is_____

I think the most important thing
for me to work on this year is_____

Ages 6, 7, 8

Name:_____ Date_____

First Conference Sheet

Last year in school I liked:

I didn't like:

One thing that I learned was_____

This year I hope _____

Make a picture of something you might build
in the block area:

Ages 8, 9, 10

Name:_____

Date:_____

THE CRITICAL PARNTERSHIP
MIDDLES 1987-88

My goal for myself this year is _____
_____

My parents' goal for me is _____
_____

My Teachers' goal for me is _____
_____

Signed: _____
_____
_____

Name of Parents:_____

Student:_____

MIDDLES PARENT QUERY: 1987 - 88

Please answer the following questions to help us plan your child's program

1) What do you feel will be most important for your child in school this year?

2) Have there been any experiences this past year (or summer) that have had a strong influence on your child? Please note any health concerns

---

NAME_____   DATE_____

MIDDLES CONFERENCE SHEET

(1) What do you think will be MOST IMPORTANT for you this year in school? Please explain your answer.
_____
_____
_____
_____
_____
_____

(2) Give the meaning of the following words (Please use your best hand-writing):

OBSERVATION: _____
_____

NECESSITIES: _____
_____

SUPPLIES: _____
_____

3) Solve ONE of following word-problems:

1. There are 24 Middles. There are an equal number of girls and boys. How many girls and how many boys in the Middles?

2. There are 24 Middles. If 1/3 of the Middles want to work on supply purchasing, how many will that be? How many are not interested in purchasing?

Appendix E
Guided Discovery

Guided Discovery is a teaching technique used to introduce materials, learning centers or processes in a classroom. It can help children make a variety of good choices, use materials successfully, and take better care of themselves, each other, and their classroom.

Goals of a guided discovery

- To excite and motivate children to explore areas and materials in their classroom with imagination, invention, industry, and joy
- To help children learn to make choices and use "choice periods" in a productive and satisfying way
- To develop children's abilities to work cooperatively in learning centers or with materials in their classroom — e.g., to be partners, to listen to each other's good ideas, to learn from one another
- To build and establish a common classroom vocabulary — all children know the names and places for materials in their room
- To develop and establish expectations and rules for taking care of materials and areas of the room — children learn expectations for independent set-up and clean-up and proper ways to handle the materials to keep them safe and beautiful

Guidelines for guided discoveries

- A Guided Discovery can be done with a whole group, small group, or individuals.
- All children will experience a Guided Discovery for a material, area or process before any children use it independently.
- All children are actively involved in generating rules, establishing vocabulary, and exploring expectations and possibilities for the material,

center or process.
- All children will have an opportunity to share work done during a Guided Discovery.

Format for a guided discovery

Pattern Blocks are the material used in this example. The whole group is sitting in circle. A Guided Discovery often includes these steps:

1. Introduction — naming
2. Generating ideas — modeling exploratory work
3. Children explore
4. Representing — sharing, comments
5. Clean-up and care of materials
6. Extensions — groups, pairs, independent work

T: signifies what the teacher might say
C: signifies what the children might say

1. Introduction — naming

Goals:
- To excite and motivate children to explore
- To build and establish common vocabulary

T: What do you think I have in this box? (Rattles small enclosed box with one of each pattern block in it.) Who has an idea?
C: Rocks, crayons, blocks . . .
T: I do have blocks in here, but now tell me more about them.
C: Is there a yellow one? Is there a square one? (Teacher brings out a block as children start to guess and name. With older children, teacher may ask for more information before bringing block out. Guessing continues until all the blocks are revealed.)
T: What do you notice about these blocks?
C: Different colors, shapes, pretty, some are bigger . . .

2. Generating ideas — modeling exploratory work

Goal:
- To demonstrate ideas and possible ways to use the material, center, or process

T: What can we do with these?

C: Build something.

T: OK. (Demonstrates making a design with blocks) What do you notice?

C: It stands up, looks like a . . .

T: If I want to build something else, watch how I will *unbuild* my construction. What do you notice about how I took it down (unbuilt it)?

C: It was quiet (tidy).

T: What else could we do with these? (May want to model other ideas children suggest or have several children demonstrate other ideas and show ways to build and unbuild with the shapes.)

C: Make a pattern, building, tower . . .

3. Children explore — "Make a beautiful design"

Goal:

• All children participate in an exploratory activity

Teacher asks every child to take the same number and shapes of blocks (two of each is a good number for this Guided Discovery) and to work in a space in front of where they are sitting.

T: Make a beautiful design. (Allow about 5 minutes, then stop and share designs.)

T: Make another design. (Children keep experimenting.)

T: Make something high, flat, that has open spaces. Make an animal, a weird thing, a wall . . . (Teacher can experiment with ideas as long as group remains focused.)

4. Representing — "Tell one thing"

Goals:

• Encourage children to share ideas
• Teach a language of sharing
• Develop active listening and noticing

After each guided instruction from the teacher, a few children (in a large group) or all children (in a small group) share their work.

Sharing:

Teacher will ask a focusing question (One thing you like, you notice, that was hard, that was tricky . . .)

T: Tell one thing that you like about your construction.

C: I like the red part, the top part, all of it . . .

Comments:
Children respond to the work of their peers, telling one thing that they see or like

T: Tell one thing that you like about _____'s design.
C: I like the way he did the windows. It looks like a . . .

5. Clean-up and care of materials

Goals:
- Establish expectations for using materials properly
- Teach children where to find and store materials
- Establish fun and instructive ways to clean up
- Establish routines for display of completed work

T: Who can show us a careful and safe way to put all the blocks away in their container?
T: Who can show us what to do while waiting for the container?
T: Who can show us how they would pass the container when they are done?
T: What's another way we could put away the pattern blocks when lots of people are using them? (Someone gets all the circles, someone else will get the squares . . .)

6. Extensions for groups, pairs, and independent work: adding concepts and skills

Techniques:
- "Copy-catting" — Children copy each other's designs (builds perceptual discrimination, visual memory, left/right directionality)
- "What's Missing?" — How did you know? (encourages shape, pattern, and vocabulary discrimination)
- Set-making (builds classification)

Extensions in pairs

Goals:
- Develop partner learning
- Model social skills — e.g., ways to be a good partner: give clues if needed, give partner time to guess, tell answers only when your partner asks for help ("I give up," "I need help," etc.)

T: Copy cat with your partner.
T: Play the "what's missing game" with your partner.

Extensions for independent work (I-work)

Goal:
- Continue to explore or discover on their own or use teacher initiatives
- Share and represent discoveries at designated times
- Continue to develop and use social skills
- Complete clean-up independently
- Place finished work in designated display area

Teacher may bring students back to the Guided Discovery process to focus on any of the goals for independent work.

T: Tomorrow make another weird design, copy your design on graph paper, make a design and write a story about it, make a design and see if your partner can copy it. (exploration and discovery)

T: Suppose someone accidentally knocks over your building, what might you do? (social skills — resolving conflicts)

T: Suppose you need more blocks and there are no more left in your bin, what might you do? (social skills — self-assertion, problem-solving)

T: Suppose some people are building and you want to join their group, what might you say? (social skills — self-assertion, ability to join a group)

T: How will you know if all the blocks are picked up? (independent clean-up)

T: Where is a good place for you to display your work? (displaying finished work)

T: What will you tell us about your work at meeting time? (sharing and representing finished work)

Appendix F
Social Curriculum Checklist

The Social Curriculum helps children gain social skills and encourages children to learn to care for themselves, each other, and their world.

Provide opportunities for children to know each other and be known in the classroom:
- Opportunities for children to be seen — notice what children do, bring into school, draw in pictures, like to do in "choice" periods
- Opportunities for children to be heard and to hear each other — sharing news from home, stories from writing, work in process
- Opportunities to be named and to name each other — greetings by teacher and classmates, naming games, names on morning charts, name cards and pictures on bulletin boards
- Opportunities to be known — "The Self Curriculum:" booklets, journals, art work that describe family facts, likes, dislikes, events, wishes for the year to be shared with teacher and classmates

Classroom activities may include morning meeting, class meeting, "choice" periods, guided outdoor group games, language arts and social studies projects featuring "The Self Curriculum."

Generate and model class rules and guidelines for expected ethical behaviors:
- The Golden Rule — children act out ways that they "bring the Golden Rule to school"
- One Rule — children think of "one rule" to make the classroom a place that is respectful and friendly
- Logical Consequences — everyone forgets rules:
  * You break it — you fix it (apology, helping hand, etc.)
  * Breach of faith — loss of privilege
  * Choose not to participate — time-out

Model social situations and practice positive behaviors to provide positive ways for children to assert their needs, resolve conflicts, make friends, etc.:

- "If someone calls you a name, what can you do?"
- "If you need something and someone is using it for a long time and won't let you use it, what can you do?"
- "If someone pushes you in line . . ."
- "If you want someone to play with and you are afraid to ask . . ."
- "If someone makes you very angry (very happy) . . ."

Model respect, friendliness, firmness of purpose, interest through teacher/student interactions by:

- Showing children what you expect
- Using affirming and encouraging language
- Stressing the deed, not the doer
- Noticing and commenting on what children do "right"
- Redirecting behavior with a firm, kind manner
- Saying what you mean, meaning what you say

Provide opportunities to participate in cooperative group activities that encourage positive interdependence by:

- Helping children learn ways to work together in small groups by dividing tasks, sharing ideas, complimenting efforts, etc.
- Planning cooperative projects in various subject areas across the curriculum
- Organizing group games for fun, not competition
- Assigning clean-up crews

Provide opportunities for children to learn constructive ways to handle controversy and differences through:

- Current events debates
- Different "right" solutions to the same problem
- Class meetings to discuss and solve problems
- Anti-bias curricula

Bibliography/References

Books and articles

Ashton-Warner, Sylvia. *Teacher.* NY: Simon & Schuster, 1963.

Bettelheim, Bruno. *Love Is Not Enough.* London: Macmillan, 1970.
Brenner, Barbara. *Love and Discipline.* NY: Ballantine, 1983.

Calkins, Lucy M. *The Art of Teaching Writing.* Portsmouth, NH: Heinemann, 1986.
Charles, C.M. *Building Classroom Discipline.* NY: Longman, 1989.
Cohen, Dorothy. *Observing & Recording the Behavior of Young Children.* NY: Teachers College Press, 1954 & 1983.

Dewey, John. *Experience & Education.* London: Macmillan, 1938 & 1969.
Doris, Ellen. *Doing What Scientists Do.* Portsmouth, NH: Heinemann, 1991.
Dreikurs, Rudolf, Bernice Bronia Grunwald, and Floy C.Pepper. *Maintaining Sanity in the Classroom: Classroom Management Techniques.* NY: Harper & Row, 1982.

Erikson, Erik. *Childhood & Society.* NY: W.W. Norton, 1963.
_____. Interviewed in "Partners for Life." *The Boston Globe Magazine* (March 22, 1987).

Faber, Adele, and Elaine Mazlish. *How to Talk So Kids Will Listen & Listen So Kids Will Talk.* NY: Avon, 1982.
Featherstone, Joseph. *Schools Where Children Learn.* NY: Liveright, 1971.

Gardner, Howard. *Frames of Mind: The Theory of Multiple Intelligence.* NY: Basic Books, 1983.
Gesell, Arnold, Frances L. Ilg, and Louise Bates Ames. *The Child From Five To Ten.* rev. ed. NY: Harper & Row, 1977.
Gilligan, Carol. *In a Different Voice.* Cambridge, MA: Howard University Press, 1982.

Ginott, Haim. *Between Parent & Child.* NY: Avon Books, 1956.
_____. *Between Teacher & Child.* NY: Avon Books, 1956.
Glasser, William. *Schools Without Failure.* NY: Harper & Row, 1969.
_____. *Reality Therapy.* NY: Harper & Row, 1965.
Glenn, H. Stephen, and Jane Nelson. *Raising Self-Reliant Children In A Self-Indulgent World.* Rocklin, CA: Prima Publishing, 1989.
Gresham, Frank, and Stephen N. Elliott. *Social Skills Rating System.* Circle Pines, MN: American Guidance Service, 1990.

Johnson, David W., Roger T. Johnson, and Edythe Johnson Holubec. *Circles of Learning: Cooperation in the Classroom.* 3rd ed. Edina, MN: Interaction Book Co., 1990.
_____. *Structuring Cooperative Learning: Lesson Plans for Teachers.* Edina, MN: Interaction Book Co., 1987.

Kegan, Robert. *The Evolving Self.* Cambridge, MA: Harvard University Press, 1982.
Kohlberg, Lawrence. *The Philosophy of Moral Development.* NY: Harper & Row, 1987.

Meier, Deborah. "Good Schools Are Still Possible" in *Conflicts and Constituencies* (Fall 1987).

Nelson, Jane. *Positive Discipline*. NY: Ballantine, 1987.

Piaget, Jean. *The Moral Judgement of the Child*. NY: Macmillan, Free Press, 1965.
Pirtle, Sarah. *Discovery Sessions: How Teachers Create Opportunities to Build Cooperation & Conflict Resolution Skills in Their K–8 Classrooms*. Greenfield, MA: Franklin Mediation Services Booklet, 1989.

Ruddick, Sara. *Maternal Thinking: Toward a Politics of Peace*. Boston: Beacon Press, 1989.

Salinger, J.D. *The Catcher in the Rye*. Boston: Little, Brown, 1951.

Audiotapes

Charney, R. *The Ethical Classroom*. Greenfield, MA: Northeast Foundation for Children, 1991.

Wood, C. *Maternal Teaching: Revolution of Kindness*. Greenfield, MA: Northeast Foundation for Children, 1991.
_____. *The Responsive Classroom*. Greenfield, MA: Northeast Foundation for Children, 1990.

Songs

Sorrels, Rosalie. "I'm Gonna' Tell On You." Timpanogas Music, 1970.

Videotapes

Clayton, Marlynn. *Places to Start: Implementing the Developmental Classroom.* Greenfield, MA: Northeast Foundation for Children, 1991.

Johnson, David W., and Roger T. Johnson. *Circles of Learning.* Edina, MN: Interaction Book Co., 1983.

Other resources

Anti-Bias Curricula — Council on Interracial Books for Children Inc., 1841 Broadway, New York NY, 10023 (212-757-5339). The Council offers "Curricula to Counter Bias in School and Society: Curriculum Guides Pre-School — High School, Film Strips & Workbooks." (Send a self-addressed business envelope and postage for 2 ozs. to the Council, PO Box 1263, New York NY 10023.)

Anti-Bias Resources — *Governor's Task Force on Bias-Related Violence.* Doug White, Chair. Division of Human Rights. 55 West 125th St., New York NY, 10027. This report provides a listing of organizations and agencies which offer materials and/or services related to anti-bias education.

Cooperative Learning — For more information about references and training workshops contact the Cooperative Learning Center, 202 Pattee Hall, University of Minnesota, Minneapolis MN, 55455 (612-624-7031).

Just Community Programs — For more information contact Dr. Ann Higgins, Department of Psychology, Fordham University, 441 East Fordham Road, New York NY, 10458 (212-579-2175). Just Community programs are currently in progress at Theodore Roosevelt High School, Bronx NY; Scarsdale Alternative High School, Scarsdale NY; and Brookline High School, Brookline MA (incorporates aspects of "Just Community" governance along with academic programs and "Effective School" program).

Mediation — For more information about references and training workshops contact Franklin Mediation Services, 97 Franklin St., Greenfield MA, 01301 (413-774-7469), Cate Woolner.